THE FAMINE
PLOT

THE FAMINE
PLOT

ENGLAND'S ROLE
IN IRELAND'S
GREATEST TRAGEDY

TIM PAT COOGAN

St. Martin's Griffin ☙ New York

To doctors Tim Fulcher and Dave Keegan and to my daughters Jackie and Olwen and granddaughters Thomond, Olwen, Fodhla, and Emma, without whose combined efforts this book would not have happened.

THE FAMINE PLOT. Copyright © 2012 by Tim Pat Coogan. All rights reserved. Printed in the United States of America. For information, address St. Martin's Press, 175 Fifth Avenue, New York, N.Y. 10010.

www.stmartins.com

All images courtesy of the National Library of Ireland

Designed by Letra Libre

The Library of Congress has cataloged the hardcover edition as follows:

Coogan, Tim Pat, 1935–
    The famine plot : England's role in Ireland's greatest tragedy / Tim Pat Coogan.
        p.   cm.
    ISBN 978-0-230-10952-0 (hardcover)
    1. Ireland—History—Famine, 1845–1852—Historiography. 2. Famines—Ireland—History—19th century—Historiography. 3. Ireland—Social conditions—19th century. I. Title.
    DA 950.7.C67   2012
    941.5081—dc23

                                                                                            2012022499

ISBN 978-1-137-27883-8 (trade paperback)

Our books may be purchased in bulk for promotional, educational, or business use. Please contact your local bookseller or the Macmillan Corporate and Premium Sales Department at (800) 221-7945, extension 5442, or by e-mail at MacmillanSpecialMarkets@macmillan.com.

First published by Palgrave Macmillan, a division of St. Martin's Press LLC

First St. Martin's Griffin Edition: September 2013

CONTENTS

Acknowledgments   vii

Chronology of the Famine   ix

Introduction   1

1   Setting the Scene   9

2   Born to Filth   19

3   A Million Deaths of No Use   31

4   Five Actors and the Orchards of Hell   43

5   Meal Use   65

6   Evictions   87

7   The Work Schemes   101

8   The Workhouse   117

9   Soup and Souperism   137

10   The Poor Law Cometh   163

11   Landlords Targeted   179

12   Emigration: Escape by Coffin Ship   189

13   The Propaganda of Famine   213

Epilogue   233

Appendix 1   237

Appendix 2   248

Appendix 3   250

Appendix 4   251

Appendix 5   255

Appendix 6   257

Notes   259

Bibliography   267

Index   273

Eight pages of photographs appear between pages 116 and 117.

ACKNOWLEDGMENTS

I WISH TO ACKNOWLEDGE THE HELP THAT I received from many individuals and institutions. As ever, the National Library of Ireland was an invaluable resource in providing both manuscripts and images. I am particularly grateful to Assistant Keeper 1 Honora Faul and Assistant Keeper 1 Ciara Kerrigan for their helpful contribution. I also wish to acknowledge the great help I received from the work of another National Library source, former Keeper of Manuscripts Noel Kissane, for his compilation of famine documents, *The Irish Famine: A Documentary History*. Thanks are also due to the courteous and efficient staff of my local Dalkey library for their assistance in procuring various texts. Dr. Críostóir Mac Cártaigh, Director of the Folklore Department UCD, was an invaluable guide to Famine material, and particular thanks are also due to Patricia Maloney of the Folklore Department for unearthing much valuable research. I owe thanks to Dr. Kevin Whelan of Notre Dame and to Michael Blanch and Mícheál Ó Shiadhal. I would also like to thank the following for their kindness in granting me permissions to quote from either their research or creative work: Dr. Evan Boland, Pete St. John, Gerard J. Lyne, Dr. Tyler Anbinder, Dr. James Murphy, Peter Grey, and the literary executors of the Paddy Kavanagh estates, Jonathan Williams and Eileán Ní Chuilleanáin. I would also like to acknowledge the kind assistance of Shane Mac Thomais of Glasnevin Cemetery and of His Excellency Mr. Altay Cengizer, the ambassador of Turkey to Ireland, and his staff for providing me with research and translations and Ciaran Wallace for reading and making helpful suggestions to the manuscript.

I would like to thank Christopher Moriarty of the Irish Quakers' Archives. A special word of thanks is also due to my friend J. J. Barrett of Tralee for his help in researching "souperism" in Dingle. And last but certainly not least I am indebted to professor Ivor Browne for his guideance on the psychological impact of the Famine.

CHRONOLOGY OF
THE FAMINE

1690

William of Orange completes process of confiscation of Irish lands begun under Normans and pursued by subsequent invaders, notably Elizabeth I and Oliver Cromwell.

1798

United Irishmen's rebellion crushed.

1800

Act of Union dissolves Irish parliament; subsumes Ireland into United Kingdom.

1845

August: Commencement of famine period with coming of potato blight.

November: English prime minister Peel reacts with relief measures such as the purchase of cheap Indian corn and the setting up of the Relief Commission.

1846

Peel continues relief efforts by methods such as passing a public works act to provide employment, the curbing of corn price escalation by the release of the Indian corn on the market at tactically calculated intervals, and above all the repeal of the Corn Laws.

June 9: Peel and the Conservatives are ousted and replaced by a Whig administration led by Sir John Russell.

July: Blight reappears and destroys three-quarters of the potato crop (compared to a third the previous year). Panic-fueled emigration occurs as mortality rates begin a climb that would last for some years.

August 17: Russell announces a change in the policy of distributing cheap corn, saying that the Whigs would "not interfere with the regular operations of merchants for the supply of food to the country."

November 13: The Quakers form the Society of Friends Relief Committee. Their operations are hampered by unusually bad weather and by ever-increasing ravages of dysentery and famine fevers that also lessen the beneficial effects of the road works relief schemes.

1847

January 1: Formation of British Relief Association.

March and April: As numbers employed on relief works pass the 700,000 mark, the works begin to be phased out and are replaced by soup kitchens.

April 27: Fever epidemic causes Fever Act to be introduced.

June 8: Some relaxation in relief regulations; a Poor Relief Act allows for outdoor relief for those hardest hit.

July 22: Poor Law Commission set up to administer Poor Law Unions.

July and August: Three million receiving soup and, though blight infestation is greatly reduced, shortage of seed at planting time results in only a quarter of normal crop being harvested.

October: As winter approaches, relief is restricted to the Poor Law Unions and the workhouses. Soup kitchens are closed.

1848

July: The abortive Young Ireland Rising and a huge fall in the potato crop, possibly two-thirds in extent.

August to December: The introduction of an Encumbered Estates Act (August 14); a cholera epidemic breaks out. The eviction rate soars, as does that of emigration.

1849

Blight reported from areas hard hit by famine in both the South and West of the country. An effort is made to increase the rate income by introducing a rate-in-aid to cover all unions.

June: Quakers defeated by scale of famine, write to Lord John Russell announcing the cessation of their operations, saying that only government aid and a reform of the Irish land system can cope with the Irish problem.

August 3–12: Some 800,000 are on outdoor relief as Queen Victoria and Prince Albert visit Ireland.

By the end of the year it is estimated that there are 250,000 people living in workhouses and that some 220,000 have emigrated. Evictions continue.

1850

Evictions are estimated at around 20,000, and some 210,000 are estimated to have emigrated.

1851

The population of the country has been reduced by death and emigration from 8,175,000 to 6,552,000. Evictions and emigrations continue.

1852

A further quarter of a million people emigrate. Evictions continue, though at lower rate than in former years.

INTRODUCTION

FLYING OVER IRELAND IN A SMALL PLANE OR helicopter, you will see tiny green fingers pushing their way into hillside heather or bogland grass. These are the remains of "lazy beds," the plots in which the nineteenth-century Irish grew their staple food, the potato. The fingerprints have left a mark not only on the bogs and hillsides but also on the folk memory of Ireland and the history of the world.

Apart from spreading death and pestilence, the Famine, which followed the potato crop's failure, set in train a tsunami of emigration that changed the course of events in countries as far apart as America, Argentina, and Australia. Where the Irish themselves were concerned, it was the influence of the emigrants, particularly those in America, who would ultimately secure their independence. The legacy of the Famine, both acknowledged and unacknowledged, has resonances for today's Ireland. The acknowledged portion of its legacy continues to impel idealistic young Irish aid workers to follow in the footsteps of medieval Irish monks who went abroad to improve the lives of others.

The influence of the unacknowledged portion of the legacy is the stark warning to today's Republic of Ireland's citizenry of what can happen when a country has no government of its own and must rely for its sustenance on the droppings from the table of a wealthy neighbor. Ireland's tragedy at the time of the Famine was that, through conquest, she had no government of her own.

As this is written, Ireland, through the corruption, incompetence, and profligacy of the then governing Fianna Fáil Party, has lost its economic sovereignty and Caitlín Ní Houlihan[1] currently stands in a dole queue in Brussels to receive handouts from the European and International Monetary Funds. At the same time a highly disturbing similarity between the famine era and the present can be seen in the existence of the National Management Agency (NAMA) in Dublin, which takes the assets of recession victims and, after what is euphemistically termed a "haircut," sells these on to well-pursed new owners at greatly reduced prices. This was the same procedure dictated by the Encumbered Estates Act during the Famine, whereby land obtained from distressed owners was sold on to wealthier purchasers with the intention of creating larger holdings and a more viable rural economy. The famine bell does not merely toll for those who died during the nineteenth century; it has resonance for those who live in the twenty-first.

The fact that people at least live in peace on the island of Ireland is an important part of the Famine legacy. It was the influence of the Irish Americans, led by the Kennedy family, whose ancestor Patrick Kennedy had fled Ireland during the Famine, that helped to bring an end to thirty years of strife and create a peace process that still holds at the time of this writing.

The Famine left other fingerprints on the folk memory of the Irish. Prior to the Famine the Irish probably had the youngest marriage rate in Europe. Too young, deprived of their staple diet, children and their youthful parents died in a holocaust of starvation and famine-related fevers. By the mid-twentieth century youthful marriage had become as rare as it once was common and there were debates in the newspapers as to whether or not the West of Ireland had the highest rates of schizophrenia in Europe. Later research showed that the West suffered not from schizophrenia but from the diseases of bachelordom, loneliness, and alcoholism.

Paradoxically, but perhaps understandably, what most survivors and their families sought to do was to exclude the Famine from their memory. And, if one visits the admirable Famine folk lore collection at the University College Dublin, one might begin to understand why survivors sought to forget. One story, for example, concerns a farmer who struck a starving woman with a stone when she attempted to pull one of his turnips from the ground.

How many other such stones were thrown? How many tens of thousands of poor farmers in afflicted areas survived because, perhaps on a daily basis, they turned people who might have been neighbours and former friends away from their doors and meagre food stores? How many doors were not even opened? As was the case of a little boy in County Wicklow who fruitlessly knocked on the doors of a village street, doors closed to the visibly dying child because he might have a fever.

The famine affected all parts of Ireland. But another one of its fingerprints, a strange reluctance to acknowledge this fact, grew among Irish historians and in various parts of the country. In the Protestant North, for example, even today some Protestants still regard the Famine as something that happened to the Catholics, God's punishment for their feckless, improvident ways. The truth was that while the northern province Ulster suffered less excess mortality per thousand at 20.7 percent than the worst-hit area, Connaught, at 40.4 percent, the Ulster percentage translates to 224,000 deaths. (Leinster's excess mortality was 8.6 percent; Munster's, 30.3 percent.)

The experience of the largest Dublin cemetery, Glasnevin, is instructive. The cemetery was and is meticulous about records, but as the Famine progressed, the sheer weight of numbers forced the cemetery authorities to choose between accepting unidentified corpses for burial and leaving them to rot outside the cemetery gates. Bodies were normally accepted for burial only when properly certified and their identity vouched for by a relative or a respected personage such as a minister of religion. In 1849, recorded deaths rose to 10,047, from 5,944 in 1845, and unidentified bodies amounted to another 10,000.[2]

The scale of the horror of the Famine was such that the English historian A. J. P. Taylor compared the state of the country to that of the infamous German concentration camp Belsen. He declared "all Ireland was a Belsen."[3] Most Irish historians would argue that Taylor exaggerated, but the honest anger of a fair-minded Englishman, who incidentally was reviewing the work of an equally fair-minded Englishwoman, *The Great Hunger* by Cecil Woodham-Smith, when he made the comparison, is preferable to the type of "colonial cringe" with which too many Irish historians have approached the topic.

The silence of Irish historians about the official hate creation and the rise in anti-Irish prejudice that accompanied the Famine was, and to a large extent still is, remarkable. Take L.P. Curtis in *Anglo-Saxons and Celts* for example: "So persistent has been the theme of English cultural superiority over the Irish that one begins to suspect the existence amongst those who tried to subdue and rule the Irish of a deep-seated need to justify their confiscatory and homicidal habits in that country." To put it mildly, Irish historians as a class have not done justice to the Famine. The colonial cringe seems to have informed the approach of many of them. From the mid-1960s onwards, as the Troubles in Northern Ireland worsened, revisionism became a matter not of revising opinions in the light of new research or new insights, but of dealing with the political climate created by the war in Northern Ireland. Irish historians would appear to have fallen in line with governmental policy, which prevented Sinn Fein spokespersons from appearing on television and the airwaves and banned any material that might have been construed as giving aid or comfort to the IRA.

Tony Blair's 1997 apology for the Famine and the subsequent ending of the Troubles in Northern Ireland stunted the growth of revisionism. Another very important factor conditioned Irish historians' approach to assessing the Famine. Professor Joseph Lee has written the following: "The external examiners in all Irish Universities came from England. Irish historians of that generation were bound to be conscious of the widespread English assumption that they might be prone to wild flights of Celtic fancy that any claims that sounded remotely exaggerated were in danger of being dismissed as extravagant. There may therefore have been a tendency to counter this image by insisting on the sobriety of one's scholarship."[4]

In evading the label of "Celtic fancy," Irish historians have also left themselves open to charges of evading the issue of British decision makers' responsibility for the Famine. Moreover, they have failed at the task that simple justice would seem to have laid upon their shoulders: describing honestly, without either malice or cap touching, how their forebears died. Take but one example: Nora Connelly. Nora was a peasant woman who, hungry and ill-clad, walked several miles over a bleak, rocky Kerry hillside to obtain food for her children from a workhouse. However, she was turned away empty-handed because her name was not on the list of those who were to be given food. When Nora eventually stumbled into her cabin once more, she found that four of her children had died of starvation. Later it was discovered that she should have been on the food list but a careless official had given her an incorrect name. There were many such officials. But for many years Irish people had only the haziest notion of what happened during the Famine or, indeed, how the Irish themselves can sometimes be blamed for what occurred. In some respects the silence of Famine survivors and that of their decedents resembles the guilty silence that the horror of the Holocaust imposed on some Jewish survivors of the camps.

Instead, budding historians of the era who came up through either British academia or Irish academia controlled by British historiography tended to challenge rather than justify John Mitchel's famous declaration that God sent the blight, but the English created the Famine. The template for the colonial cringe approach was inadvertently laid down by Éamon de Valera, circa 1943, when he laudably decreed a book should be written to mark the one hundredth anniversary of the coming of the blight in 1845. The book took some thirteen years to appear. It was called *The Great Famine* and was "edited" by R. Dudley Edwards and Desmond Williams, both professors of history at University College Dublin, part of the National University of Ireland, and both products of English university. Joseph Lee judged this to be "a great book," and another prolific writer on the Irish Famine, Cormac Ó Gráda, wrote in a foreword to the 1994 edition of *The Great Famine* that it contains "classic contributions," the whole constituting "building blocks for the future" study of the Famine.

Both these statements should be regarded more as examples of the trade unionism of Irish academic historians rather than as fully accurate assessments of the book's worth.

The book consists of a series of seven essays on aspects of the Famine, some of which, like Roger McHughes's description of what people lived (or died) on during the catastrophe, based on accounts taken from the National Folklore Collection archives at University College Dublin, are indeed very good. But the "great book" has many gaps. First, it evades the issue of who was responsible for the Famine. Professor Lee himself criticizes the absence of any contribution on the population trends. More pointedly, Dudley Edwards noted in his diary, "If it is [called] studies in the history of the famine, it is because they [the contributors?] are not sure all questions are answered. There are still the fundamental matters whether its occurrence was not due to the failure of the sophisticated to be alert."

As James Donnelly notes on the issue of culpability, the volume is evasive. Referring to the contributor who dealt with the issue of culpability, Kevin B. Nowlan, Donnelly points out that the worst sins attributed by Nowlan to the British government were its "excessive tenderness" for the rights of private property, its "different (and limited) view of its positive responsibilities to the community," and its inevitable habit of acting "in conformity with the conventions of (the larger) society." High politicians and administrators were not to be blamed; they were in fact innocent of any "great and deliberately imposed evil." Instead, insisted Nowlan, "the really great evil lay in the totality of that social order that made such a famine possible and that could tolerate, to the extent it did, the sufferings and hardships caused by the failure of the potato crop. In other words, no one was really to blame because everyone was."[5]

Another internationally respected scholar, Joel Mokyr, also took issue with one of Nowlan's judgments: "perhaps all that matters is that many died." Mokyr notes that "modern accounts dispute this, insisting that it does matter *how many* died as well as *who* died and *from what cause.*"[6] To which I might add that the nonsense of shying away from the apportionment of blame because it might arouse anti-British feeling has to be faulted on two fronts. One, it is an insult to the dignity of the unfortunates who died. As Mokyr, not an Irishman himself, has pointed out, the dead are at least entitled to an honest telling of their tale and an explanation as to why they, their children, and their parents came to lose their lives so horribly. And, two, on the score of arousing anti-British feeling the truth is that an honest account of the Famine should, as I hope to achieve here, have the effect of showing that it was not the British public or the British people either individually or collectively who should be blamed for the Famine.

Two contributors to the volume, Kevin Nowlan and T. P. O'Neill, were contributors to the *Irish Press*. Both gave me a more homely but more accurate picture of the editorial process that left glaring omissions in a work produced by Ireland's National University on the country's single greatest tragedy. Dudley Edwards' original collaborator in the Famine venture was the respected figure T. W. Moody of Trinity College, but he dropped out to be succeeded by Williams. Joseph Lee, in discussing Edwards' attainments, notes that his main field of study was the Tudors, which some might regard as a curious background for a historian of the Famine. But possibly a more decisive influence on Edwards was the fact that he was a disciple of the Whig historian Sir Herbert Butterfield, whose views he commended to his students.

The likable Desmond Williams was the epitome of the brilliant but absentminded professor caricature. He was also an *Irish Press* contributor, and one of the most disorganized men in Ireland. I once turned up, by arrangement, at the University Club in Stephen's Green, where my wife and I had been asked to dinner by him. I found him on the phone, however, apologizing to someone else for not being able to go to dinner with them because he had arranged to go to dinner with another party. When he put the phone down, I discovered that it was not I he was referring to, but a third dinner party, to which, in my folly, I actually drove him to.

O'Neill and, in particular, Kevin Nowlan told me themselves how they eventually managed to get the book through the presses, despite what Lee coyly refers to as the pair's "idiosyncrasies"; these were described by the great Irish comic writer Brian O'Nolan as "travelling in the Far Yeast."[7] A large part of the credit for the book appearing in print at all is due to Kevin B. Nowlan, then a relatively youthful figure among the historian elite. He described to me and others how, by a process of badgering and detective work, he found "chapters lying around on shelves." Eventually Nowlan succeeded in getting the book published by writing the book's foreword and affixing Edwards' and Williams' initials to his handiwork. Far from adjudging *The Great Famine* "a great book," it does not bear comparison with the *Atlas of the Great Irish Famine* produced by three geographers, John Crowley, William J. Smith, and Mike Murphy, with Cork University Press as this book was going to press. A work of this stature could and should have been produced to mark the hundredth anniversary of the Famine. I would not place "the great book" in the same category as works of the stature of James S. Donnelly Jr.'s *The Great Irish Potato Famine*, Kirby Miller's *Emigrants and Exiles: Ireland, the Irish Exodus to North America*, Peter Gray's *Famine, Land, and Politics: British Government and Irish Society, 1843–1850*, or the great pioneering work by Cecil Woodham-Smith, *The Great Hunger: Ireland, 1845–1849*.

It would be true to say that before Tony Blair's apology, the Irish abroad sought to commemorate the Famine, while Irish officialdom sought to play it down. The taxi driver Michael Blanch and the songwriter Pete St. John, as described in chapters 7 and 8 respectively, literally did more to heighten awareness of the Famine than the Irish academic and political establishment did.

"Stop Blaming British for Famine" said a headline in an Australian newspaper reporting on a speech by Avril Doyle, a Fine Gael minister of state who visited Australia for the 150th commemoration of the famine in 1996. The minister's speech reflected official Dublin attitudes to the worldwide commemoration of the Irish Famine. She spoke of the dangers that a "retreat into an idealized past would spawn racist, xenophobic and chauvinistic views and a sterile cultural framework."[8] I don't know how the Famine could be seen as forming part of "an idealized past," but she went on to say that "Irish people needed to develop a mature relationship with their past, to view the famine as a moment in history which defined a sense of human vulnerability and not as a weapon for modern political conflict." She concluded by suggesting that the Irish should view the British as taking part in a "shared experience." "Like rape?" queried a member of the audience.

With variations for local reference, this was the line pursued by the right-wing Fine Gael government during the 150th Famine Commemoration. Much of the argument of the colonial cringe variety received a death blow when Blair said he was pleased to join in remembering those who had died and suffered during "the Great Irish Famine."

He went on: "The famine was a defining event in the history of Ireland and Britain. It has left deep scars. That one million people should have died in what was then part of the richest and most powerful nation in the world is something that still causes pain as we reflect on it today. Those who governed in London at the time failed their people."[9]

Blair's declaration, it should be noted, played an important part in helping to build the trust of the Irish revolutionaries, which ultimately ended the violence in Northern Ireland with the Good Friday Agreement of 1998. Whatever befell Blair's subsequent reputation because of his disastrous involvement in the Iraq War, Tony Blair will always command an honored place in the history of Anglo-Irish relations. He deserves a large amount of credit for the vastly improved climate of British Irish relationships of which this account of what may be termed the nadir of these relationships was written.

ONE
SETTING THE SCENE

"My Lords, it is only by its government that such evils could have been produced: the mere fact that Ireland is in so deplorable and wretched a condition saves whole volumes of argument, and is of itself a complete and irrefutable proof of the misgovernment to which she has been subjected. Nor can we lay to our souls the 'flattering unction' that this misgovernment was only of ancient date, and has not been our doing . . . such a system of government could not fail to leave behind it a train of fearful evils from which we are suffering at the present day.

We have a military occupation of Ireland, but that in no other sense could it be said to be governed: that it was occupied by troops, not governed like England."

—*Extract from a speech by Earl Grey, son of a former prime minister and, during the Famine, colonial secretary, speaking to the House of Lords during the early stages of the Famine on March 23, 1846*

I N HIS GREAT NOVEL *MOBY DICK,* WRITTEN during the Famine era, Herman Melville described Ireland as a "fast fish," that is to say a harpooned whale lashed helplessly to the side of a ship waiting to be cut up by its predators. It was an apt description. The Famine cut Irish society to pieces. We can only estimate the number of deaths from the time the potato blight first struck in 1845 to the ending of the Famine period in 1851. People were buried in mass graves—appallingly, sometimes while still alive—some died in ditches and fields, by the sea and lakeshore, and, given the accompanying disruption of the population, it is hard to accept that their passing could have been accurately recorded. Historians have used the 1841 census to gauge the size of the population before the Famine hit and the 1851 census for the end date.

This placed the population of Ireland in 1841 at 8,175,124. But the figure was probably larger. The lack of roads, particularly in the West, together with the nature of much of the teeming peasantry's habitation, which was sometimes nothing more than a cave cut into a bog, would have made it nearly impossible for a census enumerator to give an accurate tally. The overcrowded slums of the cities also presented difficulties for an accurate headcount. Historiographical problems notwithstanding, it is generally accepted that during the Famine period Ireland's population fell to some six and a half million. The total given in the 1851 census was 6,552,365. But modern research, as indicated below, finds this figure masks the true extent of the population loss.

The statistics also mask the shock the famine caused Ireland. In our day we are used to reading reports of famines in the Third World, which sometimes claim hundreds of thousands of lives. These deaths occur in countries where populations are in the tens or hundreds of millions—many times greater than that of nineteenth-century Ireland. As a comparison, the terrible famine in Darfur in 2003, which claimed approximately one hundred thousand lives, did so out of a population of 27 million.

A direct result of the Famine was emigration. The hungry began to leave their homes in droves and continued to do so without interruption for some 150 years after the Famine. Ireland became a country to leave. Two highly respected historians, Joel Mokyr and Cormac O'Grada, point out that Ireland lost hundreds of thousands of people through "averted births," that is to say children who would have been born in Ireland, were it not for the Famine. Mokyr in fact calculates the figure for underreporting of those who died to be about *100 percent*. He claims that his calculations "yield a total of 1.9 million people dying in Ireland in those five years," as opposed to the official census tables which report a total of only 985,000 people dying between 1841 and 1851.[1]

The ultimate cause of these statistics was not the potato but backyardism, which dictated most of the recorded history of the relationship between the islands of England and Ireland. (Essentially, England considered its weaker neighbor, Ireland, its backyard, and therefore felt entitled to dictate what went on there.) It was backyardism that gave rise to Ireland's three damnations: colonization, proximity, and religion.

Raids by Irish pirates and disputes between representatives of the Irish church and the religious on the larger island who took their tone from Rome made minor outbreaks of hostility relatively commonplace between the two islands long before Columbus discovered America. But for our purposes it may be noted that the era of a more organized and sustained attempt at the colonization of Ireland could be said to have begun with the Normans. An Irish king, Diarmuid McMurragh, King of Leinster, invited the Normans to Ireland to help him in a dispute that arose when he kidnapped the wife of another chieftain.

The pope of the day was an Englishman: Adrian, who was advised by another Englishman, John of Salisbury. Adrian granted Henry II a Papal Bull, *Laudabiliter*, legitimizing the Norman invasion. The papal deal with Henry II in effect ushered in a prolonged era of two forms of colonialism, those of Mother England and of Mother Church. The Irish were to be saved from the barbarity of their ways by a combination of Vatican directive and Norman steel.

From the Vatican's point of view, the attraction of this arrangement lay in the fact that Rome would exert its authority through the appointment of hand-picked bishops, rather than having to struggle to assert its influence over powerful Irish abbots, who hitherto had often been appointed by their families who controlled the extensive church lands and monasteries. The attraction for the Normans was straightforward—it gave them access to Irish land which, with their advances in agriculture, they were able to exploit far more profitably than were the cattle-herding Irish. And so Christ and Caesar came to be hand in glove. Unfortunately, when Henry VIII defied the pope by divorcing his wife to marry Anne Boleyn, the gloves came off between king and pope, with disastrous results for the Irish.

From the time of Henry VIII's breaking with Rome, England became a Protestant nation and Ireland remained a Catholic one. Thus, apart from the inevitable attempts by a large country to subordinate a smaller neighbor, England's religious wars became superimposed on Ireland also. Not alone would the Catholic Irish lose their lands; they would also be forced to pay for the upkeep of the Protestant clergy. Not surprisingly in a land wherein the poet is both feared and revered, native Irish resentment at the superimposition of Protestantism found its expression in a bitter verse by Raftery, the famous blind Irish poet:[2]

> *Don't talk of your Protestant Minister*
> *Or his church without Temple or state*
> *For the foundation stone of his religion*
> *Was the bollocks of Henry VIII*

Readers may make what they will of the fact that the translation of this verse into English was made by Monsignor de Brun, a Catholic priest then president of Maynooth who later became president of National University of Ireland, Galway.

The old English Catholics, who had settled peaceably enough in Ireland from Norman days onward to an extent that it was said that they became more Irish than the Irish themselves, now became bracketed with the native Irish as objects of detestation not for merely Henry VIII, but for those who came after him, notably his daughter Elizabeth and Oliver Cromwell.

Significantly for our story Lord Chichester, Queen Elizabeth's chief advisor, wrote: "I have often said, and written, it is Famine which must consume [the Irish]; our swords and other endeavors work not that speedy effect which is expected for their overthrow."[2] Oliver Cromwell added a variant to the Chichester approach as he went through Ireland with a Bible in one hand and a sword in the other exulting in the doing of God's work by the combined slaughter of both the Irish and old English. Cromwell coined the slogan "to Hell or to Connacht" as he drove Catholics from the good lands to the barren boggy areas of the West.

If ever one required an object lesson as to the validity of a saying I first heard in Vietnam—"When elephants fight it is the grass that gets trampled and the people are the grass"—one need look no further than Ireland.

The victory of William of Orange over the Catholic King James II in 1690 at the Battle of the Boyne finally broke Catholic power in Ireland and is still fervently celebrated by the Protestants of northeastern Ireland, in the province of Ulster. This exemplifies the confusions and contradictions that can ensue when a small country gets caught up in power politics. The pope sought a Williamite victory, as part of his larger European designs (mainly against Louis XIV of France), and ordered that a *Te Deum* be rung from all churches. More importantly, Pope Innocent XI also secretly gave William large sums of money, a fact that would have shocked both Protestant and Catholic protagonists and that was withheld from the public until documents came to light in 2008. They showed that the pope had contributed some three and a half million in today's euro values toward the purchase of swords and muskets to what in effect became the enslavement of the Catholic Irish.

Ireland was both crushed and conquered. Massacres carried out in the name of religion added to the bitterness of the race memory on both sides, a bitterness compounded from the conqueror's side by the ever-present threat of Ireland being used as a springboard for invasion by one of the Catholic powers, France or Spain.

Each successive invasion, each new outbreak of rebellion had the effect of adding to this prejudice, either through reports of sanguinary far-off events in Ireland itself or by the sight of Irish mendicants torn from their homes by the upheavals in Ireland and being forced to beg on English roads and streets. As a result, as the geographers Busteed and Hodgson have noted: for the English, the Irish provided the "richest, most enduring source of nationalist demonology."[3] As we will see later, this demonology could and would be brought to life during the Famine when it suited their purposes, by British churchmen and politicians.

The demonology was multi-layered. In the first place it cast Ireland as a place of almost incomprehensible endemic political instability, warfare, and violence.

Yet despite the most ruthless application of the famine formula, accompanied by a scorched-earth policy that wiped both cattle and humans from much of the Irish landscape, England's conquest of Ireland remained partial for several centuries. Her sphere of influence largely consisted of what was known as the Pale, Dublin City, and parts of the counties immediately surrounding it. Thus Ireland became neither an integral part of England nor a developed country in its own right. The lack of a road and harbor infrastructure, particularly in the West of Ireland for example, would prove to be a major contributory factor in the Great Famine's death toll.

Irish trade was crippled by the partial conquest. Instead of being developed, valuable cattle, fishing, and woolen industries were taxed out of existence when they came into competition with either British trading interests or her military concerns, which led her to disrupt Irish trade with both France and America.

As a result, Ireland in the nineteenth century was a poverty-stricken land to which famine was a frequent visitor. Famine struck Ireland several times in the nineteenth century and even before that. One of the best-known landmarks on the Dublin coast is the obelisk on Killiney Hill, overlooking Dun Laoghaire. It was erected as a relief work, by a benevolent local landlord, John Mapas, during the famine of 1741, which was reckoned to have killed an eighth of the population. Prior to the outbreak of An Gorta Mór, the Great Hunger, in the nineteenth century, there were outbreaks of localized famine in 1800, 1817, 1822, 1831, 1835, and 1842.

Toward the end of the eighteenth century, some gleams of prosperity and, most notably, of political development had begun to shine through the murk of centuries. The country obtained a degree of legislative independence from London. It was a degree only, and the Parliament of the period was representative of the property-owning Protestant class, not of the Catholic peasantry, but it contained enormous growth potential.

The move toward legislative independence may be said to have begun when Henry Grattan in 1780 moved an unsuccessful parliamentary address to the Crown stating that the condition of Ireland was no longer tolerable, and Irish landlords began attempting to secure more powers for the impressive-looking Irish parliament in Dublin, which was in reality completely subservient to its older sister in London. Then in June 1782 a group of powerful Anglo-Irish landlords furthered Grattan's suggestion. Led by Lord Charlemont and the Duke of Leinster, they took advantage of the American and French revolutions to set up a Volunteer Army, ostensibly to help England defend Ireland as England had been forced to weaken its Irish armies to bolster its American campaign. The need to strengthen Irish defenses had been highlighted by a series of raids carried out by the American privateer John Paul Jones, "the father of the American navy," along the Scottish and English coasts, culminating in the spectacular capture of *The Ajax* in Belfast Lough.

From the outset the Volunteers made it clear that henceforth they would only obey laws passed by "the King, Lords and Commons of Ireland." Ireland would be loyal to the Crown but reserved the right to protect its own interests. Primarily these interests were those of the big landowners, the Anglican "ascendancy" as they were known, but in the eighteen years of the Irish parliament's operation the Irish economy did show an improvement. Despite the fact that competition from the more advanced British weaving industry crippled the Irish linen industry, particularly affecting parts of Ulster in the North and Connacht in the West, notably Mayo, trade and enterprise showed an upward curve. Capital was attracted to Ireland, and public works such as the building of the Newry Canal were commenced.

Cultural activity also flourished. For those with money, Dublin became an attractive place to live. Fine public buildings and imposing houses obscured the view of the teeming slums and their attendant filth, disease, and overcrowding.

The realities that lay behind Dublin's fine architecture could well have served as a metaphor for the political and economic condition of a great section of the majority of the Irish people. Through Wolfe Tone, the Protestant leader of the Society of the United Irishmen who sought to unite Protestant, Catholic, and Dissenter in the rectification of their grievances by breaking the link with England, contact was established in the late eighteenth century with the French government.

French assistance resulted in two attempts at landing French troops in Ireland. However, in the first, a protestant wind blew up in 1796 and scattered Admiral Hoche's fleet; a second force under the command of General Humbert did manage to land at Killala, in County Mayo, in 1798. Humbert's force was easily defeated by the British, but uprisings broke out in various parts of the country. However, rebellion, spearheaded by the United Irishmen, was bloodily suppressed.

At the time it was frequently said that the 1798 rebellion was secretly encouraged by direction of the English prime minister William Pitt so that it would go off half-cocked before the Society of United Irishmen could succeed in their aim of uniting Catholic, Protestant, and Dissenter against the Crown. Certainly English policy seemed directed at fermenting rather than aborting rebellion. Troops were forcibly billeted on unwilling Catholic farm owners and the yeomanry; the Protestant militia was given a free hand in oppressing their Catholic neighbors. Fair-minded Protestants were outraged at what they saw: On Easter Tuesday, April 10, in Newtownmountkennedy in County Wicklow a Protestant farmer named Joseph Holt, attending the town fair, "was sickened to witness Ancient Britons cutting the haunches and thighs off the young women for wearing green stuff petticoats."[4]

Holt subsequently became a general in the revolutionary army, but Wolfe Tone's once fair hopes of uniting Ireland's differing traditions were drowned in a debauch of blood and atrocity. A respected historian of the period has written: "1798 is the most violent and tragic event in Irish history between the Jacobite wars and the great famine. In the space of a few weeks, 30,000 people—peasants armed with pikes and pitchforks, defenseless women and children—were shot down or blown like chaff as they charged up to the mouth of the canon."[5]

One of the militia's tactics was pitch capping. A canvas crown was placed on the head of an insurgent, or alleged insurgent, and boiling tar was poured into the canvas surround. After this had had time to set, the cap was torn off, taking with it much of the "croppy's" scalp. (The term "croppy" came from the habit of some insurgents of cropping their hair in the fashion of the French revolutionists.) The hatred of the Protestants for the Catholics was such that the commanding English general Abercrombie became so revolted by the people he was defending that he had as little to do with them as he possibly could. For their part the Catholics occasionally responded to the floggings and hangings with atrocities of their own. In Scuallabogue in County Wexford for example, the insurgents burned down a church containing hundreds of captured Protestant women and children.

The killing of some Protestants by Catholics and the savageries perpetrated on the Presbyterians of Northern Ireland, by the English general Lake in particular, put the seal of death on Wolfe Tone's dreams. He was captured and cheated the hangman by committing suicide.

What the 1798 rebellion did do was to give both the pretext and the opportunity London required for snuffing out Dublin's upstart parliament. The government of William Pitt the Younger employed bribery on an unprecedented scale to cajole the Irish parliamentarians to vote for an Act of Union that subsumed the Irish parliament into the Westminster parliament. This was meant to turn Ireland legislatively into an overseas version of Wales or Scotland, that is to say a full-fledged member of the United Kingdom, but in reality spelled its legislative obliteration.

Any national parliament in Ireland with a degree of independence, no matter how restricted its franchise, contained within it a significant potential for the development of Irish interests, particularly when one considers that it was backed up by a standing army.

The zeal with which England set about stifling the parliament and, later, the brutality that it displayed toward a campaign led by Daniel O'Connell to have it restored indicate that its potential was only too well recognized in London.

Proximity both highlighted the dangers of allowing an independent Ireland to develop off Britain's shores and rendered it relatively easy to stamp out any threats. Peerages fell like leaves in Valambrossa on the shoulders of the recalcitrant and the venial alike. One of the baits dangled by Pitt, which was snapped up by the Irish Catholic hierarchy, was the lure of Catholic Emancipation. However, King George III, who had earlier lost both America and his reason, opposed this liberalization. Pitt resigned and emancipation remained an issue that would absorb Irish political energies and bitterly divide Catholics and Protestants for almost thirty years, until Daniel O'Connell succeeded in carrying it in 1829. This advance was something of a pyrrhic victory for Irish Catholics. While it did remove basic disabilities to advancement in their own country (Catholics gained entry to the higher reaches of the law and the military, and the right to enter parliament), emancipation also helped to deepen the democratic deficit caused by the destruction of the Irish parliament. The "40 shilling freeholders" lost the vote (hitherto holders of land worth 40 shillings [£2] were entitled to vote).

Now only those with holdings valued at more than £10 could exercise the franchise. This meant a reduction in the Irish electorate from 216,002 to just 37,000. Thus, the gains secured for the Vatican by O'Connell's triumph were more obvious than those for the political power of a majority of the Irish people. Under the two forms of colonization both Christ and Caesar had exacted their tributes.

Summing up the net effect of what had befallen Ireland since the Act of Union, as the effects of the Great Famine began to be felt Earl Grey speaking in the House of Lords on March 23, 1846, said: "Ireland is the one weak place in the solid fabric of British power; Ireland is the one deep (I had almost said ineffaceable) blot upon the brightness of British honor. Ireland is our disgrace. It is the reproach, the standing disgrace of this country that Ireland remains in the condition she is. It is so regarded throughout the whole civilised world" (see appendix 5 for the full speech).

The conditions in Ireland of which Earl Grey spoke are described in the next chapter.

TWO

BORN TO FILTH

"I could scarcely believe that these creatures were my fellow-beings. Never have I seen slaves so degraded; and here I learnt that there are many pages in the volume of slavery, and that every branch of it proceeds from one and the same root, though it assumes different shapes. These poor creatures are in as virtual bondage to their landlords and superiors as is possible for mind or body to be. They cannot work unless they bid them; they cannot eat unless they feed them; and they cannot get away unless they help them."[1]

—*Asenath Nicholson, American philanthropist, in*
Annals of the Famine in Ireland *(1851)*

"You cannot imagine what a complexity of miseries five centuries of oppression, civil disorders, and religious hostility have piled upon this poor people. It is a ghastly labyrinth, in which it would be difficult to try to find one's way and of which we shall only catch a glimpse of the entrance."[2]

—*Alexis de Tocqueville to his father during a*
six weeks' tour of Ireland in 1835

THE EFFECT OF THE MULTIPLE ENGLISH INvasions made the Irish peasantry the detritus of conquest. The majority of the peasantry, perhaps as many as 3 million people, lived in conditions in which a considerate owner would not have placed a dog.[3]

The bulk of the peasants' accommodation consisted of mud cabins covered in straw or what was known as "scraws" cut from the top of bogs or rough fields. Any improvements to their holdings, either to the cabins or say to the drainage of their fields, would have resulted in rents being increased. The law was on the landlords' side, and the renters of land were tenants at will who could be ejected with ease from either large or small holdings.

Moreover, the cottier and laboring class subsisted on wages that ranged between six pence and ten pence a day. Other disadvantages included having to work for free part of the time for their landlord. Food was generally not provided and in addition laborers were recorded in some instances as having to walk fourteen miles a day to their work. In order to survive, their clothes, bedsheets, and even furniture sometimes had to be pawned. Moneylenders also added to the immiseration of the peasantry. In these circumstances the standards of peasants' accommodation inevitably became the most rudimentary imaginable.

Houses generally lacked windows, and ventilation came either from the single door or through the hole in the roof through which smoke escaped. Furniture frequently did not extend much beyond a bed, an occasional chair, and, for the fortunate, a table. Occupants all slept together in the clothes they wore, on the cabins' earthen floor and huddled together for warmth, but high moral standards prevailed and commentators of the period almost universally remarked on the lack of either incest or promiscuity. Yet sex was the principal outlet of the people and early marriages were the norm rather than the exception. The peasantry reckoned that their lives could not possibly be worse married than unmarried and as a result something of a population explosion occurred. Between 1741, the date of the last big famine, and the coming of the blight in 1845 the population of Ireland *tripled*. Feeding so many was clearly a challenge.

The potato proved to be a dangerously attractive crop to grow. The tubers were sowed in what were termed "lazy beds," that is in narrow ridges about four feet in width, with a furrow between each ridge. The seed of the potato was inserted into these ridges by merely sticking a spade into the ground and dropping the seed behind the spade, which was then withdrawn, leaving the potato two or three inches beneath the soil. Sometimes poorer peasants who did not possess a spade used their hands or improvised with sticks.

Another dangerously attractive feature of potato sowing, as we shall see, was the increasing use of guano as a fertilizer in the years before the Famine, because it gave a better yield than the amounts of either seaweed or manure hitherto available. The variety of potato most favored was "the Lumper," a large ugly potato that was not particularly tasty but was highly nutritious and returned a good yield.

Subdivision of holdings compounded the problems caused by early and improvident marriage. The holders of tiny plots of say 10 acres commonly subdivided them so as to give a dowry to a daughter. It would not be uncommon for a farmer possessing 10 acres to divide eight of them among four daughters, so that they could marry. The farmer and his wife could get sufficient potatoes to live on from their remaining two acres. Any sons were expected to negotiate similar dowries from prospective fathers-in-law. Subdivision contributed to the fact that on the eve of the Famine there were some 135,000 holdings of less than one acre in Ireland. Of the remaining, roughly 750,000 holdings, half were less than 10 acres and 25 percent between 10 and 20 acres.

Famine hung over the mud cabins of Ireland like the sword of Damocles. For approximately three months of every year the average family lived in a state of continuous hunger as the old potato stock became exhausted in March or April. This was also the planting season. As the popular saying had it, potatoes planted "in for Paddy" came "up for Billy." That is to say potatoes planted before the feast of St. Patrick on March 17 were edible on the feast day of William of Orange, July 12. Near the sea the diet could be supplemented with occasional fish, shellfish, periwinkles, mussels, and barnacles found along the shore.

But inland, during these "hungry months" as they were known, it was common for some menfolk to be found lying inert in their cabins to conserve energy while the women went about their neighborhoods begging or resorting to stratagems such as boiling the yellow-flowered rape plant that grew wild in the fields, as a vegetable. The charity of the better-off ensured that a diet of vegetables such as cabbage and occasional loaves of bread were also provided. These extreme conditions have produced widely varying descriptions of how the people survived.

Giving evidence before a House of Commons Select Committee meeting on the State of the Poor in Ireland in 1825, the leading Catholic political leader of the day, Daniel O'Connell, expressed astonishment at not only how healthy people remained in these conditions but how cheerful. They made an effort to have clean clothing for Sunday and occupy themselves with pastimes such as storytelling or hurling. However, addressing the same committee, the leading clerical figure, Bishop Doyle of Kildare and Leighlin, said that he often prayed that God would take him from this life so that he would no longer have to witness the misery of his flock in County Carlow. The bishop testified that there could not be worse poverty in other parts of Ireland than in his diocese.

In fact, Carlow is surrounded by fertile land, and the conditions in any of the western counties of Kerry, Clare, Galway, Mayo, Sligo, and Donegal were often far worse. In Mayo, for instance, there were few roads to speak of. Access to the clusters of swarming mud cabins, known as clachans (too small to qualify as villages), meant negotiating reeking mounds of animal, vegetable, and human waste girding the cottages. In the circumstances one can understand O'Connell's amazement at the health of the people. Hygiene was not a priority in nineteenth-century Ireland. Some good came out of the mounds of waste because they could be used as manure.

One might combine the observations of O'Connell and Bishop Doyle before the select committee and surmise that although there was widespread depression and despair, the physique of many an Irish laborer was found to be superior to his English counterpart. Above all the most striking testimony to the strength of the Irish peasantry comes from the numbers so eagerly sought after by English recruiting sergeants. Over a third of Wellington's armies during the Napoleonic Wars came from Ireland. As we shall see later, this statistic would be conveniently overlooked when British statesmen thundered against "Irish disloyalty" during the famine.

With the coming into force of the Act of Union, Ireland became a largely rural society dependent on an inefficiently run agricultural economy.

This came at a time when, following the ending of the Napoleonic Wars, agricultural prices went up by up to 50 percent. Much of the buzz went out of Dublin, and with the transfer of powers to Westminster, talent and economic activity of all sorts followed. There was a brain drain of publishers, poets, politicians, and craftsmen. Social life declined, accentuating the trend toward absenteeism among landlords. Much of Ireland's ruling class came to take no more interest in the land they owned than they would in the affairs, say, of the South American mines in which they owned stock. Working conditions and disasters were assessed, if at all, in terms of the effect on the price of stocks and shares. Under the Act of Union some 100 Irish members of Parliament were supposed to represent the interests of Ireland, but in an assembly of over 600 MPs the Irish were ineffective lobbyists.

The management of more and more Irish estates passed into the hands of third parties, agents appointed either by the landlords themselves or by middlemen who rented large sections of land from the landlords and parceled them out in smaller and ever more costly rents to landless men drawn mainly from the small farmer and laboring class. It was here, at this level of society, that the potato would exert its catastrophic influence on the Irish population.

In this badly organized and resentful society the Catholic population probably outweighed that of the Protestants by a margin of 20 Catholics to 1 Protestant. In the North, in the province of Ulster, which had been more thoroughly planted by Protestant settlers, in particular Scottish Presbyterians, Catholics were thought to outnumber Protestants by a lesser margin of 2 to 1.

In these circumstances, the growth in the Catholic population would prove to be not a basis for economic or political growth, but a demographic disaster. By the time of the Famine, Irish society was like a pyramid at the peak of which resided the viceroy and the chief secretary who nominally controlled the country. On the higher slopes of the pyramid dwelt the landlords, some 10,000 of them. They dominated the land, although in practice many of their estates were usually mortgaged to the hilt because of their extravagant lifestyles. Only a handful of these landlords devoted the profits of their lands to improving their estates; most spent their income in London or on the Continent. An Irish middle class began to make a faltering appearance as the bigger farmers, both Protestant and Catholic, began to profit from the access to the protected British market that the Act of Union created. About 3 percent of the population could be thought of as rich farmers, and some 76 percent, mainly cottiers and laborers, lived at the base. The peasantry and the people generally had a reputation for hospitality—various writers of the period have attested to the fact that a traveler was always offered a share of whatever food was available prior to the Famine.

The privileged class attended the splendid balls and levees in Dublin Castle for which invitations were eagerly sought by a colonial society. Administrative decisions, the dispensation of patronage, and the day-to-day running of the country were all directed by the castle, which the population looked to as the government of the country, but the reins of power controlling the overall political, financial, and military situation were held in London, where all major decisions were made. Absenteeism also had the seriously harmful side effect of deepening the leadership deficit throughout the countryside. When the Famine struck, many of the class to whom both the English and the Irish looked for leadership in the relief effort were simply not there. The clergy and nuns, both Catholic and Protestant, did what they could to fill the vacuum.

There were, however, a number of areas in which the Irish most assuredly did not have a reputation for civility, principally agrarian violence and faction fighting. Faction fighting would appear to have its origins in two influences that affected the Irish character. The martial spirit of the Celts and the even more fiery spirits—often distilled from the potato—formed part of the background to the faction fights. These appear to have begun in Tipperary around the start of the nineteenth century and then quickly spread to other parts of the country. Sometimes several hundred participants took part on either side. The most famous fight at Ballyveagh Strand in County Kerry in 1834 involved some 3,000 contestants, of whom over two hundred were killed. The fighting gangs were based on extended families or on parishes, and normally fights took place either at fairs or on feast days or public holidays. The weapons were chiefly seasoned blackthorn sticks, whose lethal properties were sometimes added to by the insertion of lead in the butts. These killing instruments were the origin of the shillelaghs carried by today's leprechaun dolls. An even more deadly weapon was the whitethorn stake, a cut from which could prove fatal. Sometimes scythes and slash hooks were used. The picture painted by Martin Scorsese of Irish tribal gang warfare, in his film of the Famine period, *The Gangs of New York,* contained a core of truth. But while the deaths and injuries sustained in these fights were obviously lamented, the faction fighters tend to be remembered not as thugs, but as perhaps misguided fighters for the honor of the parish or for that of their family. Efforts by the clergy to end the fights were sometimes resisted to the point where priests were driven from their parishes. Contemporary accounts speak of clergy vainly riding through milling crowds of faction fighters lashing around uselessly with horsewhips. This flouting of clerical authority was most unusual. To the average Irish peasant the priest was the only sympathetic authority figure that he or she encountered. The Catholic clergy received no money from the State and would not have accepted it had it been offered, believing that their relationships with their flocks were strengthened by living solely on whatever the people provided.

The Protestant clergy were a race apart. They lived in bigger houses than their Catholic counterparts and, as the established church, received their incomes from the State. These incomes were considerable: the Archbishop of Armagh received £14,664 (almost thrice the salary of the president of the United States at that time); and ten other bishops received incomes varying from £7,600 to £2,310. To make matters worse in Catholic eyes, the cost of paying the Protestant clergymen at one stage fell on the Catholic population through a system known as tithes, whereby they were obliged to pay a tenth of their incomes to the clergymen of an often hostile faith. This system resulted in what was known as the "tithe war," a violent protest against the tithes. In 1838 a law was passed reducing the tithes and directing that the remainder should be paid as part of the tenant's rent to the landlord.

Faction fighting was a relatively short-lived and open form of violence. But agrarian violence, and its accompanying secret societies, was far more sinister and more widespread. Agrarian secret societies grew directly out of the appalling land situation. The powerful Caravat group, formed from landless men who wanted rents reduced and wages increased, fought with the Shanavests, who were generally representative of larger farmers and wanted to keep rents high and wages low.

By the end of the eighteenth century, secret societies were well established throughout the country, generally based on localized grievances stemming from landlordism. In the North, the largely Protestant Hearts of Oak Association objected to the cess tax, which involved doing so many days of manual and horse work without pay, or building roads, which were often constructed solely for landlords' convenience.

Bad as the situation created by British rule was, there was always an Irishman eager and willing to make things worse. A particular problem for the laborers and small farmers were the activities of "Gombeen Men," shopkeepers who cheated their customers in various ways, ranging from charging 20 percent above the normal price of goods for credit, to cheating them into accepting a lower price for their own produce if they had it. Sometimes "Gombeen Men" engaged in moneylending. Tubbercurry, in County Sligo, had a particularly bad reputation for usury. The "Gombeen Men," and sometimes the landlords, had a further black mark against them that was recorded in the oral history of the fireside and the tavern, what Liam O'Flaherty termed "the occasional exercise of the *droit de seigneur.*"[4]

The Hearts of Steel were formed in opposition to high rents, and ultimately morphed into the Orange Order. Their Catholic mirror image organization, The Defenders, joined the United Irishmen in time to be slaughtered in the 1798 rebellion.

In the South differing bands often went by the generic title of "ribbon men," from their insignia of ribbons, or "rockites." This last was a reference to the mythical and nocturnal Captain Rock, who signed threatening letters to landlords and their agents. Widespread attacks were carried out in Captain Rock's name. The most extensive association was the White Boys, so called because they wore white smocks over their heads to conceal their identities. This oath-bound organization was the most feared and most effective of the agrarian societies. A knowledgeable and sympathetic visitor to Ireland, Gustave de Beaumont, said of the White Boys:

They lived by an atrocious Savage code, worthy of a semi barbarous population, which abandoned to itself, has no light to guide its efforts, finds no sympathy to assuage its passions, and is reduced to look to rude instincts for the means of safety and protection. . . . These are banditti of a singular kind; to obtain arms, or vengeance, they commit all sorts of outrages, while they abstain from the gold and silver under their hands.[5]

The White Boys did not hesitate to use murder as a tool against informers, landlords, middlemen, or people who rented land from which a previous tenant had been evicted. One of the most brutal and unusual portions of their code included the following:

Let us strike the culpable, not only in their persons, but in their dearest interests and affections; let not only their cattle be houghed [hamstrung], their houses burned, their land turned up, their harvests destroyed, but let their friends and relations be devoted to death, the wives and daughters to dishonour.

The contents of the pre-Famine newspapers show that the White Boys' code was not mere rhetoric. They record thousands of cases of assault, animal mutilation, leveling of fences, and murder. Folk culture also contains occasional dark references to rape, which this researcher has not been able to substantiate. However, it must be acknowledged that this crime is commonly found in the wake of the dislocation caused by famine and natural disaster in other parts of the world when predators such as pedophiles emerge from their lairs. And there is the indisputable fact that the inclusion of the "dishonor" of the womenfolk of their enemies in the White Boys' oath certainly indicates at least a willingness to contemplate this crime. Overall, however, the White Boys, Terry Alts (this particular society took its name from a man named Terry Alt, wrongly accused of assault), and all the other societies never posed a serious threat either to the British Army or to the Act of Union.

The contrast between the murderous strain in Irish peasant society where their fellows were concerned and the docility and resignation with which they submitted to an unjust state attracted the attention of two experienced French observers who visited Ireland in 1835. One was de Beaumont himself, the other Alexis de Tocqueville, who had just published his famous work, *Democracy in America*. After witnessing a crowd of some two hundred starving people quietly obeying a parish priest's instructions to go home and wait until the following day when he hoped he would have food for them, the Frenchmen observed that the peasants' behavior showed extraordinary virtue.

The priest replied it was not virtue merely but also fear that motivated the people. The conditions in which the Irish peasantry lived would have caused any other European population to rise in revolt, but the Irish lived paralyzed in the ever-present shadow of the gallows or of transportation.

The priest had analyzed the peasant psychology correctly. It would take almost another century before the experiments of the American psychiatrist Martin Seligman gave a name to it: "learned helplessness." Working with dogs, Seligman discovered that dogs caged with an electrical device that was sometimes turned on at the sound of a bell learned to get away from the current when the bell rang. However, dogs that had been caged in a situation where the current still flowed, despite the ringing of the bell, made no effort to escape the shock.

It is worth noting that the two Frenchmen conducted their conversation with the parish priest some ten years before the Great Famine. In those years, as we shall see, nothing was done to prevent Irish peasant society from sliding into even greater helplessness.

But in the midst of the turmoil and the squalor of rural life, a visitor to Dublin could have observed a gilded society peacefully at play.

The landowning political and economic elite, known as the Ascendency, who controlled Ireland enjoyed lives of luxurious (albeit often debt-ridden) splendor. Lord Cloncurry described Dublin before the Act of Union of 1800 as being

> one of the most agreeable places of residence in Europe. There were no conveniences belonging to a capital in these days which it did not possess. Society in the upper classes was as brilliant and polished as that of

Paris in its best days, while social intercourse was conducted with the conviviality that could not be equaled in France.[6]

The brilliance dimmed considerably after the Union. Both before and after the Union heavy drinking was the norm. The Irish gentry seem to believe that the only proper place to dwell was beyond their means. In his famous work *The Querist,* Bishop Berkeley observed that many gentlemen in England with incomes of £1,000 a year, for example, did not have wine in the house, but that this could not be said of a gentleman in Ireland with less than £100 a year.

The famous satirist Dean Swift wrote to his friend Mrs. Delany before she married, assuring her that, as the cost of living in Ireland was a third of that of England, she could live in Dublin at least three times better than in England.

Mrs. Delany's style of entertaining validated Swift's claim. One of her menus, for a dinner for four guests, two of whom were bishops, consisted of the following first course: "Fish, beef steaks, soup, rabbits and onions, Fillet veal." Second course: "Turkey pout-Salmon grilde, pickled salmon, quails, little Terrene peas, cream Apple pie, mushrooms, crab, leveret, cheese cakes. The Dessert included: Blamange, cherries, Dutch cheese, raspberries and cream, sweetmeats and jelly, strawberries and cream, almond cream, currants and gooseberries, orange butter."

While Mrs. Delany's table might perhaps be termed exceptional, it was true, as she observed, that no gentleman earning £1,000 a year would dream of serving less than seven dishes at a course, apart from wines and champagne, and he would provide two such dinners, at least, a week.

Irish estates produced the money for these expenditures. As the mid-century and Famine approached, declining incomes and the departure of many of the "gentry" to London following the Act of Union reduced the scale of entertainment appreciably. Nevertheless, for the upper classes, Dublin was a hospitable and social place.

However, all was far from fine wining and dining in Dublin, which with 175,000 inhabitants was the United Kingdom's second-largest city, after London. Here the brutal rural contrast between Catholic peasantry and the Protestant Ascendancy continued in the contrast between the splendor of Dublin's Palladian architecture and her horrific slums.

The Rev. James Whitelaw, who carried out a survey of the Liberties area in 1798, the year of a rebellion that worsened rather than improved the condition of the people, found

> people crowded together to a degree distressing to humanity. A single apartment in one of these truly wretched habitations, rates from 1 to 2 shillings per week and to lighten this rent two, three, even four families become joint tenants. I have frequently surprised 10 to 16 persons, of all ages and sexes, in a room, not 15 ft. wide, stretched on filthy straw swarming with vermin. . . . Into the backyard of each house ordure, frequently 10 feet deep, is flung from the windows of each apartment, the stench I could scarce contain for a few minutes.[7]

During the Famine Dublin had no sewerage system, and when tenement areas flooded, as they frequently did, the halls and basement areas of the houses became cesspools several inches deep. Even the most fashionable streets had cesspools dug in front of the houses. When these were opened and emptied, there was "a horrid sight and smell." This would also prove a fertile breeding ground for fevers and famine-fueled disease.

Another evil that Whitelaw described was the enormous number of "dram-shops" in Dublin licensed to sell raw spirits, "a poison productive of vice, riot and disease, hostile to all habits of decency, honesty and industry, and in short, destructive to the souls and bodies of our fellow creature."[8] Evidence to support the good clergyman's claim abounded in the Dublin of the time. A poor woman who fell from an upstairs window while hanging out linen to dry suffered fatal injuries and lay in agony in the mud of a busy street for a day and a night suffering from breaks to her leg and thigh while people stepped over her thinking she was just another drunk.

The government encouraged distilling industries because of the revenue they created, and country landlords also favored low rates of excise duty, which led to high profits in grain. Excessive drinking was not confined to Dublin. Alcohol, which could also be distilled from potatoes, was the Irish opium and wreaked havoc on both rich and poor. The other opium of course was religion.

THREE

A MILLION DEATHS
OF NO USE

"In the present Convention, genocide means any of the following acts committed with intent to destroy, in whole or in part, a national, ethnical, racial or religious group, as such:

> (a) Killing members of the group;
> (b) Causing serious bodily or mental harm to members of the group;
> (c) Deliberately inflicting on the group conditions of life calculated to bring about its physical destruction in whole or in part;
> (d) Imposing measures intended to prevent births within the group;
> (e) Forcibly transferring children of the group to another group."

—*United Nations Convention on the Prevention and Punishment of the Crime of Genocide, Article 2*

THE LAND OF IRELAND WAS DANGEROUSLY overburdened by the weight of human stock. What was needed to avert an inevitable disaster was a humane system of assisted emigration in combination with a sustained effort at reforming the land system, developing fisheries, and building Irish infrastructure such as roads, bridges, harbors, and canals. The facts of the situation were well known in London. Throughout the nineteenth century there had been a series of inquiries into conditions in Ireland in which the facts had been clearly set forth. Mention has already been made of the Select Committee on Ireland of the House of Commons before which Daniel O'Connell and Bishop Doyle gave evidence. This issued not one but three comprehensive reports in 1830. There were also separate governmental inquiries into topics such as "Irish distress," and of course there was a constant flow of information on the state of the country from Dublin Castle to Whitehall, the seat of British administration. A comprehensive report on "Scarcity in Ireland" was laid before both houses of parliament as the effects of the blight began to be felt, detailing the many occasions that relief had had to be administered between 1822 and 1839.[1] The various counties mentioned, Cork, Kerry, Galway, Mayo, Sligo, and many others, would all become places of horror during the Famine. On the very eve of the Famine itself the prestigious Devon Commission sat gathering evidence on the failings of the Irish land system. The public hearings were attended by knowledgeable people from all over the country, and anyone reading their findings can have been left in no doubt as to what the problems of Ireland were and how they should be addressed.

However, Ireland instead went on the back burner for most of the pre-Famine decade. With the growth of English industrialization sizeable areas of urban poverty were created as people flooded into the towns. The traditional dispensers of poor relief, the aristocracy, found their pockets increasingly under pressure. Social welfare, or poor relief as it was known at the time, became the topic du jour.

Throughout the 1830s, there was a major theoretical debate among political economists, but this involved Ireland only in a peripheral and ultimately extremely harmful fashion. The major focus of controversy centered on how the English poor should be dealt with. Once a solution to English welfare problems had been decided on, attention then turned to Ireland, where a variation of the English system of welfare was applied. The finding that was decided on was irrelevant to the land situation and, when the Famine did strike, the introduction of what was known as the Poor Law to Ireland helped to worsen the horrors of famine. England had had a social welfare system since Elizabethan times, but Ireland had none and the plan imposed on Ireland had no roots in history and was largely irrelevant to Ireland's needs.

The English debate discussed not merely how or whether to assist the poor but laissez-faire, the prevailing doctrine of non-interference with trade. The debate was influenced by widespread Victorian attitudes that poverty was a self-inflicted wound, incurred through bad habits.

Political economists debated earnestly on the morality of aiding the poor because of the consequent risk of stultifying initiative and self-help among the lower orders. The real problem of course was cost, but the protagonists couched their arguments in moralistic terms. More and more as the debate progressed, one finds that the authorities cited by protagonists tended to lace their arguments with a dose of providentialism.

Providence, the divine will, was declared to have a large bearing on the subject, as it generally does when the rich debate the poor, or the strong confront the weak. It was the era in which in America the indigenous Americans were going down before a similar doctrine: Manifest Destiny.

A central figure in the debate was a classical economist. Nassau William Senior, the first professor of political economy at Oxford University, preached, among other things, that it was not the duty of the State to alleviate poverty that came about through the fault of the individual. English poor law owed a great deal to his theories and, during the Famine, Whig apologists would see to it that the idea of Irish culpability for Irish poverty would become widespread among the British public. "Lazy beds" was used as a term of derision to indicate that the Irish even brought their laziness to bear on their potato cultivation. Nassau Senior criticized Irish landlords for neglecting "the duty for the performance of which Providence created [them,] the keeping down population."[2]

A Royal Commission, of which Nassau Senior was a member, issued a report in 1834, which became the New Poor Law Act of 1834. He was a confidant of the prime minister's and cabinet members and through his writings in such journals as *The Edinburgh Review* became one of the most influential voices raised in the great debate concerning how Irish poverty should be tackled. In England, Nassau Senior is remembered as being a very pleasant man who became a lifelong friend of, among others, Alexis de Tocqueville, who was deeply sympathetic and insightful concerning Irish problems.

In Ireland, however, he is chiefly remembered for a comment passed by the great English educationalist Benjamin Jowett, the Master of Balliol, who said that he had no time for political economists since he overheard Nassau Senior say that even if one million people were to die in the Irish famine it would do no good.

Since the days of the Famine people have debated as to whether Nassau Senior's comments were either taken out of context, or whether they should be regarded as epitomizing official England's lack of feeling for Irish suffering. The latter would appear to be the case. We have the evidence of the prime minister responsible for dealing with the Irish catastrophe, Lord John Russell, to indicate that the million-deaths view was not confined to Nassau Senior but was widespread among his associates.

Many years after the Famine had ended, Prime Minister Russell wrote to his friend Chichester Fortescue MP on the improved state of Ireland at that time, 1868. He said:

> The remedies have been due partly to the divine Providence and partly to human exertions. Many years ago the Political Economy Club of London came, as I was told, to a resolution that the emigration of two million of the population of Ireland would be the best cure for her social evils. Famine and emigration have accomplished a task beyond the reach of legislation or government; and Providence has justly afflicted us by the spectacle of the results of the entire dependence on potato cultivation, and by the old fires of disaffection which had been lighted in the hearts of Irishmen, and are now burning with such freshness on the bank of the Hudson and the Potomac.[3]

Russell's comment sheds an important light on British governmental approaches to tackling Irish poverty. The potato was the cause of the Irish disaster, not misgovernment. None of the theorizing economists are remembered for addressing themselves to the ultimately fatal question: What happens if the potato fails? A mountain of corpses was of course the answer, but the public view of them was obscured by the quite obscene use of the concept of providentialism—divine Providence intervening in Irish affairs to take care of problems created by deficiencies in the Irish character. At the time of the Famine Victorian self-confidence was understandably at a high level. It was the era of the Great Exhibition, that showcase of Victorian advancement.

The African emperor Theodorus exclaimed despairingly but truly: "First come the missionaries then the traders and then the canon. I prefer to go directly to the canon." He did, and he died for it. Britain's Navy and Army, often in the wake of her missionaries, were adding fresh territories to the British Empire by the hour, and Victorian accomplishments in agriculture, engineering, and science caused many Britons to see themselves as standing at the apex of the civilized world. The contrast with shabby, inefficient, run-down, Catholic Ireland was stark. The inclination of Protestant England to take a share of blame for this contrast was almost nil.

The arch high priest of laissez-faire is generally regarded as being Adam Smith. The members of the Political Economy Club mentioned by Russell may in turn be regarded as Smith's ideological followers. Smith believed that when the individual pursued self-interest he indirectly assisted society as a whole because it created competition in the free market. This kept prices low and created the incentive for the creation of goods and services. In his celebrated work, *The Wealth of Nations*, he wrote:

> The natural effort of every individual to better his own condition, when suffered to extend itself with freedom and security, is so powerful a principle, that it alone, and without any assistance, is not only capable of carrying on the society to wealth and prosperity, but of surmounting a hundred impertinent obstructions with which the folly of human laws too often encumbers its operation.[4]

Charles Trevelyan, who, as we shall see, was effectively placed in charge of relief in Ireland, issued copies of Smith's writings to his subordinates in Ireland as guidebooks for their approach to the question of feeding the starving. Unsurprisingly the results did not err on the side of either generosity or humanity.

Jeremy Bentham, another club member, wrote: "Laissez-faire, in short, should be the general practice: every departure, unless required by some great good, is a certain evil."

Ireland did not come under the heading of "some great good." Nassau Senior shared the view of Thomas Malthus that overpopulation must lead to famine and that it was necessary for the working class to exercise restraint in matters of procreation. These men argued that extending their relief to the poor was dangerous because it encouraged overpopulation and would swallow the resources of the nation. Malthus therefore argued this of a poor man: "If he cannot get subsistence from his parents, on whom he has a just demand, has *no claim of right to the smallest portion of food,* and in fact has no business to be where he is."[5]

This view was of course of monumental irrelevance to the cottiers of West Mayo. But apart from irrelevance there was another, specifically anti-Irish element in Malthus's teachings. He continuously argued that proximity meant that there was an ever-growing threat of Irish paupers one day swamping the market and driving down wages and hampering trade. He maintained: "The land in Ireland is infinitely more peopled than in England; and to give full effect to the natural resources of the country, *a great part of the population should be swept from the soil.*"[6]

In addition to Nassau Senior and Thomas Malthus, the influential Irishman Edmund Burke also came down on the side of providentialism. He too set his face against governmental intervention when "distress" threatened: "It is not by breaking the laws of commerce, which are the laws of nature and consequently the laws of God that we are to place our hope of softening the divine displeasure to remove any calamity under which we suffer."[7]

All these theories, expounded from the lectern, in the journals where influence was made, in the clubs of the well-off, across the dining tables of the mighty, played a part in formulating the policies that would shortly contribute to ensuring that some millions of Irish would have no dinners at all.

Ireland was not entirely without friends at Westminster. The radical independent MP for Stroud, Gloucestershire, George Poulett Scrope, attacked

the Malthusian approach and that of factory farming. He continually highlighted the abuses of the Irish poor law and in his thinking was close to
Irish spokespersons as disparate as Bishop Doyle of Kildare and William
Sharman Crawford, another radical MP, high sheriff of Down, and an advocate of land reform and tenant right. This doctrine, regarded as heresy
by landlords, held that tenants should have some security in their holdings
and an entitlement to a share in the value of any improvements they made.
Both men achieved considerable publicity for the Irish issue, but it would be
stretching matters to say that they greatly influenced the course of events.
One British cabinet member who did manage to exert a benign influence
was Viscount Morpeth, a humanitarian Whig who succeeded in getting the
Quakers involved with the Irish situation. The Quakers' subsequent efforts,
as we shall see, were one of the few unadulterated pluses of the relief effort.

The Royal Commission on Poor Law in England produced a report
in 1834, however, largely written by Senior. This had more to do with the
theories of political economists than with the grinding reality of life as lived
in London slums, but it did have the merit, in governmental eyes, of sparing
the Treasury's purse. This was because the commission had enlisted the aid
of a couple of tightwads who would have literally been quite at home in a
Dickensian workhouse.

The two were the Rev. Thomas Whately, rector of Cookham and
Maidenhead, and George Nicholls, the overseer of Saltwell Parish. These
men were not only devotees of the theories of Adam Smith and the Political
Economy Club, they were also demonstrably successful penny pinchers.
They had deliberately set out to make workhouse life actively unattractive, so that only the most destitute would approach these places for relief.
Moreover, that relief would be administered only under the roof of a workhouse. Nicholls and Whately frowned on outdoor relief, which was held to
be demoralizing as it encouraged recipients not to look for work but to stay
at home in the dreaded occupation of procreation.

While these attempts to reform the English poor law situation went
forward, ultimately taking legislative shape in the English Poor Law Act of
1834, the government also turned its attention to doing something about
the intractable problem of Irish poverty. The government's motivation was

not charitable, but was inspired by proximity. There was a growing fear that if something were not done to tackle Irish poverty in Ireland, the resultant emigration would, as Malthus and company predicted, have disastrous results for England.

The government set up a Royal Commission in 1833 under the chairmanship of Richard Whately, the Protestant archbishop of Dublin who had succeeded Senior as professor of political economy at Oxford, but had resigned on being appointed to Dublin.

Like Whately, the other members of the commission were political economists and were expected to produce a report backing the ideas of Nicholls and Whately, and those who thought like them, when it came to sparing pennies on the poor. And here it should be pointed out that, if the fact is not already self-evident, the great attraction of political economists for politicians was that they stressed the curtailment of expenditure and gave the withholding of money from the poor a respectable moral dimension.

However, the commission did its work extremely thoroughly, interviewing 1,500 people and taking three years to compile a report that came up with the alarming figure that almost two and a half million Irish needed assistance for several months of every year—a fact that of course had been made known to the House of Commons by Daniel O'Connell several years earlier. Whately's commission was guilty of further heresy inasmuch as it found against the English system of providing relief within the confines of a workhouse and recommended instead that the ills of Ireland be cured by economic regeneration. They suggested that large-scale emigration to the colonies be encouraged and proposed that fisheries be developed and land reclaimed among other measures.

These were exactly the sort of measures the situation called for but not what the government had expected from disciples of Nassau Senior. The government regarded the commission's proposals as being too expensive, and significantly, Russell, who would shortly be presiding over the results of the failure to introduce these kinds of policies to Ireland, condemned the report. He felt that it should have confined itself to dealing with the problems of the destitute, not those of improving "the general welfare of the country." Nassau Senior, from whom the government sought advice, commented that it was the Irish landlords who were responsible for poverty in Ireland, not the government. Senior's argument and those who shared it would have a direct bearing on the course of the Famine. The political fiction of the time was that Ireland was an integral part of the United Kingdom, in the same way as Wales and Scotland, because of the Act of Union, but the political economists argued that it was the responsibility of the Irish population to solve its own problems. Despite the Act of Union Ireland was regarded as "their" country when it came to relief expenditures by the British government.

By this stage the dogs in the street could have informed any political economist, Treasury official, or political decision makers that Ireland needed a solution to the land problem, not a tinkering with the poor law based on a disdainful unwilling charity dependent on the introduction of the workhouse system to Ireland. Such an approach, however, would not have come within an ass's roar of the mind-set of Victorian decision makers. Apart from laissez-faire and the question of cost, the Irish landlords, though viewed with increasing disfavor, were still a force to be relied on to help subdue Ireland should rebellion threaten. Irish landlords were still a power in the House of Lords, and most importantly, some of the biggest Irish landlords were powerful members of the British government: Clanricarde, Landsdowne, and Palmerston, all of whom, as we shall see, were to exert a baleful influence on the course of the Famine.

Once more recourse was available to the arch penny pincher George Nicholls, who had the added advantage that he knew nothing about Ireland. He was appointed the first resident Irish poor law commissioner, with the assistance of four other Commissioners trained in English workhouse ways and all equally ignorant about Ireland.

Given the ineffectual state of Irish public opinion, none of the five gentlemen suffered any great pressure to take Irish susceptibilities into consideration as they introduced their schemes.

The Irish poor law came into operation in 1838. The country was divided into 130 new administrative units known as "unions." Each union would have its own workhouse, centrally situated near a market town.[8] Apart from the fact that workhouses were ludicrously insufficient to cater to the populations that they served, the union system also suffered from another crippling flaw. Some of the districts in which unions were established were too poor to make any significant contribution to relief, and good landlords who had the misfortune to find themselves located in a bad union area were dragged down by the profligacy, or simply the poverty, of bad landlords. Overall, the insufficiency of workhouses and the lack of resources for unions occurred in the districts where relief was most needed, in the areas hardest hit by famine in the West of Ireland. For example, a workhouse was built on the Martin estate at Clifden in County Galway. Martin was an eccentric figure known for his gambling, for his fearsome prowess as a duelist, and for his kindness to animals, which led him to found the Royal Society for the Prevention of Cruelty to Animals and to be nicknamed "Humanity Dick." Martin lived in splendor at Balinahinch Castle on a huge estate comprising some 200,000 acres and including parts of Mayo and most of Connemara, that incredibly beautiful, but barren area of County Galway stretching westward from Galway City along Galway Bay, skirting the coastline until it reaches the open Atlantic.

A workhouse was built on the estate, at Clifden, even though it was notorious for being crippled by debts, mainly through Martin's gambling. The "King of Connemara," as he was referred to in Ireland, had had to flee the country several years earlier upon losing his parliamentary immunity. On his death in 1834 his son Thomas became his heir. During the Famine Thomas died from a fever contracted while inspecting the awful conditions in the overcrowded workhouse, which could not cope with the demands placed upon it. The workhouse went bankrupt and had to close, with catastrophic results for its inmates, Clifden, and its environs. The Martin estate was subsequently put up for auction, and one of its principal attractions as cited by the auctioneers was the fact that none of the tenants who had lived on the estate before the Famine lived there any longer. Given the population density per acre at the time, this could have indicated a death toll of some 200,000 people. Overall Galway had the fourth-highest death toll of the Famine. (Mayo had the worst at 58.4 percent of excess mortality per thousand.)

No matter how one strains for objectivity, those percentages make the workhouse approach to the Irish situation seem nothing more than an obscene irrelevancy. Nicholls estimated that the workhouses would cater to 1 percent of the Irish poor, some 100,000 paupers. It should be remembered that the Commission on the Poor had estimated that more than twenty-five times this number required assistance in any given year. It was laid down that life inside the workhouses be made as unpleasant as possible and the work provided was to be as "irksome" as possible so as to encourage paupers to speedily quit the workhouse. The diet was made deliberately monotonous. Families only were admitted and once inside the workhouse the sexes were strictly segregated. The guiding philosophy of the poor law was that of the political economists who believed that poverty was the fault of the individual and that people should be discouraged from entering the workhouses, not encouraged to do so.

There was to be no outdoor relief and of course there was to be no "right" to relief. If a workhouse happened to be full, that was just too bad for the supplicant. As the respected famine historian Christine Kinealy has said: "Overall, both in principle and in underlying ethos, the Irish Poor Law was intended to be more stringent than its English counterpart. Its provisions illustrated an approach to policy that underpinned the government's response to the onset of the famine in Ireland only seven years later."[9]

Stringency by itself would have made the workhouse approach to alleviating the plight of those millions of Irish whose hold on life was more precarious than most of Europe's peasantry completely inadequate. However, as we shall see, the government subsequently, in the summer of 1847, would add one more brand to the burning. With the ostensible objective of forcing Irish landlords to make a contribution toward the cost of relief, a rating system was introduced. Landlords would become liable for rates on land valued at less than £4 per year. This meant that at a time of falling rents, caused by famine, cash-strapped landlords now found themselves liable to further financial burdens. The provision fell heaviest on the West of the country, where poverty, subdivision, and overcrowding have already been described. Even if they had the inclination, many landlords did not have the wherewithal to pay this tax. What they did have was an incentive to clear their tenants off the land. So pauperism was increased, not diminished, and the demand for workhouse relief, or any sort of relief, shot up. The demand for relief was further increased by what was known as the Gregory Clause, which was inserted into the poor law, as the rates legislation was being debated.

Gregory was one of the most clamorous of a group of Irish landlords who argued that there should be stringent tests for destitution and claimed that the rates bill would result in them being included among the destitute. Gregory's proposal meant that in order to benefit from relief the peasantry had to surrender any holding greater than a quarter of an acre. Gregory was the husband of Lady Gregory, one of the founders of the Abbey Theatre. Ironically, for a man who added immeasurably to the sufferings of the poor, fate decreed that Gregory himself would later lose much of his estate through gambling.

Such was the stage setting for the horror story that was about to unfold in Ireland. It is now time to turn to the role of a number of the chief actors in the drama. There were of course millions of bit players, but their lines were not listened to and echoed only in graveyards.

FOUR

FIVE ACTORS AND THE ORCHARDS OF HELL

"The General failures of which we read, are producing serious apprehensions. Yet surely the United States have little real cause to fear. If the potato were entirely extirpated, the people would enjoy an ample sufficiency of food. It is in the densely packed communities of Europe that the failure would be alarming, and in no country more, or so much, than in our own. But happily there is no ground for any apprehensions of the kind in Ireland. There may have been partial failures in some localities: but, we believe that there was never a more abundant potato crop in Ireland than there is at present."

—The Dublin Evening Post, *September 9, 1845*

OF THE MAIN PLAYERS WITH THE MOST SIGnificant roles in the Irish Famine, two were British prime ministers. The first prime minister, the Conservative Sir Robert Peel,[1] christened "Orange Peel" by Daniel O'Connell, was elected in 1842 and presided, with considerable success, over the Famine's onset. The second, who succeeded him in 1846 and remained in office until 1852, was Lord John Russell, who was anything but successful. The other main players were the chancellor of the exchequer under Russell, Sir Charles Wood, and the home secretary, Sir George Grey, an evangelical Protestant who was a strong supporter of Wood's policies toward Ireland. These policies were in large measure the creation of the man who was in many ways the key figure of the Famine story, Sir Charles Trevelyan, the assistant secretary to the Treasury and in effect the permanent head of the Civil Service. Ultimately, it was Trevelyan who had control of Irish famine expenditure—or lack of it.

This group of English decision makers and politicians may be considered the puppet masters who controlled the actions of all the secondary actors in the drama. These were the Irish lord lieutenant and the chief secretary, the relief commissioners, the coast guard, the British Army when required, the commissariat, and of course the Irish themselves, who provided an army of often not very efficient relief officials.

The leader of the Irish was the now-failing figure of Daniel O'Connell, in his day the greatest orator of them all. Very few Irish MPs of any stripe were admitted to the House of Commons. There were some 105 Irish MPs in all. These belonged roughly to the Liberal or Conservative parties, popularly known as the Whigs and the Tories. At the time of the Famine there were forty-two Conservatives and twenty-five Liberals. O'Connell's forty or so supporters were in the Liberal sphere, and he had temporarily shelved his repeal aspirations in favor of a more gradualist, incremental approach toward securing improvements for Ireland. However, O'Connell disliked Peel and took up the repeal campaign once more when the 1841 election ousted the Whigs with whom he was relatively friendly and restored Peel and the Conservatives to power. How much O'Connell secretly believed in the chances of repeal succeeding is a moot point, but he certainly mounted a spectacular public campaign to achieve it. How well founded these hopes were, or indeed his entire repeal campaign, is described below. O'Connell was a realist. His followers might sing:

We'll have an Irish parliament, fresh laws we will dictate,
Or we'll have satisfaction for the year of [98]

They might believe that repeal of the Union would bring prosperity, but O'Connell himself was under no illusions. Yeats wrote a famous poem about an incident in which a laborer is supposed to have shouted at O'Connell as he passed along the road. "Liberator, do you think we'll get Repeal?" O'Connell is said to have replied, "What does it matter to you, you'll still break stones."

There were no stone breakers in the Parliament; MPs had to have a certain income before being admitted. Feargus O'Connor, the Irish Chartist leader, was disbarred because he didn't have enough money.

O'Connell, a member of an old Kerry Catholic family, had had to be smuggled to France to obtain his education because of the Penal Laws. At their height the Penal Laws discriminated against both Catholics and Presbyterians in favor of the Anglican establishment. For example, Catholics could not own property, marry Protestants, gain an education, or sit in Parliament; they could not carry firearms, own a horse worth more than £5, or attain any position of consequence in either the law or the military. The anomaly of this last provision can be gauged from the number of Irishmen in Wellington's army.

O'Connell became one of the most successful lawyers in the history of the Irish bar. The severity with which the Penal Laws had hitherto been enforced had waned somewhat by the time O'Connell founded his political machine, the Catholic Association, in 1823. In a hard-fought campaign over the next four years the association became the vehicle he used to win Catholic Emancipation in 1829.

By this measure Catholics were allowed to enter Parliament, were given access to a variety of opportunities in the higher reaches of the law, and were allowed to enter the officer ranks of the military hitherto closed to them. O'Connell was barred from taking up his seat when first elected to the House of Commons in Clare, one of Ireland's most westerly counties, but he stood again the following year and became the first Catholic in modern history to be admitted to the Mother of Parliaments.

Although he aroused great hostility in the ranks of evangelical Protestantism and among those of Unionism, his physique, his oratory, and his durability made him one of the most commanding figures in the House of Commons. His energy was phenomenal. Apart from his legal practice and the time necessarily spent on political activity in Ireland, he had to contend with a factor not often adverted to in the history of Irish representation in the House of Commons both during O'Connell's lifetime and afterward: the stress involved in traveling between Ireland, particularly from faraway Kerry, in the southwest of Ireland, to London, to attend a far from welcoming Parliament by coach, rail, and boat, often across a stormy Irish Sea.

He was derided by his opponents as "the king of the beggars" and dismissed as a showman, both of which descriptions are accurate in terms of his methodology and the condition of the majority of his followers. But there was far more to O'Connell than either demagoguery or showmanship. He deserves to be regarded as the founder of the modern peaceful civil rights movement. His hatred of oppression was universal. "My heart walks abroad," he said, "and wherever the miserable is to be succoured, and the slaves to be set free, there my spirit is at home, and I do like to dwell."[2]

In America he was deified by the anti-slavery movement for his speeches in their favor and for the manner in which he turned down substantial money offers from slave owners who commanded twenty-seven votes in the House of Commons during the emancipation battle, saying: "Gentlemen, God knows that I speak for the saddest people the sun sees, but may my right hand forget its cunning and may my tongue cleave to the roof of my mouth before, to help Ireland, I keep silent on the negro question."

He denounced George Washington for owning slaves, a stand that brought him into serious conflict with powerful politico-religious figures like Archbishop Hughes of New York, who condemned him for interfering in America's domestic affairs. Some newspapers attacked him. The *New York Herald*, for example, falsely accused him of having a stable of concubines and a crop of illegitimate children whom his wife had to look after in their home.

Over a century and a half later, the *New York Times* recorded a more fitting testimonial for O'Connell. As this book was being written, during his June 2011 trip to Ireland, President Obama acknowledged the influence that O'Connell had on Frederick Douglass, the great abolitionist. Douglass was so impressed with O'Connell that he spent months in Dublin listening to his speeches and studying his methods.

O'Connell was nearing the end of his life when he took up the attempt to repeal the Act of Union. This campaign alone was an important event in Irish history, but it may have had a sinister side effect that has not hitherto been much adverted to by historians of the Famine. Documentary evidence suggests that the assistant secretary to the Treasury, Charles Trevelyan, a principal actor in the Famine drama, may have become prejudiced against the Irish cause from seeing the repeal movement in action at first hand.

Throughout 1843 Ireland witnessed an extraordinary phenomenon, what the London *Times* described as "monster meetings." These were held throughout the country and demanded repeal of the Act of Union. On April 19, 1843, 120,000 people attended a meeting at Limerick; five days later, on April 24, the crowd at Kells, County Meath, had grown to 150,000. By May 9, Peel, who had become prime minister two years previously, was sufficiently exercised to inform the House of Commons that he would not hesitate to seek additional powers to defeat the repeal movement. Shortly afterward, on May 21, a crowd of 300,000 was reported at Cashel in County Tipperary and 500,000 at a meeting in Cork. On August 15, O'Connell held a meeting at Tara in County Meath that was attended by 750,000 people, a gathering that was not surpassed in Ireland until the Eucharistic Congress held in Dublin in 1932.

Tara had been deliberately chosen. It was the ancient seat of the High Kings of Ireland, and "King Dan" was now the uncrowned king of Ireland. The "monster meetings" had been extraordinarily peaceful. International observers commented on the sway O'Connell held through his presence, his eloquence, and the sheer power of his voice, which reached a great distance into the crowds before his words were passed on through the further rows of spectators by stewards. The excellence of the stewarding and the complete absence of drunkenness impressed everyone who witnessed the meetings. Nothing even remotely resembling faction fighting occurred. Apart from O'Connell himself, one other figure has to be given credit for the success of the meetings: Father Matthew, the Capuchin monk who preached temperance to such effect that not one drunken shout could be produced by Dublin Castle note takers as evidence that the meetings were a danger to public order. Nevertheless, as O'Connell's meetings reached a crescendo, British fears and anger at the threat to the Union mounted accordingly.

O'Connell planned to hold the most significant meeting of all on October 8 at Clontarf, on the northern shores of Dublin City, the site visible from the battlements of Dublin Castle, where another Irish king, Brian Boru, had defeated the Vikings in 1014. O'Connell and the organizers had intended that the meeting would follow the pattern of those that had gone before: marshaled by priests, characterized by the saying of Mass and the presence of women and children, a melange of picnicking, politics, and religion, the whole entirely peaceful.

However, on the eve of the meeting, October 7, the British banned it. Heavily armed detachments of troops were mustered and warships were anchored in the bay with their guns trained on the gathering site. Had the meeting gone ahead, a bloodbath would have ensued. O'Connell bowed to the ban. He was subsequently sentenced to a year's imprisonment on a charge of conspiracy. He served only four months and those in conditions more akin to a hotel than a jail—the authorities feared to mistreat him, knowing the respect in which he was held.

But the strain of the obloquy he endured from his younger and more fiery followers, who reckoned that Ireland would have got more from defying the British, no matter what the bloodshed, together with the effects of his stressful life, his trial, and his imprisonment, took their toll. Four years later O'Connell would be dead, his political following in disarray. His last political effort, at the age of seventy-two, was a vain plea before an unsympathetic House of Commons for help for his helpless country. Benjamin Disraeli's scornful description of O'Connell's last speech summed up the diminished stature of the former Irish Titan. All he remembered of the occasion was "a feeble old man muttering before a table."[3]

His death would come to symbolize both the tragedy of the Famine and the enduring impetus it gave to the Irish physical force tradition. More than a century later, when the provisional IRA killed Lord Mountbatten, the organization cited the Famine as one justification for their action.

The man ultimately responsible for the banning of Clontarf was Sir Robert Peel, the Conservative prime minister. His treatment of O'Connell notwithstanding, Peel was a forward-looking man, if a cold and not very likable one. He was a reformer and an innovator. Using Ireland as a laboratory, as did many British decision makers in the nineteenth century, he set up the first Irish police force, the Irish Constabulary, in 1822, which ultimately

became the Royal Irish Constabulary in 1867. Its success led to the formation of the London Metropolitan Police and to the replication of the RIC in
colonies as far apart as Australia and Trinidad.

Before becoming prime minister, Peel had been chief secretary of
Ireland for six years and had shown himself an enemy of Catholic Ireland.
He had opposed Catholic Emancipation—although in later life he would
increase the grant for St. Patrick's College, Maynooth, the major Irish
Catholic seminary—and responded to Whiteboy activities not as indicators
of the need for reform of the land system but as signs that the Irish needed
more and tougher coercion laws, which he duly gave them.

By way of emphasizing where his sympathies lay, he used to stand on a
chair with one foot on the table after dinner and propose the Orange Toast,
of which there were, and are, at least two versions: "To the glorious, pious,
and immortal memory of the good and great king William, who delivered
us from Popery, slavery, arbitrary power, brass money, and wooden shoes."

The second version concludes with: "And here's a Fart for the Bishop
of Cork."

History is silent on the subject of which version Peel favored, but it
does show Peel in the 1840s with two major crises on his hands, the Corn
Laws controversy and the onset of famine in Ireland. One crisis, that of the
Corn Laws, directly militated against the solution of the other. As a result,
the verdict on the Tories' efforts of famine relief are reminiscent of that on
the curate's egg which, we are told, was "good in parts." That said, however,
it must be acknowledged that Peel did a lot better than did the Whig prime
minister, Lord John Russell, who succeeded him.

The Corn Laws debate, which led to Russell's replacing Peel, was one
of the most divisive to affect England since the Civil War in the seventeenth
century. Apart from the virulent opposition of the Whigs led by Lord John
Russell, Peel faced fervent internal opposition in his own Tory Party, whose
"Squireocracy" profited from the laws by keeping out foreign grains and,
at the same time, setting a high price for English- (and Irish-) produced
grains. The effects of this were felt most severely by the laboring classes
now flooding into the burgeoning Victorian industrial cities and forced to
contribute to the wealth of the landlord class through higher bread prices.

Peel himself was anti-protectionist and saw the removal of trade barriers as being essential for economic growth. He was a devotee of laissez-faire, but by October 1845 long-threatening disaster was coming at last, and Peel was grappling with the onset of famine in Ireland. By then he had in hand the multivolume report of the Devon Commission, which he had set up two years earlier, in 1843; the report contained glaring evidence that the land system in Ireland was rotten to the core and was a disaster waiting to happen. Famine had recently visited Ireland yet again, in 1839. The visitation had demonstrated, for anyone who wished to take note, the limitations of the theories of political economists and of the workhouse approach in the alleviation of "distress," as the effects of starvation were described.

Potatoes would have to be replaced by grain and food made available to the starving. On October 15, 1845, Peel wrote to the Lord Lieutenant, Lord Heytesbury, saying flatly, "The remedy is the removal of all impediments to the import of all kinds of human food—that is, the total and absolute repeal for ever of all duties on all articles of subsistence."[4] With these words Peel signaled that he was about to begin one of the great parliamentary battles in English history—the repeal of the Corn Laws. Critics have questioned his commitment to famine relief, but the record shows that Peel did attempt to alleviate the situation. He faced up to the challenge of Corn Law reform by saying to his cabinet: "Can we vote public money for the sustenance of any considerable portion of the people on account of actual or apprehended scarcity and maintain in full operation the existing restrictions on the free import of grain? . . . I am bound to say my impression is we cannot."[5]

Some eighty-one workhouses had been built in various parts of the country but not in the worst-hit areas, the counties of Kerry and Mayo, where conditions had become even worse than those described in chapter 3. Clare, which was also stricken, had only one workhouse, at Kilrush. However, the prevailing wisdom made outdoor relief in any form anathema. The governing precept was that only the workhouse, with all its grimness and deterrents to entrance, was the true test of destitution. How the test was to be applied in an area in which near-starvation was clearly present, but workhouses were not, was not explained.

Peel was one of the first people in England to realize that the problem required not an explanation couched in economic jargon but an answer applicable to the real world. Early in August 1845 he received a letter from the Isle of Wight, an island in the English channel, a market-garden area and a fertile place for potato growing, alerting him to the fact that a strange disease had struck the potato crop. A few days later the disease was reported on the English mainland at Kent, Sandwich, Maidstone, and Gravesend. At the same time reports reached London that the blight had been recorded in France and Holland.

Peel immediately grasped the significance of the reports. They bore dire implications for England, where expensive bread and low wages were increasing the dependency of the laboring classes on the potato, but the reports of blight portended calamity for Ireland. David Moore, the curator of the Royal Dublin Society Botanic Gardens at Glasnevin, alarmed at the reports from England and the Continent, began watching out for signs of the disease. On August 20, 1845, he began finding them in and around Dublin. *Phytophthora infestans* (potato blight) had arrived in Ireland.

The fungus attacked with astonishing ferocity and speed. The initial symptoms of infection appear on the stems and leaves and spread quickly during damp weather. Patches form at the edges of the leaves, gray-green at first then brown, causing them to dry up or rot. A white fungal coating forms on the underside of the leaves. *Phytophthora infestans* spreads via spores, which use a germ tube to penetrate the plant tissue. The fungus spreads mainly on the wind or is washed into the soil by rain, where it also infects the tubers, whose flesh turns brown and quickly rots to a stinking mush.

Phytophthora can overwinter in the tubers, and a single infected tuber planted in the spring is all it takes to cause an epidemic in the potato crop. Prior to the arrival in Ireland of the disease *Phytophthora infestans*, commonly known as blight, there were only two main potato plant diseases. One was called "dry rot" or "taint" and the other was a virus, known popularly as "curl." *Phytophthora infestans* is an oomycete or a water mold and although it resembles a fungus its characteristics place it in the kingdom of *Stamenopila* or *Chromista* with brown and golden algae.

When blight first struck the lumper in 1845, a warning peal of doom sounded over Ireland. In my mother's novel, *The Big Wind*, there is a passage describing the effect that the discovery of blight in their potato patch had on a peasant couple:

"There's something wrong with my potatoes!" he sobbed at the first drill. There was no tobacco smoke to kill the stench that rose and smote him to the earth. Nonnie found him there when she came to call him to the watery porridge. He refused to stir and lay babbling. Stiffly, like an old woman she stooped and pulled a stalk from the earth. It was laden with fine potatoes. She gripped one. There was a squelch as her fingers closed over slime. She took her hand away from it, from the abomination, the stench. Before her eyes, the mess that had been a firm potato dropped into a gaping hole. She screamed. It was a haunting! The orchards of hell were forcing their evil fruit up through the earth. She fled.[6]

This heightened, fictional account would prove to be an all too factual depiction of what happened all over Ireland, but not just yet. Some counties suffered less from the blight onslaught than others. In fact, a loss of more than a third of the crop was reported from only six counties, Roscommon, Kilkenny, Louth, Limerick, Wexford, and what was then known as Queen's County, today's Laois. The *Dublin Evening Post* confidently asserted on September 9, 1845: "We believe that no apprehension whatever is entertained even of a partial failure of the potato crop in Ireland." However, a rather more informed journal, *The Gardeners Chronicle*, widely read among Victorian England's considerable gardening class, stopped its presses four days later, on Friday, September 13, to publish a special announcement: "We stop the press with very great regret, to announce that the Potato Murrain has unequivocally declared itself in Ireland. The crops about Dublin are suddenly perishing. The conversion of potatoes into flour, by the processes as described by Mr. Barrington and others in today's paper, becomes then a process of the first national importance; for where will Ireland be, in the event of a universal potato rot."

Where indeed? Unfortunately, we today know the answer to that question all too well. For, despite the entire claptrap about political economy, the imperfections of the Irish character, and the invocation of Providence, the reality of the situation was that at the moment of the blight's discovery, and at every stage of the subsequent disaster, Ireland had no shortage of food. The problem was that people had no money to buy it. The Irish food produce would not have replaced the potato, but had the food that was exported all through the Famine been retained in Ireland, it would have greatly alleviated the situation.[7] Table 4.1 shows the statistics for food production during the relevant period.

TABLE 4.1

Year	Oxen	Sheep	Swine	Wheat Quarters	Oats
1846	186,483	259,257	480,827	419,228	1,348,458
1847	189,960	241,793	106,457	221,356	723,649
1848	196,049	255,682	110,787	221,936	1,691,876
1849	201,811	241,001	68,053	249,489	1,007,364
TOTALS	734,403	1,080,119	766,164	1,209,080	4,771,347

Peel set up a scientific commission headed by Sir John Lindley, professor of botany at the University of London, to investigate the causes of the blight. Lindley thought the disease was due to wet weather. The other commission members came up with no better solutions. They were Professor of Chemistry at Apothecaries' Hall Dublin, Robert Kane, who offered his services free, and one Lyon Playfair, whose services were not free. Dr. Lyon Playfair was a chemist, a friend of Peel's, and an enthusiastic joiner of any commission that offered a fee. He got three guineas a day for his services, which turned out to be of absolutely no value in detecting the cause of the disease and hence, of course, its cure. However, the research of another man, G. H. Fitzgerald, who was not a member of the commission, might conceivably have either averted or greatly alleviated the disaster had it been possible for Patrick Kavanagh to pen the following lines in the mid-eighteenth century rather than in the nineteenth.

Spraying the Potatoes
Patrick Kavanagh

> *The barrels of blue potato-spray*
> *Stood on a headland in July*
> *Beside an orchard wall where roses*
> *Were young girls hanging from the sky.*
> *And I was there with a knapsack sprayer*
> *On the barrel's edge poised. A wasp was floating*
> *Dead on a sunken briar leaf*
> *Over a copper-poisoned ocean.*

Had Fitzgerald been listened to, many wasps would have drowned in the watery graves described by Kavanagh and the lives of many humans been spared.

He noticed the similarity of the disease to wheat bunt and treated the potato seed as he did wheat, steeping it in a solution of bluestone copper sulphate and water. The potatoes remained healthy and Fitzgerald decided that the potato blight was a fungus that could be treated. His letter of February 1846 to Dublin Castle detailing his experiments was ignored by the chief secretary. On March 14 he published his discoveries in the *Limerick Chronicle*, where they caught the attention of officialdom and were forwarded to Dublin Castle again. This time they were brought to the attention of Kane, who thought nothing of them and did not even draw them to the attention of Lindley, who was at the time publishing every theory that emerged in *The Gardeners Chronicle*, including a report stating that potatoes in the vicinity of the copper smelting works near Swansea were free of disease. Following the discovery in 1882 by Professor Pierre Millardet of the effects of copper spray on vines, the first fungicide to be used worldwide, known as the Bordeaux Mixture, was invented. Although the spraying of potatoes with this copper sulphate, hydrated lime and water solution to prevent the spread of blight would one day become commonplace, in 1846 Fitzgerald, not being a professional man, became discouraged at the silence of the scientists and abandoned his experiments, eventually losing his estate as the blight progressed. His experiments, had they been acted on, would probably not have been in time to greatly affect the course of events in 1846, but they might have prevented, or at least greatly alleviated, the horrors of what, as we shall see, became justifiably known as "Black '47."

Peel also experienced severe discouragement in his attempts to grapple with the blight. His protectionist Tory Party was so enraged at the prospect of the Corn Laws being repealed that the very existence of a famine in Ireland was questioned. In Liverpool, a town with a large Irish population, the Tory mayor refused to call a meeting for the relief of Irish distress. It was said that similar meetings in Dublin, which had led to the setting up of a major relief committee known as the Mansion House Committee, "had the object not of relief but of spreading false alarms."[8] The reports of the blight were dismissed as "the invention of agitators on the other side of the water"; others knew better. The chemists Dr. Lindley and Dr. Playfair officially reported on November 15: "We can come to no other conclusion than that one half of the actual potato crop of Ireland is either destroyed or unfit for the food of man. We, moreover, feel it our duty to apprise you that we fear this could be a low estimate. We would now add, as melancholy as the picture is, that in all probability the late rainy weather has rendered the mischief yet greater."[9]

Peel knew just how "melancholy" the picture was. On October 24, a couple of weeks before receiving the chemists' report, he had been warned by an unquestionably authoritative source, Lord Monteagle, a former member of both the cabinet and the London Political Club, who was also—that rare being—an improving Irish landlord, that he did not "recollect any former example of a calamitous failure being anything near so great and alarming as the present. . . . I know not how the peasantry will get through the winter in very many cases."[10]

And there was even more ghastly news in the pipeline on the day Peel wrote to the lord lieutenant declaring that the way forward lay in the abolition of food tariffs. Peel had received a disturbing report from the medical officer at Coleraine workhouse: "Famine must be looked forward to and will follow, as a natural consequence, as in former years, typhus fever, or some other malignant pestilence."[11]

Faced with the implications of these reports while at the same time attempting to deal with the incessant opposition to Corn Law repeal, Peel suffered greatly: "I never witnessed such agony,"[12] the Duke of Wellington declared. However, with a courage not always acknowledged in Ireland, Peel persisted. He succeeded with the Corn Laws but not in a manner that benefited the Irish crisis, as the lowering of tariffs took some three years to come fully into operation. One bold stroke of Peel's deserves to be mentioned here as it illustrates both the difference in the approach to relief under the Conservatives and the Whigs, which will be discussed in more detail in the next chapter, and the greater authority that Peel exercised over his cabinet than did the man who replaced him as prime minister, Lord John Russell, the Whig leader.

Without either consulting his colleagues or seeking Treasury sanction, in 1845 Peel made £100,000 available for a secret purchase of Indian corn (maize) in America through the Baring Brothers Bank. It could not be argued that the importation of Indian corn was a breach of the Corn Laws as there was no trade in maize at the time. Nevertheless, the Barings were sworn to secrecy, and the first shipments of corn arrived in Cork Harbour some weeks before their existence became generally known. The Barings at least appreciated the seriousness of the situation and, in addition to maintaining secrecy, greatly reduced the bill for their services. The corn was intended to be used to keep prices down by putting it on the markets when prices rose unduly. The estimated value of the lost potatoes was some £3.5 million, so there was no question of £100,000 worth of corn replacing that amount of food. But, in fairness, Peel can be absolved of much of the guilt of the charge that can more appropriately be leveled at the Whig followers of Adam Smith, Thomas Malthus, and other doctrinaires of the London Political Club.

On December 5, 1845, Peel found that opposition in his cabinet to Corn Law repeal was such that he resigned. Queen Victoria sent for the leader of the opposition, Lord John Russell, and asked him to form an administration. But after ten days of frenetic negotiation, Russell found he could not form a government either so the queen sent for Peel once more and asked him to form another administration. He did so, but it could only be made to last for six months. The protectionists within his own party hated him, and the allegedly free-trading Whigs resented his bringing forward a policy that they considered their own. Moreover, not only were relationships between the two parties bad, but those between Russell and Peel were poor also. The Conservative Benjamin Disraeli took advantage of Russell's antagonism to convince him that the Whigs should combine with the protectionist Tories to overthrow Peel on an Irish issue.

Disraeli had no love for the Irish. In fact, in 1836 he delivered one of the more resounding pieces of anti-Irish prejudice of the era, declaring: "The Irish hate our order, our civilisation, our enterprising industry, our pure religion. This wild, reckless, indolent, uncertain and superstitious race have no sympathy with the English character. Their ideal of human felicity is an alternation of clannish broils and coarse idolatry [Catholicism]. Their history describes an unbroken circle of bigotry and blood."[13]

One would have thought that the author of such sentiments would have been in favor of a measure that sought to curb manifestations of Irish hatred for the English, but politics are politics, and Disraeli persuaded the Whigs to vote with a segment of his own party against a Coercion Bill giving the police extra powers and supported by Peel to deal with the agrarian violence in Ireland that was worsened by the failure of the potato crop. Ironically, the Coercion Bill, the seventeenth introduced to Ireland since the Act of Union, came before the House of Commons just as the Corn Law reform was passed into law by the House of Lords on June 25, 1846. It was a parliamentary ambush laid by MPs who had never before shown any interest in Ireland and, as was said of them at the time, most had "as much to do with Ireland as Kamchatka."

Peel didn't have to resign, but after all that had passed, he did so anyhow. The Coercion Bill maneuver, coming at the end of the bitterly divisive Corn Laws debate, would form the backdrop for major changes in English politics, the emergence of the modern Conservative Party, and a general lowering of party discipline that also affected the Whigs. This imposed a limit on Russell's ability to curtail the activities of members of his cabinet during the crisis and prevented him from bringing forward the more humane policies that he sometimes advocated, but for Ireland the division bells in the House of Commons that night tolled a *de profundis*.

It would not be completely unfair to say of Lord John Russell that he was a small man who did big damage to Ireland. Certainly it would not be inaccurate. Russell was not innately prejudiced against Ireland or the Irish; in fact, he was so friendly with the Irish lyric poet Tom Moore that after Moore's death, it was Russell who finished the poet's autobiography. Politically, Russell had flirted with supporting O'Connell. In 1835 the Whigs and a group of radicals had met with O'Connell at Lichfield House, London, and agreed to the Lichfield Compact, whereby the Whigs agreed to cooperate with O'Connell in securing an amendment of the Irish Reform Act of 1832, which would have reformed both municipal government and the tithe issue. In return, O'Connell was pledged to help bring down Peel, who was replaced by Lord Melbourne and remained out of office until 1841.

In the days of the Lichfield House Compact, O'Connell was so close to the Whigs that he became a founding member of the London Reform Club, wherein today one is still greeted by a magnificent full-length portrait of O'Connell that was commissioned as a result of his support for the Reform Bill. The Whigs' subsequent treatment of Ireland and of O'Connell is one of history's object lessons that eaten bread is soon forgotten. Once in office, the Whigs would evince a limited inclination to provide food for O'Connell's starving people.

After the 1847 general election returned a high proportion of MPs hostile to the idea of spending money on Irish relief, Russell either could not or would not bring his former liberalism to bear on the alleviation of Irish agony. His cabinet was riven by faction and at the same time committed to laissez-faire and the theories of political economy described in the discussion of the great debate in chapter 3. As a result, one of the best historians of the period, James S. Donnelly Jr., has judged: "Even though Russell denounced clearances and supported various proposals for government intervention in Ireland, Cabinet divisions often thwarted him and made a shambles of his ineffective attempts at leadership."[14]

It was not only "Cabinet divisions" that thwarted Russell; a figure who was not in the cabinet and who, strictly speaking, would normally have been described merely as a senior civil servant also played a vital role in influencing Irish policy and must bear an unusual burden of responsibility for what happened. This was Charles Edward Trevelyan, a man who calls to mind Yeats's description of Kevin O'Higgins in "The Municipal Gallery Revisited" as being "a soul incapable of remorse or rest."[15]

According to Joseph M. Hernan, who has done some of the best research on Trevelyan, a stained-glass window in a church on the Trevelyan estate in Northumberland captures the image of Trevelyan as he saw himself. It depicts him as St. Michael the Archangel in golden armor. Trevelyan is wearing a royal blue sash inscribed "VERITAS" and holding a golden shield inscribed "SCROTUM FIDEI." The Holy Ghost in the form of a dove hovers above him and below there is a quotation from St. Paul: "I have fought a good fight, I have finished my course." Trevelyan's "course" began in 1807 when he was born into what he himself described as "one of the oldest and best" families in England.[16] He became Sir Charles Trevelyan because of the Famine and was dubbed "A Victorian Cromwell" by his historian grandson, G. M. Trevelyan, and by his brother-in-law Thomas Babington Macaulay, "for his attempt to bring order from chaos with no thought of self-advancement." In fact, the record shows that Trevelyan was immensely courageous and tenacious in fighting his corner when he chose to. He was deeply concerned both with his image and with retaining his control of all the levers of power. Some have disputed the Cromwellian appellation, but I believe the record shows that it is not inappropriate. Neither is it possible to say of Trevelyan that he was merely a civil servant and that policy was decided by his political masters. As we shall see later, he very often devised both the policies and their implementation.

Trevelyan's mother, Harriet, was a daughter of Sir Richard Neave. His father, George Trevelyan, was the archdeacon of Taunton. His family was part of a group of neighbors and friends known as the "Clapham set" that included Zachary Macaulay and William Wilberforce, who led the successful campaign to end the slave trade. Trevelyan himself was a devout Protestant much given to Bible reading. He entered the Indian Civil Service in 1826 after studying at Charterhouse and Haileybury. On arrival in India with perhaps appropriate symbolism, he speedily became known as a leading exponent of the "sport" of spearing wild boar from horseback. At the age of twenty-one, he soon gave evidence of both administrative efficiency and moral courage.

To the outrage of Delhi's English society, he accused the Resident Commissioner of Delhi, Sir Edward Colebrooke, of corruption and after a period of ostracism won his case, causing Colebrooke to be dismissed. In India, Trevelyan was at the heart of a group of young administrators who sought to reform the Indian Civil Service. He later did just that with the British Civil Service, co-authoring the Northcote-Trevelyan Report in 1853, which is generally regarded as the foundation document of today's British Civil Service.

Trevelyan showed himself to be no friend to what Rudyard Kipling termed the "lesser breeds without the law" where Ireland was concerned. By contrast, during his Indian sojourns he took the trouble to learn a number of local dialects.

Trevelyan described himself as belonging to "the class of reformed Cornish Celts" who "by long habits of intercourse with the Anglo-Saxons have learned at last to be practical men."[17] I believe Hernon to be correct in his judgment that "racialism and economic dogmatism are intertwined in his dealings with the Irish." He could also have added anti-Catholicism to Trevelyan's attitudinal catalogue. That catalogue is glaringly revealed in a submission to the *Morning Chronicle* by Trevelyan himself that led to a clash with both Peel and his immediate superior, Sir James Graham, the home secretary (see appendix 1). With the exception of Cecil Woodham-Smith, who devoted a paragraph to the episode, it has been largely overlooked by his historians, but I feel that the article which caused a row is sufficiently indicative of Trevelyan's attitude as to merit reproduction in full and it is included (see appendix 1). The *Morning Chronicle* incident of course also speaks volumes for the strength of the Trevelyan personality, which enabled him to display such arrogance to the home secretary and prime minister of England and get away with it.

The episode began when Trevelyan gave a confidential briefing to Graham and Peel on his return to London from what appears to have been an extensive tour of Ireland that ended only days before Peel and Sir James Graham, the home secretary, banned O'Connell's Clontarf meeting. After giving a confidential briefing to Graham and Peel, Trevelyan wrote a lengthy two-part letter to the editor of the *Morning Chronicle* suggesting that the repeal movement had become a front for military operations directed by the clergy. The first part, which appeared four days after Clontarf was banned, was signed Philalethes (lover of truth), but a furious Peel immediately recognized the author and complained to Graham: "How a man after his confidential interview with us would think it consistent with common decency to appeal to the editor of the *Morning Chronicle,* and the world, all he told us, is passing strange. He must be a consummate fool. Surely he might have asked *us* what we thought of his intended proceedings?"[18] Peel's relationship with Trevelyan never recovered from the letter episode. One can't help speculating in retrospect that Ireland would have been spared much misery and tragedy and Anglo-Irish relationships would have been greatly improved had Peel chosen to sack Trevelyan over the episode, rather than merely to subsequently mistrust him.

Trevelyan gave no ground to Graham, saying that though he might have erred in writing to the *Chronicle,* "I think there cannot be a doubt that now the first portion of the letter has been published it would be better that the second portion should be also." To fully grasp Trevelyan's mind-set toward Ireland, his lurid letter is best read in its entirety, but a few of the points he made are indicative of the attitude of the man who effectively controlled British famine relief to Ireland. Its imperialist viewpoint comes through loud and clear.

He began by stating his credentials. The letter was "from one who for six weeks past has seen, read, thought, enquired, and spoken nothing but Ireland." As a result, he judged that "one of the greatest of the delusions which have been put into the heads of peasantry is that they are *a nation.*" He declared that his trip to Ireland had confirmed views he held before he ever visited the country. "Before I left England," he said,

I took great pains to form a just opinion as to the real nature of the popular movement in progress in Ireland [repeal], and the conclusion I came to was the same which as I believe, has been arrived at by the best informed persons of this country. The whole affair appeared to me to be a gigantic piece of Blarney on O'Connell's part. I believed it to have its roots in the vulgar, but nevertheless, very powerful emotion of saving himself from pecuniary ruin. Besides this, every demagogue is, from the necessity of his position, obliged to go forward. He is by profession a fisher in troubled waters. The demagogue thinks into insignificance just in proportion as public affairs settle down into tranquillity.

O'Connell, no doubt, also aimed at upsetting the present government, and getting some instalments for Ireland; but that a shrewd person like O'Connell, who has attended Parliament year after year and who knows the power and resources of the British nation, and the fixed determination of the great majority, in numbers, wealth, and intelligence, not to submit to a dismemberment of the Empire, should seriously believe in the possibility of Repeal, is so unlikely as to be really incredible. . . .

It soon became apparent to me, after my arrival in Ireland, that this view of the case was perfectly correct as far as O'Connell was concerned, the matter had taken much deeper root. Other leaders beside O'Connell will either appear on the stage, skulk behind-the-scenes; and above all that the great mass of the Roman Catholic peasantry had thoroughly taken the matter to heart. . . . The plans of operation with which the heads of peasantry were filled did not originate with themselves but that they had emanated from some common source, and were in fact, the instructions of superior minds, afterwards disseminated by means of some established organisation among the people.

Trevelyan said that he found widespread plans among the people for attacking barracks, "a perfectly correct military idea." In view of what was to befall—and the calculations of the London Political Club—one of the conversations he claimed to have had with a passerby on the street had a particularly ominous ring:

I encouraged him to speak out, he proceeded to say that there were 8 million of them, that the land was not able to bear them, that one or 2 million might be spared with advantage, and that the country would be for the survivors. I afterwards heard the same idea, either in whole or in part, in a variety of forms, but the burden of the song always was, Protestant and Catholic will freely fall, and the land would be for the survivors.

The Catholic clergy were Trevelyan's particular target. He said:

There cannot be a doubt that the great body of the Roman Catholic priests have gone into the movement in the worst, that is, in the rebellious sense. . . . The priests have given to the repeal movement all the weight of a religious cause in the eyes of a superstitious people. . . . The women and children are sent out of Chapel once the services are over, and the men are lectured on political subjects, and have treasonable papers read to them, often for an hour altogether.

The primary object of the priest is, no doubt, to get the temporalities of the established church; but they have also a further object, which is much nearer to their heart, which is to make Ireland a Catholic country. . . . The result is, that we are standing on the verge of religious and agrarian war, which would unite with the horrors of the Jacquerie and St Bartholomew. . . . O'Connell has for some time past been aware of this fact, and nobody has been more alarmed at it than he has been. He has whipped his horses and they have run away with him, and now, to his dismay, he finds that he is not his own coach man. He has a gentleman on the box, dressed in black.

The anti-Irish sentiments expressed above may have seemed worthy of only a paragraph to the otherwise extremely perceptive Cecil Woodham-Smith, who judged that during his Irish visit Trevelyan had fallen victim to Irish informants whose sense of humor had led them to fill his head with alarming information about immediate and bloody insurrection. His views could have been dismissed as mere ill-founded expressions of racialist prejudices. But they assume a sinister significance when one sets Trevelyan's views not as a mere observer of Irish affairs in 1843, but as, literally, having the power of life and death over huge numbers of starving Irish, and he did utter the following: "The judgement of God sent the calamity to teach the Irish a lesson, that calamity must not be too much mitigated. . . . The real evil with which we have to contend is not the physical evil of the Famine, but the moral evil of the selfish, perverse and turbulent character of the people."

In the succeeding chapters we will see how Trevelyan did his best to help God teach the Irish a lesson.

FIVE
MEAL USE

"The Vulgar sham of the pompous feast
Where the heaviest purse is the highest priest
The organised charity, scrimped and iced
In the name of a cautious, statistical Christ."[1]

—*John Boyle O'Reilly*

AN ASPECT OF FAMINE RELIEF THAT CAUSED great offense to more-radical Irish spokespersons like John Mitchel was its "crumbs from the rich man's table" nature. Mitchel and the Young Ireland group, who coalesced around the weekly newspaper called *The Nation*, did not want charity. They favored the measures proposed by the deputation led by O'Connell; this group met the Irish viceroy, Lord Heytesbury, in Dublin just three days after Peel had told his cabinet of his plans for Ireland and the central fact that these involved repeal of the Corn Laws.

This meeting glaringly exposed the fatal consequences of the loss of the Irish parliament and the introduction of the Act of Union. On November 3, 1845, O'Connell led an outstanding deputation to ask Heytesbury to introduce a series of emergency measures to deal with the Famine. The deputation included the Duke of Leinster, Lord Cloncurry, Sir J. Murray, Henry Grattan's son Henry, who was at the time lord mayor of Dublin, and over a score of other distinguished personages. The list of proposals drawn up by O'Connell involved stopping the export of food, especially corn, which he asked should not be used for either brewing or distilling. The members of the deputation also asked that there should be free importation of food, rice, and Indian corn from the colonies. He proposed that food stores be set up throughout the country and people deployed to maintain the stores and disperse the food. There was to be a program of public works. A tax of 10 percent was to be deducted from the rent rolls of landlords, rising to between 20 and 50 percent in the case of absentees. A loan of £1.5 million was to be raised against the security of Irish forests.

Lord Heytesbury received the deputation "very coldly." He had just received Peel's letter apprising him of the intention to remove the Corn Laws and was aware of the high politics and parliamentary warfare that lay ahead. What the Irish delegation proposed was what the situation called for, but Heytesbury knew, given the depth of opposition to repealing the Corn Laws, that what Ireland would likely get would be an ineffectual creation fashioned from economic dogma as seen through the workhouse window. Accordingly, the deputation's proposals were not discussed.

Heytesbury read from a dispiriting prepared script. It was through him that London had received some of its most accurate and apocalyptic reports. Nevertheless, his script claimed that the reports on the potato crop failure were so contradictory that the full extent of the problem would not be known until the crop was harvested. Much of what the delegation proposed would require new legislation. The proposals would be brought immediately to the government's attention, but they would have to be "maturely weighed." As soon as he had finished reading, Heytesbury began to bow his guests out of the room and out of hope.[2]

Heytesbury's behavior was typical of the high-handed approach of many British officials throughout the Famine. He and his like were the proconsuls of the dominant imperialist power of their time—innovative, pioneering, and above all, successful. In the eyes of many, the Irish were the *Untermenschen* who would pay the penalty for the crime of being weak. The very bad electoral bargain that Britain had imposed on Ireland as part of the price for Catholic Emancipation had been somewhat mitigated by the Irish Reform Act (1832), which partially reformed the electoral system and increased the electorate from 37,000 to 92,141. But this was still only 1.2 percent of the population. In effect, just 1 in 115 people in Ireland was enfranchised compared with 1 in 24 in England. The fragmented Irish representation in the House of Commons rose from 100 to 105. O'Connell, the leader of the largest group, was now an aged and broken man. Militarily, England held the country in an iron grip.

James Donnelly Jr., a fair-minded historian who is always willing to re-examine and, if possible, refute charges that the Famine was the outcome of deliberate attempts at genocide by British officials such as Sir Charles Trevelyan, assistant secretary to the Treasury, and to quote laudatory judgments on relief operations, nevertheless wrote, "It is no doubt true that the forced retention in Ireland of the entire grain harvest of 1845, or even the prohibition of the export of oats and oatmeal alone, would have been sufficient to offset the partial loss of the potato, but only if the government had been prepared to subsidise the purchase of higher-priced native produce. Thus oatmeal, costing around £15 a ton in the spring and summer of 1846, was about 50% more expensive than Indian meal."[3]

The government was not prepared to pay the higher prices, the grains were not retained, and though the crumbs from the rich man's table were few and slow in dropping, they were all the Irish peasantry would get. Laissez-faire thinking held Irish famine relief in its deadly grip.

Peel persevered with his interventionist relief schemes in the eight months that elapsed between his informing his cabinet on October 31, 1844, that he intended to repeal the Corn Laws and his leaving office the following June. A Relief Commission for Ireland was set up under the chairmanship of Sir Randolph Routh. Routh's experience had been gained with the commissariat, the British Army's supply unit. The commissariat would provide much of the Relief Commission's infrastructure and manpower, food depots, and distribution mechanisms. Apart from Routh, the Relief Commission consisted of the chief executives of the Irish government departments involved in the relief effort: the chairman of the Board of Works, the inspector general of the coast guard service, Edward Twisleton, the resident Irish poor law commissioner, and the inspector general of the police force. The chairman was Edward Lucas, former undersecretary at Dublin Castle, and the secretary—and the most interesting figure—was John Pitt Kennedy, who had been secretary to the Devon Commission and had gained some fame by writing a pamphlet that suggested a revolutionary approach to solving the problems of the Irish peasant. That was not to hang, jail, or transport them, but to give them employment.

Unfortunately, such thinking was in very short supply in the Ireland of the 1840s. It was Peel himself who partially corrected the short-sighted vision of those responsible for assembling the official Relief Commission when he pointed out that it did not contain a single Catholic. This was corrected by appointing the Irish scientist Professor Robert Kane. The commission was to supervise the operation of local committees consisting of the leading people in the district, local proprietors, clergy, magistrates, and so forth. These people were to collect subscriptions which would fund the distribution of alms and food.

Another prestigious relief committee was set up in London under the chairmanship of Thomas Baring at the offices of the financier Baron Lionel de Rothschild; it worked assiduously to collect money in conjunction with other relief organizations such as that of the Quakers. This committee, known as the British Relief Association, met every day and worked hard and diligently; it included some of the top business leaders of the day. One name that deserves to be mentioned is that of Count Strzelecki, whose administrative areas covered some of the worst hit of the West and Northwest. The count was a Polish nobleman living in England who had become a naturalized Englishman. He is still remembered with gratitude in the annals of the Famine, not only for his hard work but for his empathy with the suffering. From the moment he arrived in Westport, he exhibited a strong feeling for with the famine victims. He wrote, "You may now believe anything which you hear or read, because what I actually see surpasses what I have ever read of past and present calamities."[4]

Another name worth mentioning in the sphere of relief is the only too aptly named Sir Edward Pine-Coffin, the deputy commissioner of the official government relief agency, the Relief Commission for Ireland, which came under the direct control of Trevelyan. Pine-Coffin had already distinguished himself by combating hunger in Scotland; when the potato failed there, his reaction was to commandeer a warship, fill it with food, and send it around the distressed areas. He is remembered in Ireland for having displayed the same dash and humanitarian instinct, but he was hampered by having to operate under Trevelyan's iron control and had to suffer the mortification of seeing ships laden with food sailing from Irish ports during the Famine.

From the outset, Trevelyan laid it down that there was to be no interference with food exports: "Do not encourage the idea of prohibiting exports . . . perfect Free Trade is the right course."[5]

He reprimanded Routh in a Treasury minute telling him that he was asking too much for Ireland. Scarcity of food, he was reminded, extended over the whole of Western Europe and the United Kingdom, and nothing ought to be done for the West of Ireland that might send prices, already high, still higher for people "who, unlike the inhabitants of the West Coast of Ireland have to depend on their own exertions."[6] His reaction to the likelihood of public protest was summed up by something he said in September 1846: "Food riots are quite different from organized rebellion and are not likely to be of long duration."[7]

This continued to be Whig policy throughout the Famine. There were ineffectual riots and gestures of despair such as cutting the traces of horses pulling food carts for the export market, but food continued to be exported, sometimes under military and naval escort.

What do Irish historians say about food export during the Famine? The most respected domestic historian of the Famine is Cormac Ó Gráda, professor of economics at University College Dublin. His scholarship is beyond reproach; however, I do question his judgments on food exports during the Famine. Ó Gráda argues that the retention of the exported food would have made little or no difference in making up for the loss of the potato: "Thus the 430,000 tons of grain exported in 1846 and 1847 must be set against the shortfall of about 20 million tons of potatoes in those same years."[8]

Ó Gráda estimated that the exported food would only have amounted to one-seventh of the value of the potato crop that failed. But how many lives would this have saved? The political economists may argue that the exported food was negligible, but how many lives constitute a negligible saving? The economists make reasonable points, qua economists, but the fact is that food exports formed part of a flint-edged policy that was aimed at land clearance. And though given the scale and problems of want and, above all, distribution in parts of the country where roads were scarce, to save some would have been better than to save none. And no amount of economic jargon can quell the emotions stirred by the sight of food sailing from a fertile but famine-stricken island. But what about other exports such as meat, butter, and eggs? As early as 1800 the Irish economy was supplying British cities with 83 percent of their beef, 79 percent of their butter, and 86 percent of their pork.[9] Granted that in good times those who starved to death during the Famine would never have had access to such luxuries as pork, beef, and so forth, had they been made available in bad times, they would surely have made some inroads into the death toll. And what about the psychological impact?

A people seeing food flowing along Irish roads to be exported from Irish ports, very likely under the guard of Irish soldiers in British uniforms or Irish men in the police force as their fellow countrymen died horribly in ditches along the roads, does not have its anger abated by references to economic theory. Ó Gráda also bolsters the case for allowing food exports to continue by alluding to the possible reaction of some half a million Irish farmers if their market was interfered with or their prices affected. That was an argument that also appealed to Trevelyan, and he would certainly have used his influence, as would Sir Charles Wood, the chancellor of the exchequer, to prevent funds from being devoted to buying up the food and distributing it to the starving. Nevertheless, to a starving people, the sight of a single sandwich being exported was an inflammatory gesture, and some better means to combat famine than shipping out food that might have fed the people surely outweighs the theoretical arguments of the well-fed in a lecture hall.

Sir Charles Wood, who was Trevelyan's immediate superior, privately donated £200 toward famine relief. However Trevelyan, who disapproved of the collection, gave only £25. Queen Victoria gave £2,000 and the pope £1,000. Both the pope and the queen subsequently issued letters of appeal

to their followers for famine relief. The people of Rome contributed generously, as did a few cardinals, but no masterpieces from the Vatican's art collection were removed for sale to help supplement the appeal, and it is likely
that the amount of money that was collected came mainly not as a result
of the pope's letter but from the generosity of the Irish Catholic diaspora,
particularly from America.

In fact, at the height of the Famine it was the Irish who sent money to
the pope. In 1849 the pope was "on the run" because republican forces had
temporarily driven him from the Vatican. The Irish bishops were ordered to
take up a collection to help defray papal expenses. To judge from a letter of
the Archbishop of Dublin Dr. Murray, this appeal must have realized much
more than the pope's gift of £1,000. Writing to Cardinal Antonelli expressing sorrow and sympathy for the pope's plight, Murray states that "so far the
Dublin collection has realized £2,700." Murray encloses a draft of £1,500
and writes that when he hears of its safe receipt he will forward the remainder.[10] One of the more intriguing donors was Sultan Abdülmecid of Turkey.
He was reported to have wanted to subscribe £10,000, but was apparently
informed by the British ambassador that, as the queen had given only £2,000,
he could not exceed her gift and so he gave £1,000. It is also said in Ireland
that Sultan Abdülmecid followed this up by sending three or five shiploads
of grain to feed the starving, and there is a plaque to this effect on the wall
of the hotel in Drogheda in which the Turkish sailors are said to have stayed
while unloading the grain. The then president of Ireland, Mary MacAleese,
made a grateful reference to the Turkish assistance during a visit to Turkey in
March 2010. Subsequently, however, in fairly classical Irish fashion, objec-
tors began making claims that the grain ships never arrived and that there is
no mention of grain being unloaded in the meticulous harbor records kept
by the British at the time. This argument could be countered by pointing
out that this was a semi-clandestine operation and that the commemorative
plaque speaks of the grain being unloaded by Turkish sailors, not by Irish
dockers. Apart from the plaque, there is also a large illustrated scroll signed
by local dignitaries thanking Turkey for its assistance hanging in the Turkish
embassy in Dublin. In a further twist to the story, it is said that the Turkish
captain attempted to land first at both Dublin and Belfast and only landed

at Drogheda as his third choice. By way of further embellishment, some tellers of the tale say that the real reason for the story of the grain ships lies not in the sultan's concern for the starving Irish but in the fact that he and Queen Victoria "had a thing going"! How far one should go in pursuing this particular line of inquiry is not clear, but documentary evidence of the actual landing of the grain is certainly difficult to come by, as is irrefutable proof such as a captain's logbook. However, this may simply be because as a Turkish embassy official put it to me, if such evidence exists, it lies under an ocean of documents in the Turkish foreign ministry.

The fact that the Turkish sultan did send a sum of money to the Irish in their time of need is still remembered to the credit of the Turks at the time of writing, whereas no animosity remains for the casualties that the Turks inflicted on Irish Volunteers in the British Army during the botched British landing at Gallipoli. Peel visualized the committees organizing local employment schemes with the help of the landlords, who were expected to give increased employment on their estates. Employment was also expected to come from the Irish Board of Works through road building. A further prudent, but ominous, measure was a direction that workhouses were to provide fever hospitals in their grounds.

These proposals drawn up in London appeared both practical and enlightened on paper. On the ground in Ireland, however, they immediately collided with reality. The two essential planks of Peel's policy were the workhouse and the landlords. The workhouse presented difficulty because Edward Twistleton, the poor law commissioner, pointed out that under the Irish poor law, relief could be given only inside the workhouse, not outside of it. To provide outside relief would be illegal; thus the poor law officials who had been relied upon to help in the distribution of relief were not forthcoming, and greater reliance was placed on local committees, which were often staffed by people with no expertise. Education and managerial training were in short supply all over the country, but particularly in the parts where distress was most severe, such as the West of Ireland. Outside of the church, society had very little organization. Local leadership and expertise were severely limited and of a quality that can be gleaned from the letter from a Mayo parish priest to the Relief Commission that is reproduced below.

Louisburgh, Westport, April 27, 1846

Sir, I beg to acknowledge the receipt of your letter of the 24th instant conveying to me the request of the Commissioners to communicate with the Lieutenant of the County Mayo with a view to his appointing a committee of relief for this distressed district.

I beg to state for the information to the Commissioners that we do not know the address of the Lieutenant of this county; we are informed that he is, at present, in some part of England. I beg further to say that I deplore the existence of any necessity to urge the Commissioners to give such directions, as the destitution and wretchedness of the people are so very close upon us, and have been already felt by many of the people, that relief should be given promptly and immediately; the small quantities of potatoes that are for sale have reached already a famine price. Typhus fever, diarrhoea and dysentery are rife amongst the people, many of whom have fallen victims to their virulence. There is but one resident gentleman in this parish—Mr James Garvey of Tully; there are no magistrates, none but the clergy to convey the wants of the people. Under these circumstances, a committee has been formed today, composed of individuals best qualified to administer to a suffering people the relief of government, viz: Mr James Garvey, Doctors Fergus and Durkin, Messrs John Comber, George Lynch and Michael Carroll, along with the local clergy.

Now, I beg most earnestly to submit that we have done every thing in our power to meet the reasonable wishes of the Commissioners. In the absence of any of the magistracy—in the absence of the Lieutenant of the county, and with absentee landlords, we do not see what else we could do but what we have done. We beg, therefore, most earnestly of the Commissioners not to suffer the people to starve. We seek not alms, we solicit employment. But, whatever the mode of relief be, we again repeat our hope that the people will not be allowed to starve.

I have the honour to be,

Sir, your obedient servant, Patrick MacManus, Parish Priest of Kilgeever[11]

The road system in the West was so bad that grain had to be sent in ships. Apart from the fact that the shipping provided turned out to be particularly slow, the undeveloped state of the notoriously treacherous West Coast meant that there were very few harbors available.

This lack was not ascribed to its true cause—colonial policies such as those under the Tudors that had destroyed the Irish fishing industry and crippled maritime activity under the Penal Laws—but to Providence. Sir Randolph Routh complained to Hewetson, "It is annoying that all these harbours are so insignificant. It shows Providence never intended Ireland to be a great nation."[12] Providence would be invoked to explain Irish misery many more times in the future.

The foregoing circumstances meant that the relief operation had to be reorganized almost as soon as it began in January 1846, with the result that both administrative and policy control were placed even more firmly in the hands of Trevelyan.

Peel had centered his "main reliance" on the landlords for the creation of employment. How he, or his officials, could have come to rely so greatly on the landlords is difficult to understand. The government had hard evidence from the earlier famines mentioned in the preceding chapters that either through indebtedness or unwillingness, the Irish landlord was a broken reed. The officer engaged in relief during the 1839 famine reported following a tour of the entire West, Northwest, and South of Ireland that in every distressed district he found that aid had been provided by the government, not by the landlords; only a matter of weeks before Peel announced his scheme, Dublin Castle officials confirmed that the same pattern was being followed by the landlords.

On January 10, 1846, at Kilkee, County Clare, after a local relief committee had been set up—and a fairly chaotic and inefficient body it was—local landlords issued a statement saying: "Under their present difficulties and in the apprehension of those which may come on them in the spring, they neither can advance funds now nor can they offer any sufficient security for the payment by instalments hereafter."[13]

But months later Peel was still claiming that the main source of relief must be the landlords. Speaking in the House of Commons on April 17, he made a statement that shows either a confused state of mind or a complete absence of knowledge about the attitudes of the Irish clergy and of the landlord class, although each category looked on the issue from different perspectives. He said that he had received "an entreaty that for God sake the government should send out to America for more Indian corn. . . . If it were known that we undertook the task of supplying the Irish with food we should to a great extent lose the support of the Irish gentry, the Irish clergy and the Irish farmer. It is quite impossible for the government to support 4 million people. It is utterly impossible for us to adopt means of preventing cases of individual misery in the wilds of Galway or Donegal or Mayo. In such localities the people must look to the local proprietors, resident and non-resident."[14]

Although Peel was the English politician who had done the most to alleviate distress, that statement was in effect a sentence of death pronounced upon the hungry in the "wilds" of Galway and Mayo. Most of the landlords in those areas had neither the inclination nor the means to help the starving tenants. Readers will remember for themselves the case of "Humanity Dick," the biggest landlord in not only County Galway but probably in the entire country.

The other plank of Peel's policy, "relief works," generally translated as road building; the Board of Works, charged with this responsibility, had vast experience in this area and warned that most of the areas affected by the loss of the potato were in bad boggy land where there were no roads other than the tracks leading to farms. To improve these would be to benefit individual farmers unduly, and major road works were outside their financial capabilities and the tenets of laissez-faire. The result of this dilemma would pass into Irish folklore as *"bóithre an ocrais,"* or "roads of hunger," as they were known, which led nowhere and served no useful purpose. These roads could be taken as a metaphor for the entire famine relief approach. The roads led nowhere except to bogs or rocky plateaus constructed not with a view to developing infrastructure but to avoid interfering with private enterprise.

The problem with supplying food to the needy was that the bulk of those most affected didn't have any money. They didn't live, or die, in a money economy.

By March 1846 people were beginning to starve. A leading Irish member of parliament, William Smith O'Brien, reported that in Limerick he saw people eating rotten potatoes that no Englishman would give to his pigs. His report was corroborated by one from Lord Monteagle, the Irish landlord mentioned in chapter 4, who said that in Clare he saw people eating food that was "so putrid and offensive an effluvia issued that in consuming it they were obliged to leave the doors and windows of their cabins opened."[15] Sir James Graham, the home secretary, told the House of Commons on March 13 that in almost every county "dysentery had made its appearance, attended by fever in many instances."

In these circumstances the principal bulwark against starvation was the maize that Peel had surreptitiously ordered through the Baring Brothers Bank. The corn got off to a bad start with the people because of its yellow color and because, in some districts, unscrupulous suppliers unloaded diseased corn on the hungry. In Waterford deaths were attributed to eating the corn. For all the fuss about the Corn Laws, the British literally did not know a great deal about corn, certainly not of the Indian variety. It was not until January 5, 1846, that an American diplomat stationed in Brussels wrote to the Barings alerting them to the fact that Indian corn, or "hominy grits," as it was known in America, was so hard that it was not ground in the ordinary way but chopped up in a steel mill. Moreover, the corn was sensitive to sweating and overheating. If it was to be subject to long sea voyages before reaching the port of Cork, the main Irish grain port, it would have to be taken off the ships immediately and ground at once. The problem was that, as Ireland depended on potatoes rather than grain, there was very little milling capacity available, something on the order of one-tenth of what was required to process some 350,000 bushels of corn.

Cecil Woodham-Smith describes the laborious procedures that were devised to make up for the lack of milling facilities. The corn "was to be unloaded at once, and to prevent heating dried in kilns for eight hours, being turned twice, to avoid parching. Next it was to be cooled for 70 hours, dressed and cooled again for 24 hours before sacking. Ordinary millstones would have to be used, but to produce a reasonably fine and digestible meal the corn was to be ground twice."[16]

By now Trevelyan was exercising increasing control over the Irish relief operation. One of his first actions on Peel's departure in June 1846 symbolizes the attitude he was to adopt throughout the Famine—he canceled a shipment of grain on its way to Ireland. He wrote to Thomas Baring on July 8, 1846: "The cargo of Sorciére is not wanted . . . her owners must dispose of it as they think proper." Baring replied congratulating him on "the termination of your feeding operations."[17] From his work on the relief committee Baring must have known that the feeding operations were far from successful. But he probably also knew that Trevelyan had been extremely successful in making himself in effect the czar of Irish relief operations. By this time, as Peel's biographer Douglas Hurd says,

The import of maize continued through that summer of 1846. The Government began to consider whether more maize should be bought to maintain supply to the food depots which Sir Randolph Routh had set up. By this time Peel was fighting for his life at Westminster, and Sir Randolph had to reckon with the Treasury in its purest and least merciful form, embodied in the Assistant Secretary Charles Trevelyan. Young, handsome, an intense evangelical, Trevelyan was wholly devoted to hard work. By his outstanding ability he quickly came to dominate the organization of relief. Trevelyan's integrity and energy masked two difficulties: he did not approve of the Irish, and was dogmatically devoted to the doctrines of the free market. He was not on good terms with Peel, whom he had annoyed three years earlier by publishing under a pseudonym in the *Morning Chronicle* two long letters based on an earlier visit to Ireland. Peel too believed in free trade and the functioning of the market, but people were suffering, these benevolent forces took time to muster their strength, and meanwhile Peel bought maize for Ireland in 1845 and 1846, just as he had mobilized help for Paisley in 1842. These were the limited concessions he was ready to make at the expense of his theoretical beliefs to relieve human hardship. It is hard to believe that if Peel had retained power he would have allowed Trevelyan to close the food depots and refuse any further purchase of maize. The new Whig Government was more to Trevelyan's taste and fully approved his determination to wind up the relief effort.[18]

When the complexity and the time-consuming nature of the corn pro-
cessing was brought to his attention, Trevelyan made two decisive interven-
tions. First, he wrote to the Barings temporarily cutting back on the corn
supply by 50 percent and asking that henceforth, whenever possible, Indian
cornmeal should be sent rather than unprocessed grain. Second, he decreed
that there was no need for the Indian corn to be ground twice. In a letter
to Routh he summed up his attitude to relief. It was that of the workhouse:
"We must not aim at giving more than wholesome food. I cannot believe it
would be necessary to grind the Indian corn twice. . . . Dependence on charity is not to be made an agreeable mode of life."

In Ireland in early 1846 there was very little danger that the poorer
classes would find dependence on Peel's yellow meal "agreeable." The milling deficiencies and the fact that, through hunger, many of the recipients did
not give it sufficient cooking time, made for severe and widespread bowel
complaints, particularly among children. Hence the meal quickly became
known as "Peel's Brimstone." Both adults and children found the transition
from potatoes to meal difficult to make. But by June, General Hewetson, an
important figure in the commissariat, could advise Trevelyan that there were
"scarcely any" gastric complaints and that "the general health of the people
has wonderfully improved."[19] Hewetson said that "the whole sum and nutritious quality of the meal . . . was superior in every point of view to the
potato" and went on to compliment ministers who in the face of "abuse" had
done so much to avoid "horrors and misery." Hewetson was the man who
had advised Peel to buy the Indian corn in the first place, and he deserves
to be well remembered for the suggestion, which undoubtedly saved many
lives. But it may also be fairly assumed that he was anxious to place the food
in the best light possible, and his letter sounds no warning notes as to what
might be expected to happen should demand increase and milling capacity
continue to fall short. But this, unfortunately, is what did happen.

The 1846 potato crop failed on a far greater scale than did that of 1845.
Apart from the obvious pressure this placed on milling facilities, two other
factors have to be borne in mind. One was a combination of laissez-faire
and, ironically, the fact that there was a good grain harvest in Ireland that

year, which meant that in the autumn, mills were busily grinding privately owned corn, much of it for export, while the government hesitated to interfere with the markets by demanding preference for its Indian corn. The other was the cause of the good Irish corn crop, the fine weather, which added to the problems by drying up many of the streams normally used for milling.

Trevelyan tried to make up the shortfall by having the corn ground at Admiralty facilities in England and even in faraway Malta and having the meal shipped in naval vessels to Ireland. Casting around for some method of solving the milling problem, Trevelyan came up with the idea of using hand mills. He borrowed one mill from India House, picked up a traditional Irish quern from the starving West of Ireland, another type from the more prosperous area of Wick in England, and asked the experts to come up with something. A little factory for the manufacture of hand mills was actually set up in Kilkee in County Clare that November. However, the mills cost fifteen shillings each, an impossibly large sum for laborers used to being employed, when they were employed, at around ten pence a day. The few mills that did go into circulation were bought by charitable organizations.

The month before the factory opened, Hewetson once more acted as a cheerleader for Indian corn. He circulated relief committees with a potentially dangerous and certainly misleading memorandum on the virtues of the food: "Indian corn in an *unground* state affords an equally wholesome and nutritious food."[20] In fact, Indian corn in an unground state, even after prolonged boiling, is so sharp and indigestible that it can cause intestinal damage, especially in children, and when fed to starving people could, at best, be expected to produce very severe cramping.

However, Hewetson's memo advised that the corn could be used "in two ways, the grain could be crushed between two good sized stones and then boiled in water, with a little grease or fat"—"if at hand," he added prudently. "Or," he suggested, "it could be used without crushing, simply by soaking all night in warm water, changing this, in the morning, for clear, cold water, bringing to the boil, and boiling the corn for an hour and a half—it could then be eaten with milk, with salt, or plain. . . . Corn so used will be considerably cheaper to the committee and the people than meal, and will be well adapted to meet the deficiency of mill power." The memorandum particularly recommended boiling without crushing, a procedure highly unlikely to have been commonly used in the Hewetson household.

Yet, its deficiencies as a food notwithstanding, the Indian corn did stave off starvation in the 1845–1846 period. When it arrived in Ireland, it was stored in commissariat depots and sold by commissariat officials to local relief committees at a price based on the recovery of costs. As some of these depots did not open until the month of May, people were on the verge of starvation when the corn was distributed, particularly in the remote areas of the Southwest and the West. The amount of corn involved was estimated as providing a pound of meal a day for half a million people for three months, barely enough to sustain life, but Peel's measures did keep famine at bay. The amount of corn involved was not great, but by placing it on the market in a concentrated way—in the months of May, June, July, and August—the corn had a stabilizing effect on prices. Unfortunately, this very success was anathema to orthodox Whig thinking as, in their eyes, the government was tampering with market forces, something they would not do when their turn came to deal with the failure of the potato.

It should be stressed that even under Peel and the Conservatives, the result of the race between governmental efforts and famine had been a close thing. The first of the Indian corn went on sale on March 28, more or less simultaneously in Clonmel, Cork, and Longford. However, the supply was highly problematic in some of the more remote western areas where need was greatest and access most difficult because of the condition, or complete absence, of roads. Mayo in the day before the potato failure has already been mentioned. Its condition after the blight struck was nearly indescribable. People were said to look like "living skeletons." But conditions were deplorable all over the country as even the most cursory examination of distress reports filed on the significant date of March 28 shows. For example, in my own district of County Dublin, now known as Dun Laoghaire, but then called Kingstown, a dormitory area for Dublin, then very much smaller than it is now, a distress report dated March 28 stated: "695 persons are now suffering privation from the high price of provisions: 317 are in the extreme distress, the means of buying food being more inadequate than that of the others."[21]

In County Leitrim, Mohill Poor Law Union reported "that the cottiers at present are almost destitute. Lord Clements states that parties have visited the houses of dealers in oatmeal for the purpose of forcing them to lower their charges."

Mullingar Poor Law Union reported from Westmeath that "Poor labourer supply of potatoes in many instances already exhausted, and unless immediate relief is given, the consequences will be awful; 350 labourers are unemployed in Barony."

Clogher Poor Law Union reported that by the end of that month, there would be no sound potatoes left.

From the village of Freshford in County Kilkenny the Rev. Luke Fowler reported, "Distress and disease spreading . . . Amounting to all but starvation; priests house daily beset by starving people; impossible to provide even a scanty supply for the numbers famishing."

A particularly telling report came from the Mountmellick Poor Law Union:

The number of decent women with families, amounting to 80 human beings, applied to the guardians for relief, they being without food or sufficient employment; these applications form but a small proportion of those actually subsisting on food made from "'the wash'" of the starch yard [liquid waste left when starch is extracted from corn or potatoes], food but indifferently suited for pigs.

The situation didn't get any better in subsequent months. In May, the *Freeman's Journal* sent a reporter to study conditions in County Clare, in the West. He reported from Tulla (on May 7) on what he had found in the villages of Gurtnaglee and Doonass. The account could be taken as a template for the image of the Famine that would strike into the folk memory of Irish Catholics over the centuries: the starving people, the faithful clergy, and the absent, or at least impotent landlord.

At Gurtnaglee the reporter found "about 30 houses here, and not a single potato . . . with any of the people. They at present subsist on Indian meal purchased in Limerick; but the means of the people are nearly exhausted, and they are in the utmost consternation at the prospect of utter destitution which is staring them full in the face."

He said of Doonass: "A great portion of the property about here belongs to Sir Hugh Massey. At the village of Doonass, I found over 300 families— principally women, young and old—assembled around the petty sessions home, where the Reverend Mr McMahon, PP, and one of his assistant curates, with two gentlemen belonging to the neighbourhood, were giving out Indian meal to the starving people. It was a melancholy sight and perhaps one of the most touching I yet beheld. There were the representatives of at least over 1000 human beings collected about the place, all eager to get their bags filled with meal, in order to carry it to their famishing children and families. Would that some landlords and legislators have witnessed the scene. . . . The faithful clergy assisting their flocks in their trying hour of need, whilst the landlords who are morally bound to take care of the persons from whom they derive their incomes, remain in listless apathy, and leave the people to their fate."

A different viewpoint came from Cork City. Possibly for political reasons, or possibly simply because Cork City was where the Indian corn was landed and the city therefore benefited from ease of access, the State Grand Jury of the City of Cork on July 25, 1846, passed a unanimous resolution "to be respectfully presented to the Right Honourable, Sir Robert Peel and the members of Her Majesty's late government for the timely and judicious aid afforded to the distressed population of Ireland, during a period when the deficiency of the ordinary food threatened them with serious privations." But even in passing the laudatory, and unusual, resolution, the Grand Jury also called on the government to avert "impending calamity" by providing "extensive employment for the labouring classes, by the construction of useful public works."

The Cork resolution had spoken advisedly of "impending calamity." Terrifying new reports of blight had begun to circulate in that month of July, and other developments conspired to ensure that henceforth there would be very little cause for Irish public bodies to pass resolutions praising the British government's humanity.

Trevelyan was a Whig, although as a civil servant he was supposed to have no politics. This fact and episodes such as the *Morning Chronicle* affair had not worked to create a good relationship between him and Peel. Consequently, Trevelyan was much more at home with the members of Lord John Russell's administration than with those of Peel's administration and the Conservatives. Famously, he wrote to Routh on July 6 telling him approvingly, "The members of the new government have begun to come in today to the Treasury. I think we shall have much reason to be satisfied with our new masters."[22] He followed this up a week later in an even happier mood: "Nothing can be more gratifying to our feelings than the manner in which the new Chancellor of the Exchequer has appreciated our exertions."[23]

The new chancellor, Sir Charles Wood, was a worshipper at the shrine of laissez-faire who shared Trevelyan's views on relief and on much else concerning Ireland and political economy. In his six years at the Treasury, Wood ceded almost dictatorial powers to his driven assistant secretary. Alarming new reports of potato blight in Ireland were beginning to filter through to London as Woods and Trevelyan commenced their partnership. Trevelyan decided that the way to counter the looming disaster was to *end* relief. He reasoned that once it became generally known that the blight had struck again, the people would turn to the government to be fed. Both he and Woods recoiled from this cost.

One of Trevelyan's first actions after the Whigs' coming to power had enormous symbolic significance. Only two days after Woods and his people took over at the Treasury, Trevelyan reversed Peel's policy on grain shipments. He literally stopped the supply of food to Ireland by writing to Baring on July 8 to cancel a shipload of Indian corn. Baring, as we saw, replied congratulating him on "the termination of his feeding efforts." And terminated they were, although not in the circumstances that Baring envisaged. A few days after writing to Baring, on July 17, Trevelyan told Routh to begin winding up his feeding operations: "Whatever may be done hereafter these things should be stopped now, or you run the risk of paralysing all private enterprise and having this country on you for an indefinite number of years. The Chancellor of the Exchequer supports this strongly."[24]

The use of that accusing "you," with its clear threat that Routh would be held responsible for bringing "this country" down on him should the starving continue to be fed, stifled any prospect of rebellion from either Routh or his staff who were daily dealing with a rising tide of human misery. The bureaucrat uses "we" or even "I" when things are going well but "you" when the possibility of blame looms. Of even more significance was the declaration that the chancellor of the exchequer "*supports* this strongly." Perhaps unconsciously, perhaps deliberately, Trevelyan was reminding a subordinate of the identity of the architect of famine policy and the fact that he had official backing. Trevelyan had already been in a controlling position before the advent of the Whigs. In succeeding years, he became even more powerful, with Woods depending on his advice and Russell dependent on Woods.

Following the Trevelyan communication to Routh, Russell made a statement in the House of Commons (*Hansard* [the official report of the proceedings of the Parliament] on August 17, 1846) laying down the policy the Whigs intended pursuing toward relief: "We shall still take care not to interfere with the regular operations of merchants for the supply of food to the country, or with the retail trade, *which was much deranged* by the operations of last year. With regard to relief committees, we propose that they should for a time be constituted, taking care to avoid those errors which have hitherto from want of experience, and guided by the lights we have received from the practices hitherto established. In particular we shall endeavour to avoid the giving of tickets, by members of the relief committees, to persons who are not in need of relief."

The last sentence requires some explaining. It refers not merely to a desire to prevent undeserving people from gaining government assistance, but to one of the guiding precepts of the relief operation, namely that aid was to be given only to people who were in need because of the failure of the potato, not those suffering from the common or garden variety of "distress" caused by endemic poverty. In practice this distinction was nearly impossible to make as famine affected ever greater numbers. In order to ensure that everyone connected with famine relief would be clearly "guided by the lights," Trevelyan authorized a Treasury minute on August 21 stating:

> In order to keep in check, as far as possible, the social evils incident to an extensive system of relief it is indispensably necessary that the relief committee should not sell the meal or other food provided by them, except in small quantities to persons who were known to have no other means of procuring food, that the price at which the meal is sold should, as nearly as possible be the same as the market prices which prevail in the neighbourhood; that the committee should not give higher rates of wages, nor exact a smaller quantum of work on any works carried on by them from funds at their disposal than is the case in respect to the works carried on under the superintendent of the Board of Works and that work should be carried on by them only to the extent to which private employment is proved not to be available. . . . The strictest regard being at the same time paid to the pledge which is being given, not to interfere in any case in which there is a reasonable expectation that the market would be supplied by mercantile enterprise.[25]

It was laid down from on high that, henceforth, the doctrines of "a cautious statistical Christ" were to be closely followed. In their wake, another trade would follow and flourish—that of the evictor.

SIX

EVICTIONS

"Undoubtedly it was the landlords right to do as he pleased, and if he abstained he conferred of favour and was doing an act of kindness. If on the other hand he chose to stand on his right, the tenant must be taught by the strong arm of the law that they had no power to oppose or resist. . . . Property would be valueless and capital would no longer be invested in cultivation of land if it were not acknowledged that it was the landlord's undoubted, indefeasible and most sacred right to deal with his property as he wished."

—*Tory Lord Brougham*

"The people were all turned out of doors and the roofs of their houses pulled down. That night they made a tent or shelter, of wood and straw, but however the drivers [bailiffs] threw them down and drove them from the place. . . . It would have pitied the sun to look at them, as they had to go head first into the storm. . . . It was a night of high wind and storm, and wailing could be heard at a great distance. They implored the drivers to allow them to remain a short time as it was so near that time of Festival [Christmas] but they would not. Previously 102 families had lived in the area but after the eviction only the walls of three houses remained."

—*James Hack Tuke*

THE FAMINE BURNED A NUMBER OF TERMS into the Irish folk memory: coffin ships, emigration, food exports, starvation, landlords, evictions. Of these, "evictions" is probably the most resonant since it touches on all the other terms. The word, far from unknown previously, began searing its way more prominently into the Irish lexicon early on in the tragedy as, for different reasons, landlords began taking advantage of the situation to get rid of unwanted tenants.

Lord Lucan, for example, systematically evicted 400 families, comprising some 2,200 people, from his Mayo estates, clearing wide areas around the Ballinrobe district in particular for sheep grazing. His Lordship's clout ensured that his flocks were not reduced by theft, as happened with smaller sheep graziers in other parts of the country. Between sheep and cattle rearing, combined in some cases with the renting of land to "strong farmers" for grazing purposes, Lord Lucan did very nicely out of the Famine. In fact, in the point-counterpoint nature of the Anglo-Irish relationship, Lord Lucan's clearances, while spreading desperation and death among the Irish, produced exactly the type of farming at which Sir Charles Wood, Sir Charles Trevelyan, Lord Palmerston, and the rest were aiming behind the cloaks of moralism and "providentialism."

Sometimes, however, as we shall see in the case of Ballinglass, County Galway, landlords evicted their tenants for less obvious reasons. But before going on to examine Ballinglass and some other examples of what can only be described as the landlords' cruelty, it is necessary in the interests of accuracy and fairness to emphasize that not all landlords were monsters. At least not entirely, as an eyewitness, John Mitchel, the bête noir of revisionists, pointed out: "Irish landlords are not all monsters of cruelty. Thousands of them indeed, kept far away from the scene, collecting their rents through agents and bailiffs, and spent them in England or in Paris. But the resident landlords and their families did, in many cases, devote themselves to the task of keeping their poor people alive. Many remitted their rents, or half their rents, and ladies kept their servants busy and kitchens smoking with continual preparations of food for the poor."[1]

However, from early 1846, when it was obvious that the peasantry had neither food nor money to pay the rents, some landlords began clearing the wretched from their estates to prevent arrears from mounting. What distinguished Ballinglass from this process was the fact that the tenants were apparently *not* in arrears. The village was a model of its kind. It consisted not of mud huts, but of sixty-one stone-built houses, all solid and well kept. The tenants lived under the rundale system, a system of land division where discontinuous strips of land were leased to tenants who held it in common and holdings therefore could include a small amount of fertile land with a strip of outlying bogland, foreshore, or less fertile rough or mountain grazing. The tenants had managed to clear some four hundred acres of bogland so that the place was a little haven of prosperity, or what passed for prosperity in the West of Ireland in those days. But the landlord or -lady, a Mrs. Gerrard, decided that she wanted to move into the realms of "high farming" and adapt her land for grazing purposes.

On the morning of March 30, 1846, a detachment of troops and police turned up to eject the people from their homes. Their belongings were thrown out and the roofs of their houses tumbled. It was made clear to the people in surrounding areas that if they took in the evictees, they would suffer the same fate. And so the evicted people passed from door to door vainly seeking shelter. In desperation they erected temporary shelters in ditches or constructed what would become a common sight that year across the Irish countryside, "scalps." These consisted either of poles covered by sods that were stretched across a ditch or, if the ditches were filled with water, as they frequently were, they simply dug a hole in the ground or in the shelter of a gable end of their tumbled house and covered this with sticks and sods. But in Ballinglass, as elsewhere, the bailiffs returned in the days following the evictions to destroy the "scalps" and move the people off the landlord's land.

Needless to say, all this happened in the years before waterproof rain gear became common, and the three hundred or so men, women, and children affected by the eviction were frequently barefoot and hopelessly ill-clad to withstand the rigors of a March night spent under the open skies of Ireland, when either rain or frost would not be uncommon. At the time, the reports of the weeping, the desolation of the people as they clung to the doors of their ruined homes or tried to rescue a blanket or a cooking pot before being driven away by the bailiffs, made a great impression on the public, and the question was raised in the House of Lords. But as the Famine worsened, the public became inured to even worse occurrences, evictions that could at least have been described as premeditated manslaughter and, at worst, as culpable homicide.

The latter term could certainly have been applied to a set of evictions carried out by a landlord called Walshe in the Belmullet district of Mayo shortly before Christmas 1847. There were three villages, or hamlets, of the straggling, unplanned, unhygienic sort frequently met with in Mayo and described in earlier chapters, on a bleakly beautiful peninsula known as the Mullet. Even in summer the wind blows cuttingly here, ruffling the sea-spray–tinted brown grass that grows sparsely on bad boggy land.

On the December day that Walshe himself led the eviction at the largest of the three villages, Mullaroghue, the wind blew at gale force. Eyewitnesses later testified to clergy and to a poor law inspector named Hamilton that Walshe had been implored to delay the evictions until after Christmas but refused. The cabins were destroyed and people driven from the district. The other two villages, Tiraun and Clogher, were systematically destroyed on succeeding days. One of the most meritorious figures in the Quaker effort, James Hack Tuke gave an account of what took place at Mullaroghue: "The people were all turned out of doors and the roofs of their houses pulled down. That night they made a tent or shelter, of wood and straw, but however the drivers [bailiffs] threw them down and drove them from the place. . . . It would have pitied the sun to look at them, as they had to go head first into the storm. . . . It was a night of high wind and storm, and wailing could be heard at a great distance. They implored the drivers to allow them to remain a short time as it was so near that time of Festival [Christmas] but they would not. Previously 102 families had lived in the area but after the eviction only the walls of three houses remained."[2]

As in Ballinglass, the proceedings horrified the British officer in charge of the troops involved, Captain Glazebrook of the Forty-ninth Regiment. In the days after the evictions Walshe tried to get the troops involved in driving the evictees from the district, but Glazebrook found various excuses for re-fusing his request. Similarly, at a place called Guitmore in County Tipperary, members of the Seventy-second Highlanders, perhaps moved by similar occurrences in Scotland, went far toward belying the Scots' reputation for meanness by openly declaring that they hated being involved in the eviction of several families and gave money to the evicted people.

An Englishman called Higgins, a member of a British Relief Association, who witnessed the aftermath of the Mullet evictions, wrote, "The horror of that wretched place you can never describe."[3] He said that he would like to have been made dictator of the district "with power to shoot." Hamilton, the poor law inspector, created a "feeding station" for the inhabitants of the ruined villages. (The term was probably used to get around Trevelyan's ban on providing outdoor relief.) Here he ministered to some three hundred people, whom he described as being "in various stages of fever, starvation and nakedness."[4] Many of these people were too weak to stand, so they lay on the ground, but they at least had the strength to make it to what must have been one of the last means of survival on earth. Hamilton noted that many more were too weak to leave their various shelters and ditches and died unfed and unseen.

The eyewitness accounts came from reputable, responsible people. James Hack Tuke, who had been powerfully affected by the sight of the traumatized evictees wandering about the ruins of their former homes like birds fluttering about pilfered nests while what remained of their belongings rotted in the rain, afterward wrote to the Society of Friends in London about a dinner that Walshe gave on the night of the first eviction: "I feel that it is utterly beyond my power to describe the full of misery of this and similar sights. At a dinner party that evening, the landlord, as I was told by one of the party, posted that this was the first time he had seen the estate or visited the tenants. Truly, their first impression of landlordism was not likely to be a very favourable one."[5]

How many perished through Walshe's evictions we will never know. Even for another Mayo tragedy of the same period that attracted international attention, accounts of the death toll vary. This was the Doolough Lake incident, which could equally well be called the Louisburgh walk of death. There are differing versions of what happened, but all agree on the fact that people died by the side of the road or soon after returning home from their fruitless but agonizing walk from Louisburgh.

The incident took place on March 30 and 31, 1849. A large group of people who had been instructed to turn up at Louisburgh to be examined to determine whether they qualified for tickets for relief from the Westport Union assembled at Louisburgh on March 30. However, they were informed that there had been some mistake and that the poor law commissioners were at Delphi Lodge, some sixteen kilometers away. After a night spent in the open, the starving people, between four and six hundred of them, although some accounts say the crowd was considerably larger, set off on foot for Delphi Lodge. When they got there, they were told that the commissioners were eating and could not be disturbed.

When the commissioners did meet the gathering, they informed the people that they did not qualify for tickets for relief and that they had no food to give them. The weakened people helplessly attempted to remonstrate but were driven away by the guards at the hunting lodge and set off back to Louisburgh. The crowd divided on the way home, some taking a route along the seashore, others following a track along Doolough Lake. The bodies of at least seven of these people were later discovered by the side of the lake. Others are said to have been swept into the lake by a mudslide, believed to have drowned when they fell into the water in their weakened state. Another version of the story is that the bodies of several of those who took the sea route were later washed up along the shore. Either way, a monument stands today to commemorate those who perished there. The inscription also pays tribute to the Choctaw Indians who, having survived a horrific march from Mississippi to Oklahoma in 1841, identified with the Louisburgh marchers and somehow managed to collect $700 for them from their meager resources.

I visited the memorial on a July day. The sunshine was countered by a cutting breeze that whipped around the mountains, and it was bitterly cold. After pausing for a few photographs, I was only too glad to get back into the car and turn on the heater. How the barefoot, half-naked starvelings felt during the hail and snow showers of March 1849 is best left to the imagination.

Even before the Famine the conditions in Mayo militated against accurate statistical compilation. During it, record keeping became an almost impossible task so that myth and reality often intertwined like the roots of a tree.

A group of the starving is said to have set off from the Erris district in impossible weather conditions to try to reach the workhouse in either Ballina or Westport; this involved treks of sixty and eighty kilometers, which would be more than a day's march for a skilled and healthy walker. The group probably came from caves cut into the bog and would almost certainly have been barefoot and dressed in rags. Famished and hallucinating from the effort of trying to cope with the march and the elements on stomachs that had been empty for days, the group were halted as night drew on by what appeared to them a ghastly apparition: it was a thorn tree, its branches lashing in the gale. The group fled in terror and their fate is not known. They simply perished into the oblivion of the still only guessed-at death toll of County Mayo. The story may be taken either literally or allegorically as an indication of the differing British and Irish attitudes to the Famine.

> At a lunch I attended in Boston, a prominent academic quoted a descrip-tion of "a monster," which he claimed he had been given by an English cabinet minister, who was at the time dealing with Irish affairs—a tree! Neither the Englishman or the American academic had ever visited the barren areas of Mayo and would not have known that there were no trees and a people who normally never moved much beyond 6 or 7 kilometres from their birthplace would have found a tree a very disturbing site in-deed—particularly if it was dusk and they were starving.
>
> —*Tory Lord Brougham*

After the Ballinglass evictions in 1846, for example, the Tory Lord Brougham answered critics of what had happened in Ireland by trumpeting the cause of laissez-faire and the rights of landlords in the terms previously quoted: "Undoubtedly it was the landlords right to do as he pleased, and if he abstained he conferred of favour and was doing an act of kindness."

Unfortunately, throughout the Famine many a landlord did "as he wished," thus making a sizeable contribution toward turning Ireland into a giant charnel house. However, to be fair, it should again be stressed, as John

Mitchel pointed out, that not every Irish landlord behaved in that fashion. Following Brougham's declaration, one of the largest landowners in Ulster, Lord Londonderry, condemned what had happened at Ballinglass and, in the House of Lords on March 30, asked, "Was it to be wondered at . . . that deeds of outrage and violence should occasionally be attempted?"

Lord Londonderry was speaking from an area of the country, Ulster, where there was a semblance of a decent relationship between landlord and tenant, largely because of the existence of the "tenant right," a custom whereby tenants who improved their holdings enjoyed the benefit of their initiative instead of being penalized for it, as happened in other parts of the country. It was the power of Lord Brougham's "strong arm of the law" that bore down on most Irish tenants in four separate ways: (1) the legal system governing evictions; (2) the £4 valuation rates levy on landlords; (3) the introduction of the Gregory Clause, which denied relief to anyone who owned more than a quarter acre of land; and (4) the Encumbered Estates Act, which raises very uncomfortable memories for Ireland.

At the time of writing, as a result of a crash in property values, a bad situation is being made worse by people being forced by creditors to sell their homes and businesses at knockdown prices that meet the needs of neither owners nor creditors. So it was during the Famine. The government made an attempt to create a market in farmland by the Encumbered Estates Act of 1849, which made it compulsory for land to be sold on the petition of either the owner or a creditor. The result was a series of fire sale auctions that caused further clearances and increased poverty. The speculators and gombeen class who did well out of buying land for a fraction of its worth proved to be even harsher landlords than the previous landowners, and evictions multiplied, with no immediate benefit to the overall situation.

As indicated earlier, most of the bill for securing Catholic Emancipation was paid for by the Irish peasantry. The price of the deal for the Irish, an increase in the property qualification from forty shillings to ten pounds, meant that the numbers entitled to the franchise in Ireland had fallen to 37,000. Prior to emancipation, the landlords had an inducement to allow subdivision to continue and the numbers of their tenants to multiply because they controlled their votes. The pendulum then swung the other way as, along with the diminished franchise, there arose a phenomenon already referred to: "high farming." This involved more scientific farming methods, the increased use of horses, steam, a concentration on growing cereals and green crops, and above all, larger fields involving fewer laborers and far fewer small holdings.

Prior to the Famine, a steady stream of legislation that encouraged the development of high farming had been enacted. One landlord spoke in 1820 of cheap ejectment as having been "found highly beneficial" and said it was therefore "desirable that same should be extended." The net effect of all this legislation, which applied only to Ireland, was to ensure that it made it both cheap and easy for a landlord to eject his tenants. A sheaf of summary ejectment could be secured from a judge at Quarter Sessions for a few shillings on the uncontested word of a landlord, or his agent, that a tenant was in arrears. Armed with these writs, the bailiffs speedily moved in, supported by the police and, if thought necessary, by the army, destroying homes quite legally.

Landlords didn't even have to carry out evictions legally. If they were powerful enough, they could bypass the law and eject tenants at will. Such an eviction occurred on the Blake estate in Galway on New Year's Eve 1848 and aroused such indignation that it was raised in the House of Commons on March 24, 1849, by the Radical MP George Poulett Scrope, supported by former Prime Minister Sir Robert Peel, who read into the record a horrific report on the incident by Major McKie to the poor law commissioners that deserves to be read in full:

It would appear from the evidence recorded that the forcible ejectment's work is illegal; that previous notices had not been served; and the ejectments were perpetrated under circumstances of great cruelty. The time chosen was, for the greater part, nightfall on the eve of the New Year. The occupiers were forced out of their houses with their helpless children, and left exposed to the cold on a bleak Western shore in a stormy winter's night; that some of the children were sick; that the parents implored that they might not be exposed and their houses left till the morning; that their prayers for mercy were in vain; and that many of them have since died. I have visited the ruins of these huts (not at any great distance from Mr. Blake's residence); I've found that many of these unfortunate people were still living within the ruins of these huts, endeavouring to shelter themselves under a few sticks and sods, all in the most wretched state of destitution; many were so weak that they could scarcely stand when giving their evidence. The site of these ruins is a rocky wild spot, fit for nothing but a sheep walk.[6]

However, despite the intervention of a former prime minister, nothing was done about Blake. The attorney general, Sir John Jervis, informed the House "that it was not usual in this country, *certainly not in Ireland,* to make any amount of private wrong the subject of a public indictment." Sir John was not entirely accurate. If one of Blake's Catholic tenants had committed a "private wrong," it would not have been merely usual but the norm to have proceeded with indictment backed up by such indispensable aids to the administration of justice as jail, transportation, or even the scaffold.

The £4 valuation charge and the Gregory Clause had devastating consequences. The former worsened the landlords' financial position and created the image that these feckless, reckless, and incompetent lords of the soil were going to provide monies essential for the provision of relief. Unions, as the groupings of parishes were termed, did not have the resources available to them to carry out the duties designed by Trevelyan and Wood and assigned to them by the British government. Worse, this shortfall was greatest in the areas that most needed relief, the impoverished West and Southwest of Ireland. As already noted, the Gregory Clause meant that to establish their destitution, tenants had to hand over their slivers of land before being deemed eligible for relief, thus swelling the numbers of paupers, removing any prospect of self-sufficiency, and putting further pressure on already scarce resources, forcing the Treasury to reluctantly put its hand further into British, not Irish, pockets. The inspiration behind the term "United Kingdom" had been that it would provide England with a tranquilized, non-threatening neighbor who would supply her with an inexhaustible supply of cannon fodder for her armies and an equally inexhaustible supply of cheap food for her citizens. The payment of a seemingly inexhaustible supply of

Irish food and medical bills had not formed part of the script. Grossly inadequate provision was made for the former and, sadly, as we shall see, even less for the latter.

The economic moralizing described in chapter 3 certainly formed part of the reason for the parsimonious approach, and several examples of a sanctimonious nomenclature of "providentialism" can and will be given to illustrate the mind-set of the London decision makers. But these attempts to show that it was God's hand working through mounds of rotting potatoes, and even more odoriferous rotting corpses, were akin to the claims of divine oversight made by Cromwell for his slaughters at Drogheda and elsewhere, or to the cry of "manifest destiny" that justified the slaughter of the North American Indians as the wagons rolled westward.

Trevelyan could cloak government policy in the language of morality better than most, as in the following extract from a letter he wrote to Lord Monteagle:

> I think I see a bright light shining in the distance to the dark cloud which at present hangs over Ireland. A remedy has been already applied to that portion of the maladies of Ireland which was traceable to political causes, and the morbid habits which still to a certain extent survive are gradually giving way to a more healthy action. The deep and inveterate root of social evil remains, and I hope I am not guilty of irreverence in thinking that this being altogether beyond the power of man, the cure has been applied by the direct stroke of an all-wise Providence in a manner as unexpected and unthought of as it is likely to be effectual. God grant that we may rightly perform our part and not turn into a curse what was intended for a blessing. The ministers of religion and especially the pastors of the Roman Catholic Church, who possess the largest sphere of influence over the people of Ireland, have well performed their part: and although few indications appear in many proceedings which have yet come before the public that the landed proprietors have even taken the first steps of preparing for the conversion of the land now laid down to potatoes to grain cultivation. I do not despair of seeing this class in society still taking the lead which their position requires of them, and

preventing the social revolution from being so extensive as it otherwise must become.[7]

Thus, a pity about the landlords, but the government believed that divine Providence sanctioned "high farming." In October 1846 the worst effects were about to manifest themselves. *The Times,* publicly viewed (correctly) as the voice of the establishment and privately a mainstay of Trevelyan and Wood's spin-doctor activities, had given vent to the following sentiments a month earlier, on September 22, 1846: "For our parts, we regard the potato blight as a blessing. When the Celts once cease to be potatophagi, they must become carnivorous. With the taste of meats will grow the appetite for them. With this will come steadiness, regularity, and perseverance; unless indeed the growth of these qualities be impeded by the blindness of Irish patriotism, the short sighted indifference of petty landlords, or the random recklessness of government benevolence."

There is no need to belabor the point, which would be immediately obvious to readers, that both the letter to Monteagle and *The Times*'s leader have resonances of Trevelyan's own versions on Celts and his *Morning Chronicle* epistle. However, it is appropriate to point out that behind the moral smokescreen there lurked a ruthless imperial attitude and an equally ruthless individual self-interest. Apart from an imperialist outlook, most members of the cabinet shared a common bond of being members of the aristocracy. Their power was such that their fathers bought parliamentary seats for them when they attained their majority as easily as they bought racehorses. Power, privilege, and a worldview were things they shared and guarded.

Some of the most disreputable and inexcusable events of the 1840s were the opium wars with China. Using modern naval technology, the British forced the Chinese to accept the opium trade, which made millions for British traders and destroyed the lives of millions of Chinese.

The chief architect of Britain's gun boat diplomacy in China was Viscount Lord Palmerston, a member of Lord Russell's cabinet and, like his colleague the Marquis of Clanricarde, the postmaster general, and Lord Lansdowne, had huge estates in Ireland. The deaths of the Irish cottiers weighed about as heavily on the consciences of these men as did the deaths of the Chinese in the opium wars. By March 1848 the evictions had so outraged Russell that he referred to the "lynch law of the Irish landlords." Complaining to the Irish Lord Lieutenant Lord Clarendon about the eviction policy, Russell, who at the time was bringing forward legislation proposals that, had they passed into law, would have rendered the eviction process more humane, said, "The murders of poor cottier tenants are too horrible to bear, and if we put down assassins, we ought to put down the lynch law of the landlord."[8]

Like Russell, Lansdowne had been a friend of Moore's and helped the Irish singer to live out his days in some dignity by giving him a house to live in on his enormous estate Bowood in Wiltshire. The marquis would prove himself less tender-hearted at the cabinet table when matters arose affecting the tenants on his large Kerry estates. Like many another Irish landlord, Lansdowne used emigration to clear his land. But it was said of his former tenants, who mainly congregated in New York's noisome Five Points district, that they were the most ragged and ill-clad of all the Irish emigrants who fled the Famine.[9]

On March 31 Russell gave vent to his feelings on eviction before his cabinet, whom he hoped to persuade to support a bill curbing evictions. However, another Irish landlord, Palmerston, had circulated to his colleagues a memorandum that, in effect, set forth what became the core policy of the British government toward the Irish land problem: "It was useless to disguise the truth that any great improvement in the social system of Ireland must be founded upon an extensive change in the present state of agrarian occupation, and that this change necessarily implies a long continued and systematic ejectment of Small holders and of Squatting Cottiers."[10]

Clanricarde made similar statements and, it is said, "a general shudder" went around the cabinet table.[11] The Palmerstonian viewpoint was shared by other Irish landlords, even by one of the most humane, Lord Monteagle. After Russell's bill had cleared the House of Commons, Monteagle, in particular, declared war on it in the House of Lords.

The upshot was that the bill was so gutted that by the time it passed into law, it was virtually irrelevant to the evictions policy. For example, one of its provisions said that pulling down the roof over somebody's head only became illegal if the person was in the house at the time. Nighttime evictions were also precluded, as were evictions on Christmas Day or Good Friday. With colleagues like Palmerston and Monteagle and company, that was the best Russell could do.

SEVEN
THE WORK SCHEMES

"It was melancholy in the extreme to see the women and girls labouring in the gangs on public roads. They were employed not only in digging with the spade and pick, but also in carrying loads of earth and turf on their backs and wielding barrels like men and breaking stones, while the poor neglected children were crouched in groups, about the bits of lighted turf in the various sheltered corners along the line."

—*William Bennett, in Tubbercurry, County Sligo*[1]

SOME HISTORIANS HAVE ARGUED THAT IT IS unfair to blame Sir Charles Trevelyan for the Famine as he was only a public servant executing the government policy. However, even though Trevelyan's station was officially merely that of civil servant, albeit an exalted one, while the Irish Famine was being hammered into being on the anvil of Whig policy, it cannot be denied that it was Trevelyan who enthusiastically swung the hammer. Even today his role is recognized by the Irish all over the world. Weighty historians, writing in different eras, in different countries, and with differing methodologies, like James Donnelly Jr. and Cecil Woodham-Smith, have stressed the extent to which he both initiated famine policies and was given carte blanche to carry them out.

He is most clearly remembered, more in sorrow than in anger, in a remarkable song composed by Pete St. John in 1979 that, thanks to television and the Internet, is sung by the Irish worldwide, especially in the unlikely setting of rugby and football matches. "The Fields of Athenry" has been adopted as the anthem of the great Irish rugby province of Munster and is also sung by Leinster supporters and rings out during moments of excitement at international games. In addition, it is sung as "The Fields of Anfield" by supporters of the Liverpool soccer team, a club that, of course, has roots deep in the Irish experience. Probably the most remarkable use of the song came, however, in the Euro 2012 Championship. Tens of thousands of Irish supporters who, in the teeth of recession, had made their way to Poland to support Ireland were devastated by the unexpectedly poor performance of their side—the first team to be knocked out of the competition. But instead of rioting or venting their anger on the team, the Irish fans stood together long after the match had ended, belting out "The Fields of Athenry." The message of this remarkable tableau, which was captured on television to be seen all around the world, emanated from deep in the Irish folk memory and said in effect, "We survived the Famine and we will get over this also."

The Fields of Athenry
Pete St. John

By a lonely prison wall
I heard a young girl calling
Michael they are taking you away
For you stole Trevelyan's corn
So the young might see the morn.
Now a prison ship lies waiting in the bay.

Low lie the Fields of Athenry
Where once we watched the small free birds fly.
Our love was on the wing we had dreams and songs to sing
It's so lonely 'round the Fields of Athenry.

By a lonely prison wall
I heard a young man calling
Nothing matters Mary when you're free,

Against the Famine and the Crown
I rebelled they ran me down
Now you must raise our child with dignity.

Low lie the Fields of Athenry
Where once we watched the small free birds fly.
Our love was on the wing we had dreams and songs to sing
It's so lonely 'round the Fields of Athenry.

By a lonely harbor wall
She watched the last star falling
As that prison ship sailed out against the sky
Sure she'll wait and hope and pray
For her love in Botany Bay
It's so lonely 'round the Fields of Athenry.

"Whig policy" is usually taken to mean the fidelity to the Protestant virtues of thrift, hard work, self-reliance, and charity for the "deserving poor only." This created a strongly sympathetic milieu for Trevelyan, but three points can be validly made here. First, readers' attention is called again to his letter to the *Morning Chronicle;* this reeks with anti-Irish and anti-Catholic sentiment and moreover is highly inaccurate in its judgments. The Catholic clergy, for example, far from seeking "the temporalities" of their Church of Ireland counterparts, were resolutely opposed to state subventions as they feared it would cut them off from their flocks. Second, O'Connell was in no danger of having his carriage of repeal hijacked by the priests. He used the priests purely as educated marshals of his followers, and though a devout Catholic himself, he led rather than followed bishops and senior clergy. O'Connell, for example, was far less inclined to accept the government's proposals on the university question than were the bishops, for all their seeming opposition to "godless colleges." The controversy centered on the setting up of a National University for Ireland, with constituent colleges and centers such as Belfast, Cork, Dublin, and Galway, and passed into law in 1845. While the bishops were concerned with the teaching of religion, the Protestants opposed the giving of grants for Catholic education. O'Connell was concerned with the issue of Anglicization and the possibility that the colleges might be used as centers for spreading colonial doctrines. He understood Westminster and English politics better than they and could see pitfalls and traps if the type of colonizing propaganda used in primary education (described in chapter 9) was carried into the tertiary sphere.

Third, apart from prejudice, Trevelyan was fundamentally destructive and obstructive toward any substantive proposal to build up the Irish economy, as opposed to merely clearing the land and putting the English food supply on a better footing.

Trevelyan's policy and that of like-minded powerful supporters, such as Sir Charles Wood, the Marquis of Clanricarde, the Marquis of Landsdowne, Lord Palmerston, and Sir George Grey, took a firm hold in the fault lines of the clash of cultures between Whig orthodoxies and Irish realities. A clash of cultures is said to have occurred when Ireland was examined through this prism. The Irish were seen as feckless, lazy, and wallowing in a mess of potatoes and priest-craft. Throughout the Famine they would certainly be portrayed as such, but behind the rhetoric of Whiggery and the jargon of political economy there lay the brutal, unacknowledged realpolitik that Palmerston had articulated: Famine was at long last dealing with the Irish land problem. A surplus and unwanted population was being disposed of. It cannot be too often stated that sitting alongside Palmerston were men like Clanricarde and Lansdowne, all of whom had a vested interest in the Irish situation through their vast Irish estates. One wonders if they joined in the shuddering.

Palmerston was the son of an Irish peer and had extensive estates in one of the worst-hit counties, Sligo. He was a ruthless exponent of gunboat diplomacy, undermining foreign governments to further British interests. He moved easily between Tory and Whig cabinet posts but used his vast English political influence merely to help him shrug off well-founded criticisms that he treated his Irish tenants badly and shipped them across the Atlantic in particularly inhumane conditions. Hubert George de Burgh-Canning, better known as the Marquis Clanricarde, had a 50,000-acre estate in the Portumna district of County Galway and was known not merely through the Famine but throughout much of the subsequent decades as a particularly exploitative absentee landlord. So far as Lansdowne's Irish land-owner's hat was concerned, there was a thin man, or at least the semblance of a decent one, trying to get out of the fat reality of his role as an Irish landlord and the Earl of Kerry. But as we will see in chapter 12, "Emigration," his human qualities did little or nothing for his Irish tenants during the Famine.

Sir Robert Peel's efforts to stave off famine were appreciated by the poor. Sir Edward Pine-Coffin, a commissioner general of the Relief Commission, reported that there was a general awareness that "only for the government meal, thousands would have been now dying by the roadside." Peel's biographer Douglas Hurd, himself a former Tory home secretary, would later claim that under Peel, no one died of starvation. Would that a similar judgment could have been passed on Russell's administration!

Peel's approach had been two-pronged. On the one hand, he had quietly arranged to have some twenty thousand tons of Indian corn and oatmeal shipped into the country and stored at a series of distribution depots. Under the tutelage of the relief commissioners, local committees then arranged for the sale and distribution of this food at cost price. The money to subsidize this was collected locally from landlords and others, and by a government subvention. The scale of this assistance was not large—£68,000 cash—but it had a markedly beneficial impact in combating hunger. The food was released onto the market in a concentrated period between mid-May and mid-August 1846, thus keeping food prices down. Had the government retained the Irish production of oats and oatmeal in the country that year, this alone would have helped balance the loss of the potato. But such a course was unthinkable in the laissez-faire climate of the day.

The second prong of Peel's approach had been an attempt to spend money on permanent improvements such as harbors and land drainage. Some of Peel's ideas (based on his own firsthand knowledge of the country's needs) could have been of benefit to Ireland even as this is written. For example, money was to be spent on developing the fishing industry: providing better boats, nets, and equipment. There was also an imaginative scheme to link up the lakes of Connacht and Ulster that could have benefited either nineteenth-century transportation of goods or twenty-first-century tourism. But too little money was offered to encourage the adoption of either of these improving schemes and, overall, much too little local initiative was forthcoming. Instead, public works expenditure largely degenerated into road works.

There were two principal reasons for this: the method whereby the schemes were financed and the bureaucratic procedures governing the sanctioning of schemes. The road schemes, whether they involved improving existing roads or building new ones through landlords' properties, were immediately popular because they qualified for a 50 percent grant. Loans were available for other works, but these had ultimately to be paid for out of local resources.

The scheme designed to pay for these works and, insofar as possible, keep down their costs was cumbersome and time-wasting in the extreme. An area seeking assistance had to begin the process by sending a petition to the lord lieutenant. The petition, or Memorial, as it was termed, was then forwarded to the relief commissioners and to the Board of Works for inspection. Next it was sent to a local surveyor. The surveyor then sent a report on the validity of the scheme to the Board of Works, which, if it accepted the surveyor's findings, then made a recommendation to the lord lieutenant, who then sought permission where it counted—from the Treasury.

The scheme was a microcosm of how Ireland was governed in the nineteenth century. Genuine attempts to improve the lot of the people were befogged by a miasma of prejudice, interest, lack of capital, and a stultifying of local initiative. In a word, the scheme embodied all the corruption and delay involved in administering what was supposed to be a full partner in the Union of England, Scotland, Wales, and Ireland but was in fact a badly run, resentful colony kept in check by force, or the threat of force. By the end of 1846, famine would cruelly expose that unlovely reality.

Things were already bad at the beginning of the year, particularly so in the counties of Cork, Kerry, Clare, Galway, and Mayo, where people were already living in hunger and a growing terror of starvation. Peel had introduced his relief measures to Parliament in January, but the system described above ensured that relief only began in March. In parts of Mayo, work did not begin until June and in Tubbercurry in Sligo not until July. Meanwhile, the failure of the potato was having all sorts of consequences on health, on the food chain, and on the economy. Deprived of the cheap source of feed provided by the potato, pig rearing fell off. Deprived of the profit from pig rearing, cottiers' rent paying fell off, and evictions followed. Hunger also caused a decline in sheep rearing as farmers found that their flocks were being raided at night. The resultant switch to cattle rearing helped to further increase evictions as farmers began requiring more space for grasslands.

Even potatoes that had appeared sound when stored in 1845 were found to be diseased when the pits were opened. Although they were clearly unfit for human consumption, these were frequently eaten by the desperate, who attempted to make them edible by cutting away as much of the diseased portion as possible. Further long-term disaster was guaranteed when starvation forced people to eat their stores of seed potatoes. Contemporary accounts describe people fighting off this last fatal step, sometimes going without food of any sort for days before being forced to eat the seed. For such people and their families, death's visit was subjected to but a brief postponement. The small amount of potatoes planted in the spring guaranteed shortage and starvation in the autumn.

By August 1846 the various relief schemes are reckoned to have employed some 140,000 people at wages of nine to ten pence a day. It is generally estimated that when family numbers were included, some 700,000 benefited from the schemes. For all their manifest faults, the schemes succeeded in their primary objective of staving off famine.

But it was the question of deficiencies, not of distress, that engaged Trevelyan's attention—and his anger. His objections were twofold: philosophical and practical. His overall attitude to relief was contained in the letter he wrote to Sir Randolph Routh on December 1, 1845, in the early days of the crisis: "That indirect permanent advantages will accrue to Ireland from the scarcity, and the measures taken for its relief, I entertain no doubt. . . . Besides, the greatest improvement of all which could take place in Ireland would be to teach the people to depend upon themselves for developing the resources of the country, instead of having recourse to the assistance of the government on every occasion. . . . If a firm stand is not made against the prevailing disposition to take advantage of this crisis to break down barriers, the true permanent interests of the country will, I am convinced, suffer in a manner which will be irreparable in our time."[2]

Decoded, one can see in the passage echoes of Trevelyan's 1843 Philalethes contribution to the *Morning Chronicle;* a desire to make those responsible in Ireland, the landlords, shoulder their own burdens; and an inclination to, at best, push Ireland toward "high farming" and, at worst, take advantage of the crisis by letting nature take its course in helping to clear surplus population off the land.

Captain Edmond Wynne, Board of Works inspector for West Clare, earned himself an unenviable reputation in the history of the Famine for the ammunition he furnished Trevelyan in furthering his objectives. Wynne, whose activities have been chronicled by Ciarán Ó Murchadha for the number of faults he found with the work schemes, is credited—discredited would be a better term—with providing Trevelyan with the reasons he needed to close down the schemes completely.[3] Afterward, the chameleon Wynne, probably to distract attention from his handiwork, affected to be moved by the suffering this caused and produced what to the uninitiated could be taken as a genuinely sympathetic description of the misery caused by the closures:

> I confess myself unmanned by the extent and intensity of the suffering that I witnessed more especially amongst the women and little children, crowds of whom were to be seen scattered over the turnip fields, like a flock of starving crows, devouring the raw turnips, mothers half-naked, shivering in the snow and sleet, uttering exclamations of despair while their children were screaming with hunger.[4]

As Peel's relief scheme lumbered into operation, Trevelyan's opposition to a number of the salient features grew exponentially. In April 1846 Trevelyan drew up and issued a Treasury report that contained a number of serious criticisms of the scheme: The wages were too high. He would have preferred to have seen food given in return for work, but if wages were to be paid they should be at a lower rate than the normal levels obtained in any neighborhood. Reverting to the basic workhouse approach to the Irish relief package, Trevelyan declared that wages should only aim at keeping a laborer and his family from starvation. He claimed that the existing rates of pay (nine to ten pence a day) were diverting laborers from normal farm work, and he bolstered this argument by pointing to the fact that, in some areas, seasonal migration to England had stopped. He also objected to the fact that payment was made on a daily basis, not for task work, and claimed that this acted as an inducement to make public works both slow and expensive.

The report, which was drawn up on Trevelyan's own initiative without reference to the government, was condemned by the man who was supposed to be his political master, chancellor of the exchequer Henry Goulburn, and by other members of the government as interference in government policy, but no action was taken against him. One reason for this immunity, apart from the formidable character of the man himself, was the fact that, unfortunately, Trevelyan had good grounds for criticizing some aspects of the relief scheme's workings.

He could see at a glance that many of the schemes put forward were aimed not at succoring the people but at providing local interests, mainly landlords, with a share of the grants. Evidence of patronage, graft, and corruption was not difficult to find. The tickets necessary to enable a laborer to take part in the work scheme sometimes fell into the hands of profiteers, who sold them to the desperate. Patronage, or bribery, sometimes allowed unqualified persons to put their hands into the public purse. Only the destitute were supposed to be employed in the work schemes, but there is evidence that some small farmers were placed on the schemes by landlords in order to ensure that they paid their rents.

Overall, the work schemes were a shambles. The Whig objection to interfering with market forces had to be met, which meant in effect that most of the work undertaken had either no benefit or, worse, a harmful effect. "*Bóithre an ocrais*" (roads of hunger) were built going nowhere, petering out in bogs or rocky plateaus. Holes were dug in existing roads and then filled in again. Hills and hollows in roadways were meant to be leveled out but frequently became traffic hazards; reports of carriages losing wheels and accidents occurring on what had hitherto been safe roads became commonplace.

Ironically, this waste of resources came about because Trevelyan, consistently and relentlessly, deployed his formidable intellect in finding arguments against spending money in Ireland on even the most worthwhile and productive of projects. Lord George Bentinck, speaking in the House of

Commons on February 4, 1847, pointed out quite correctly, at a time when the country was crying out for assistance of any sort, that there were "500,000 able-bodied persons in Ireland living upon the funds of the state . . . commanded by a staff of 11,587 persons, employed upon works which have been variously described as 'works worse than idleness' . . . as 'public follies' and as 'works which will answer no other purpose than that of obstructing the public conveyances.'"[5]

Bentinck's eminently practical suggestion for improving this state of affairs was to build badly needed railways in Ireland, for which the government should raise a loan of £16 million at 3.5 percent, the loan to be repaid with interest in thirty-seven years and the railways taken as security. Trevelyan objected to the proposal, arguing: "The only item of railway construction requiring unskilled manual labour was earthworks, and that expenditure was only one-third of the whole. The most distressed of the population would not be reached, because railway lines were not constructed through impoverished districts, and far from giving employment to the helpless and destitute the object of railway companies is to select the ablest labourers who will give the best return for their wages."[6]

The American entrepreneurs who linked the East and West Coasts of America with railways were apparently unaware of Trevelyan's pronouncements concerning the lack of need for unskilled laborers. They built the transcontinental railway by employing vast armies of not only unskilled Irish laborers but Chinese workers, and they accomplished one of the great engineering feats of nineteenth-century America (the Irish laid the track from the East and the Chinese laid it from California).

When Peel's government fell in the summer of 1846, Trevelyan, working with a like-minded chancellor of the exchequer, Sir Charles Wood, was in a position to exert even greater influence on Irish relief, and he set about incorporating what he saw as reforms into both the ideological and practical spheres. Stringency and Whig ideology, not humanity, were to be the watchwords from here on.

With the second failure of the potato in 1846 the period of "distress" may be said to have given way to that of the Famine. Coroners' juries began to bring in verdicts of "willful murder" against Lord John Russell's government. The core of Trevelyan's policy was contained in a catchphrase that was frequently to be heard in decision-making Whig circles: "Irish property must pay for Irish poverty." There were to be road works again, but this time there were to be no grants. The government would advance loans to enable the works to be carried out, but the money had to be repaid by the counties where the works took place. Interest was charged at a rate of 3 percent per annum.

This stipulation, combined with the Gregory Clause, was to give a literally fatal stimulus to evictions. Another of Trevelyan's innovations also had the effect of pushing up debt rates. He made it a condition of employment that work should only be paid for on a task basis. The scheme was administered by the Irish Board of Works, which was swamped by the number of applicants and had only a limited number of engineers to measure up and cost the tasks, with the result that, as in the first scheme, there were long bureaucratic delays before it went into operation.

As was the case with the first scheme, the task work, apart from its primary function of filling empty bellies, was intended to do a number of other things. According to Trevelyan, it would promote feelings of self-reliance and banish indolence. It can be said to have failed on all fronts. Sometimes the laborers didn't have the picks, the shovels, or the wheelbarrows necessary to carry out their allotted tasks. Not only did such people, coming from the type of barren mud cabin already described, not have shovels and other implements, but they were often lucky to have a shirt on their backs. Every other article of clothing had generally been either pawned or sold.

Delays in paying these people added to the misery; some of the delays may have been caused by the heartless incompetence of pay clerks. But graft and corruption, those two inevitable outriders of any large-scale calamity, were also present. The following is a brief abstract from an account written by the most effective and knowledgeable relief organization that attempted to alleviate the Famine, that set up by the Society of Friends, the Quakers. A full list of the abuses may (and should) be read in appendix 6.

There were instances of clearances by landlords as ex-officio poor law guardians refusing to recommend their tenants to outdoor relief unless they gave up their holdings; the dead were left unburied, "so contrary to the Irish reverence for funeral rites"; landlords were not interested in taking advantage of the Improvement Act to get their lands drained; only the able-bodied men and boys could participate in the government's public works scheme—the aged, infirm, widowed, and disabled were excluded. Landlords took little interest in the schemes. Apart from the problem of absentee landlords and lack of resident gentry in some areas, towns owned by the Ecclesiastical Commission were precluded by an act of Parliament from granting aid, and these suffered terribly.

The worst culprits, of course, were those landlords and bigger farmers who sought to avoid paying anything toward relief. One of the most egregious offenders was Lord Lucan, who said that he would not pay "paupers to breed priests."[7] He holds an unenviable place in Irish history because of the thousands he evicted from his vast estates. However, in his guise of concerned citizen, Lucan wrote to the lord lieutenant complaining that the relief committee in the Foxford area had allowed on to the work scheme "forty nine persons who had between them upwards of 200 cows, 50 horses and asses, several sheep and a quantity of oats."[8]

As a result of such claims and the experiences of the previous scheme, the Board of Works issued directions that sought to ensure that only the "deserving poor" were employed. Lists were to be prepared for scrutiny by the responsible engineers to weed out the unsuitable. But who was to weed out the weeders? Patronage, a culture of "jobs for the boys," is deeply rooted in the Irish tradition.

From Sligo came complaints that pay clerks included the sons of clergymen and a magistrate. However, such cases were defended on the grounds that pay clerks needed a knowledge of accounts and sureties (two of £400 each) that their salary of £2 a week would not meet. What the inducements were to take the jobs in such circumstances we can only speculate. What is known is that schoolmasters were criticized for being double jobbers, neglecting their pupils by somehow managing to get themselves hired as stewards and other functionaries of the relief schemes.

There were other drawbacks to the public works relief scheme, but the most serious was the low level of wages: ten pence a day or thereabouts. This was insufficient to keep a man and his family alive in the best of times.

But these were the worst of times, and scarcity was driving up food prices. By November, Indian meal was selling at 2 pounds 2 shillings a stone, or 6.35 kilos, in Tipperary. (One pound equaled 20 shillings, and there were 12 pence to the shilling.) A relief official's report stated that the people were "in great distress [and] ten pence a day will, I believe, only give one meal a day to a family of six persons."[9] By December, the meal was selling at 3 shillings and 4 pence in Roscommon and at around 2 shillings and 8 pence in Limerick, Clare, and Galway, and in Meath, the most fertile county in Ireland, at 3 shillings. Moreover, delays in the allocation of task work meant that though the job might be measured and approved, its cost might not be, and payment of even the slender wages was held up. It is a matter of record that men died of starvation while waiting for wages owed to them.

Reports similar to the following (from West Clare) reached Dublin from all over the country. Laborers arriving for work were described as being so weakened that they were staggering when they arrived at the worksite: "Hundreds of them are never seen to taste food from the time they come upon the works in the morning until they depart at night."[10]

Lieutenant-Colonel Harry Jones, who was in charge of the Board of Works, noted that this was no isolated incident. He said, "In some districts the men who come up to the works are so reduced in their physical powers to be unable to earn above four pence or five pence *per diem*."[11]

To make matters worse, the skies literally closed over Ireland in that awful winter of 1847. Fierce showers of sleet and thunderous rain swept across fields filled with the blackened potato stocks. There were heavy frosts and huge falls of snow. Trevelyan saw the arrival of bad weather as an opportunity to save money. He greeted the arrival of the frosts in December by telling Lieutenant-Colonel Jones, "Now that the hard weather is here, you will, I presume, act upon the rule long ago settled by you with the Lord-Lieutenant that on days when the weather will not permit the people to work, they will receive but a proportion of what they would otherwise earn, that is clearly the right way of meeting the exigency."[12]

The Board of Works officials who administered the relief schemes were like the meat in a sandwich caught between the horrors of famine and the in some ways greater horrors of political economy. It was they who felt and bore the brunt of the laborers' anger at the introduction of piecework. It was they who suffered threat and intimidation as desperate men sought work for themselves or, sometimes, members of their families. And it was they who had to cope with the conflicting demands of the vast tide of human misery flowing onto the works and the penny-pinching demands of the Treasury.

Fudge and compromise was the outcome of the clash between the two forces. When the "hard weather," as Trevelyan called it, arrived, the work schemes notionally went ahead, though what work could be carried out by starving people on roads subject to heavy frost and snow that was sometimes several feet deep, it is difficult to imagine. But when falls of several feet of snow occurred, as happened in parts of the worst-affected areas of the West such as Clare, Mayo, Sligo, and Donegal, it became impossible to pretend that road work was continuing. As a result, not only were starving men deprived of their pittances, but they and their children were evicted into these arctic conditions for non-payment of rent.

One method of dealing with the crisis was to allow stone breaking to be considered a relief work. Another was to admit women and children to the works. This resulted in scenes like the following recorded by a William Bennett in Tubbercurry, County Sligo, which introduces this chapter: "It was melancholy in the extreme to see the women and girls labouring in the gangs on public roads. They were employed not only in digging with the spade and pick, but also in carrying loads of earth and turf on their backs and weeding barrels like men and breaking stones, while the poor neglected children were crouched in groups, about the bits of lighted turf in the various sheltered corners along the line."[13]

Yet even though the numbers employed in the works mushroomed to a total of over 700,000 at peak, by the time the works schemes ended, they had alleviated only a fraction of the crisis they were allegedly meant to solve. For example, around Tubbercurry, from whence came that heartbreaking account of the women and children breaking stones, distress was particularly acute, but the work scheme proved singularly inadequate to deal with it.

Liam Swords, one of the most authoritative commentators on the Famine in the West of Ireland, noted that "a petition from Bohola in the middle of November at the beginning of '46, signed by the parish priest, curate and a number of other prominent inhabitants complained that of the population of 4,800, three quarters of whom were in 'the most frightful destitution' only 230 were employed which was about one in every 16 required. In the parishes of Swinford, Kiltimagh and Bohola, with a combined population of almost 22,000, not more than one in 10 of those requiring relief were employed . . . only one fifth of those in Ballaghaderreen who needed it were given employment."[14]

Swords quotes the parish priest of Ballaghederreen who wrote to the lord lieutenant in October 1847 saying, "The awful scenes I have this day to communicate are heart rending. Two persons have died today from starvation. One of them, declared a few hours before his death that he had not eaten a full meal for 12 days previously. I had over 200 persons at this my house today crying out for work or food. Their patience is great considering their wants. . . . Their appearance is frightful. We have only two principal lines here where the people are employed and one quarter of those who want work are not on them. If the Board of Works does not provide work . . . we will have to record in dozens the deaths of the people."

The people of the district were not given work, and deaths were recorded "in dozens." All over the country graveyards filled up as, increasingly, potholes did not. One of the worst winters in recorded Irish history bore down with pitiless severity. In a remarkable article, written to commemorate the 150th anniversary of the Famine, the historian Laurence M. Geary notes the extraordinary similarity between the effects of famine on the Irish and on the half million Jews in the Warsaw ghetto who were systematically starved by the Nazis in 1942. Hunger changed "active, busy, energetic people into oppressed, apathetic, sleepy beings, always in bed, hardly able to stand up to eat or go to the toilet."[15]

There were indeed striking similarities in the effects of hunger on both the Irish and the Jews. There was, however, one difference: in that winter of 1846–47 many of the Irish did not have beds. They were driven from their homes to face the elements by evicting landlords or their agents and by "middlemen." In many cases death was the inevitable consequence of eviction. Death was not caused directly by starvation, but by related disease. Under Peel's administration it had been recognized that it was a near certainty that if famine struck, it would inevitably be accompanied by disease, and a number of measures were taken to curtail the spread of fevers.

In March 1846 the government set up the Central Board of Health to improve facilities for dealing with fever. Fever was already endemic, although relatively controlled among the urban poor and in the congested districts of the West, Northwest, and Southwest. At that time there were only twenty-eight fever hospitals in the country. In addition, there were some five hundred dispensaries for outpatients, and the workhouses were provided with some rudimentary facilities. The Central Board of Health was attempting to improve these facilities when Peel's government fell. Regime change, a good summer, and, ironically, the fact that Peel's measures had just about managed to stave off famine and, consequently, disease meant that the board was wound up.

The ghastly events of the winter of 1846–47 caused it to be reconstituted in February 1847. Deprived of the regular supply of vitamin C contained in a potato diet, the starving people became susceptible to diseases of all sorts, particularly among the young and the elderly. They were also carried off by familiar diseases ranging from the common cold, to influenza, to tuberculosis and painful stomach disorders caused by eating badly cooked Indian meal. But the mass killers were those fevers normally contained in their lairs amid the poor and now unleashed all over the country: typhus, relapsing fever, and bacillary dysentery (the "bloody flux") were joined by outbreaks of scurvy, pellagra, and smallpox. Typhus and relapsing fever are spread by the human louse; bacillary dysentery, by human contact, by eating diseased food, and by lack of hygiene. This will be dealt with in chapter 8.

Hordes of dispossessed people wandering from house-to-house, village to town in the vain hope of finding either food or employment became unwitting but ideal vectors for the spread of disease. The crowded soup kitchens and the overcrowded workhouses meant that places like Skibbereen became charnel houses, all combined with enforced mobility to ensure that the greatest number of deaths during the Famine were caused not by starvation itself but by the agonizing diseases that accompanied "the Great Hunger."

A typical Irish cottage of the period (sketched by Arthur Young in 1780). Smoke escapes through a hole in the roof. Potatoes grow in the lazy beds in the background.

The Gardeners' Chronicle.

SATURDAY, SEPTEMBER 13, 1845.

MEETINGS FOR THE TWO FOLLOWING WEEKS.
WEDNESDAY, Sept. 17—South London Floricultural   .   1 P.M.

COUNTRY SHOWS.
WEDNESDAY,   Sept. 17 – Hexham Floral and Horticultural.
FRIDAY,   Sept. 19 – Devon and Exeter Botanical and Hort.
THURSDAY,   Sept. 25 – Surrey Horticultural and Floral.

WE stop the Press, with very great regret, to announce that the POTATO MURRAIN has unequivocally declared itself in Ireland. The crops about Dublin are suddenly perishing. The conversion of Potatoes into flour, by the processes described by Mr. BABINGTON and others in to-day's Paper, becomes then a process of the first national importance ; for where will Ireland be, in the event of a universal Potato rot ?

Recognizing the seriousness of the coming of the blight, the influential London publication The Gardeners' Chronicle *stopped the presses during a print run to include a "Stop Press" notice on its front page.*

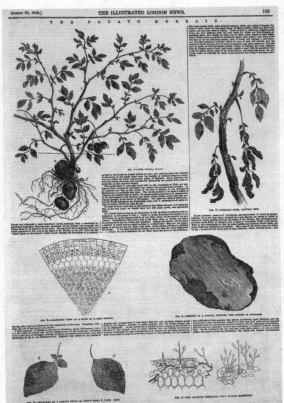

A fatal diet: a tuber-bearing potato plant.

The notorious Clifden, County Galway, workhouse, which went bankrupt with disastrous consequences for the starving paupers of the district.

A death cart in operation. This lithograph was created by Lord Dufferin, one of two young aristocrats (the other was the Hon. G. F. Boyle) who published an account of their journey from Oxford to Skibbereen during 1847 and on their return to the university took up a collection for the starving that netted £50 sterling.

The day after ejectment: a London Illustrated News *sketch of a man and members of his family on the day after they had been evicted from their home.*

A "scalpeen." This London Illustrated News *sketch of 1849 shows a typical example of the type of dwelling that evicted tenants tried to establish within the walls of their unroofed cottage.*

The village of Moveen in County Clare as it looked after bailiffs had evicted the people and removed the roofs of the houses.

In lieu of rent, landlords were entitled to seize cattle, crops, or other valuable possessions from their tenants who could not, or did not, pay their rents. This London Illustrated News *sketch from 1849 shows drovers driving seized livestock at Oughterard, County Galway.*

one out of the group on the floor in the Ballinaboy school opened 4 months on 10 Aug

Oh' some of them are too Naked to stand up.

Starvation or nakedness? This sketch of a starving child sitting on the floor of a school in Ballinaboy, County Galway, is thought to have been made by a Protestant visitor to the school in August 1850, four months after the school had been opened during the Protestant-Catholic educational controversies of the period. The irrelevance of the controversy to those most concerned, the children, may be judged from the fact that the child, like many encountered by the artist, was sitting on the floor either out of hunger-induced weakness or to hide his or her lack of clothes.

Sir Robert Peel, the Conservative prime minister who attempted to avert the famine.

Lord John Russell, the Whig prime minister whose administration presided over the famine.

Lord Palmerston, the English statesman and Irish landlord whose views on land clearance caused his cabinet colleagues to shudder and, ultimately, acquiesce in his view.

Lord Lansdowne, cabinet member and man of refinement. His Kerry tenants were the shabbiest emigrants to land in New York.

Lord Monteagle, a cabinet member and Irish landlord who did make some efforts to alert his colleagues to the sufferings of the peasantry.

John Mitchel, the Irish rebel journalist and polemicist, was the principal exponent of the theory that held that God sent the blight but the English sent the famine.

Daniel O'Connell, the Irish Catholic leader who died as the worst of the famine struck. His advice, which if accepted would have greatly limited the famine's impact, was greeted with indifference by the House of Commons.

Charles Trevelyan, knighted for his famine contribution, as he appeared in 1865. Courtesy Multitext Project in History, University College Cork.

EIGHT

THE WORKHOUSE

"Every system of poor relief must contain a penal and repulsive element, in order to prevent its leading to the disorganization of society. If the system is such as to be agreeable either to those who relieve or to those who are relieved, and still more if it is agreeable to both, all test of destitution must be at an end."

—*Sir Charles Trevelyan to Lord Monteagle, October 9, 1846*[1]

T HE *FREEMAN'S JOURNAL* REMARKED PRE-sciently on April 22, 1847, that political economy was a science that looked at things "in the long run," but that "life or death depends on the short run." By December 1849, when the Famine had had not a short but an altogether too long run, the London *Times* quoted a report from the *Limerick Chronicle* that the union workhouse proposed under the Irish Poor Law Provisions was so inappropriate and cruelly irrelevant that the following conditions were observed in Kilrush workhouse: "Money and credit are all gone, and starvation has literally set in among the paupers in the workhouse; the inmates having been sent to bed on Thursday night without having eaten any dinner—the only remedy that the guardians could suggest to numb the sense of hunger."

Here it might be remarked that the impact of these awful conditions and what gave rise to them was not confined within workhouse walls. Moral

as well as physical degradation, even today, makes for uncomfortable conversations, particularly in the Irish countryside. We get glimpses of some of
the sources of discomfort from the records of the priceless National Folklore
Collection at University College Dublin (UCD). The archive owes its existence to another, more successful initiative by the then Irish taoiseach, or
prime minister, Éamon de Valera, who wanted the centenary of the Famine
marked in a commemorative book, *The Great Famine*. As a result, in 1945 a
team of Irish-speaking researchers was established with the mission of seeking out elderly people who might have firsthand recollections from parents
or grandparents of what had happened during the Famine.

In those days of petrol shortages and woefully inefficient public transport the collection of archival material was literally a labor of love. The ar-
chivists were not well paid and did not always own cars. The two collectors
assigned to Kerry and Donegal had to traverse their mountainous districts
on bicycles. Their recording equipment weighed twenty-five kilograms and
could record only eight minutes of conversation at a time before reels had
to be replaced. One man, Michael J. Murphy, had a bad leg and did not
possess a car. As the director of the folklore archive Críostóir MacCartaigh
said truly, "As he covered most of Northern Ireland, he often had to make
extremely complex travel arrangements." How complex for a man with a bad
leg may be gauged from the fact that twenty-five kilos is more than the bag-
gage allowance on many airlines today. The invaluable collection, taken from
the more remote parts of the country, is in Irish, accessible only to scholars
with a good knowledge of the language.

The archive literally tells us how people both survived the Famine and
then tried to erase the survival methods from the folk memory. One finds
a girl who was seven when the blight came, describing how she went with
her father through a blackened field, picking out diseased tubers, and how
they cut off a healthy portion to provide desperately needed nourishment.
Nourishment of another sort brought shame: a woman from Kilworth,
County Cork, recalls her mother telling her how members of families who
were "big people" availed of soup kitchens, but for unexplained reasons "don't
like to be reminded of that now." Unfortunately, there were far worse reasons
for omertà than mere embarrassment at one's ancestors' poverty. There were

reports of neighbors whose children went to school with adjoining farmers and who chatted with them at Mass and on other such occasions but who then took advantage of the Famine to grab land, causing the sitting tenants to be evicted. In the folklore records at UCD one comes across incidents of cruelty such as the following description, collected in 1945, which was unfortunately typical rather than exceptional: "the awful cruelty practised by farmers who were fairly well off against the poorer and less comfortable neighbours. The people who were old when I was young, I'm sixty-six, were never tired of discussing how some of those, taking advantage of the poverty of their neighbours, used to offer rent of their farms to the landlord, the rent which the owners could not pay, and grab their farms adding some to their own farms.

"Several people would be glad if the Famine times were altogether forgotten so that the cruel doings of their forebears would not be again renewed and talked about by the neighbours."[2]

In natural disasters all over the world, aid workers dealing with the aftereffects of famine, tsunami, or war automatically take steps to protect women and children from predators, along with providing them with food and medicine. But in Ireland accounts of such predation are scant. One certainly does not come across them in the official folklore archive. No queries about these aberrations appear on the questionnaire to which respondents replied, although I did come across an account by a woman of her father and uncle watching the graves of relatives until after nine days had passed. However, Shane Mac Thomás, the historian of Glasnevin, the largest cemetery in Ireland, could find no evidence of cannibalism cases involving the cemetery. Body snatching for research purposes ended when lookout towers were erected on the cemetery walls in the nineteenth century. Mac Thomás hazarded a guess that people might have sat up to protect their loved ones' corpses from thieves who might have desecrated the bodies by removing teeth or some such. While evidences of cannibalism are hard to find, rumors are found flickering in the folk memory like disturbing shadows moving outside the light of a campfire. Eavan Boland's famous poem "The Famine Road," which uses the metaphor of a barren woman comparing her body to a hungry road, also touches on the idea of cannibalism during the famine.

"Idle as trout in light Colonel Jones
these Irish, give them no coins at all; their bones
need toil, their characters no less." Trevelyan's
seal blooded the deal table. The Relief
Committee deliberated: "Might it be safe,
Colonel, to give them roads, roads to force
from nowhere, going nowhere of course?

"one out of every ten and then
another third of those again
women—in a case like yours."

Sick, directionless they worked fork, stick
were iron years away; after all could
they not blood their knuckles on rock, suck
April hailstones for water and for food?
Why for that, cunning as housewives, each eyed—
as if at a corner butcher—the other's buttock.

There are at least two recorded incidences of cannibalism in the provincial press of the time.[3] One came to light when John Connolly was brought before a court in the West of Ireland charged with theft. He pleaded that the theft arose from his circumstances, which were so desperate that his wife had eaten some flesh off the leg of her dead son. He was discharged when the body of his son was exhumed and his story verified. There is also on record a deeply disturbing letter, "The State of Ballinrobe," on the subject of cannibalism from a Protestant clergyman in the West of Ireland, Rev. James Anderson:

"My lord," says the rev. gentleman, "I have yet other woes to mention, so truly horrifying, that former tales are as nothing in comparison, and possibly they may put an extinguisher for ever upon that left-handed policy, and that base niggard economy, which are gnawing out the vitals of the country. 'Horresco refereus.' Well, then, my lord, in a neighbouring union a ship-wrecked human body was cast on shore—a starving man extracted the heart and liver, and that was the maddening feast on which he regaled himself and perishing family!!!

"Is the English exchequer so paralysed as that it can afford no better food for the famine-stricken, emaciated Irish peasant than the putrid hearts and livers of his fellow mortals? or is it really the desire of the government to see the entire population of Ireland 'disposed of' in this quiet way? The picture drawn by the Rev. Mr. Anderson, in the remainder of his letter, is certainly a fearful one, but, alas! no less fearful than true. One word and we have done. How long does Lord John Russell intend that such a state of things continue?"[4]

It's not surprising that the references to cannibalism should occur in the Mayo area; readers are already familiar with the conditions in that county. The evidence of Mr. O'Shaughnessy, assistant barrister for the county, given before the Commons Poor Law Committee bears out the horrors of life in Mayo on a day-to-day basis and is recorded in the *Ballina Chronicle* on June 6, 1849:

The peasantry of the county with which he stands judicially connected had really no alternative but the commission of crime. In passing, along the roads; in going from one town to another, it was quite afflicting to see the state of the children—they were nearly naked, with a few rags upon them; their hair standing on an end from poverty; their eyes sunken; their lips pallid, and nothing but the protruding bones of their little joints visible. I could not help exclaiming as I passed them, "Am I living in a civilized country and part of the British empire?"

The evidence of the Rev. Sydney Godolphin Osborne corroborates the evidence of O'Shaughnessy. He has recorded that he saw no effort made to comfort dying children: "I never saw one solitary instance of anyone attempt to cheer these little ones, in any one of the very many ways in which we know children, sick and dying can be cheered."[5]

One of the most famous Irish ballads, "Revenge for Skibbereen," concerns a father who did manage to take his child away from such horrors. The phrase "Revenge for Skibbereen" encapsulated the anger of Irish emigrants for decades after the Famine had ended. It was one of the first songs I heard my mother sing, and in its day the ballad was the most popular song of the Irish diaspora, particularly among Irish Americans. Skibbereen, a small market town in pleasant West Cork, came to epitomize not merely the horrors of famine but those of the workhouse system and its inadequacy in stemming the course of the Famine.

> *Oh! Father dear, I often hear*
> *You speak of Erin's isle,*
> *Her lofty scenes and valleys green,*
> *Her mountains rude and wild.*
> *They say it is a lovely land*
> *Wherein a prince might dwell;*
> *And why did you abandon it?*
> *The reason to me tell.*
>
> *My son! I loved my native land*
> *with energy and pride*
> *'Till the blight came all over my crops*
> *My sheep, my cattle died.*
> *My rent and taxes were to pay,*
> *I could not them redeem,*
> *and that's the cruel reason why*
> *I left old Skibbereen.*
>
> *Your mother too, God rest her soul,*
> *fell on the snowy ground.*
> *She fainted in her anguish at*
> *the desolation round;*
> *She never rose, but passed away*
> *from life to mortal dream,*
> *and found a quiet resting place*
> *In the abbey near Skibbereen.*

And you were only two years old
and feeble was your frame.
I could not leave you with your friends—
you bore your father's name;
I wrapt you in my cota mor
at the dead of night unseen,
I heaved a sigh and bade goodbye
to dear old Skibbereen.

O' father dear! The day is near
When in answer to the call,
Each Irish man and woman
will rally one and all;
I'll be the man to lead the van
beneath the flag of green,
When loud and high we raise the cry;
"Revenge for Skibbereen."

The extent of the inadequacy of the workhouse system came home to me on a warm sunny day in July 2009. I stood with other members of the National Famine Commemoration Committee amid a crowd that had gathered on the first National Famine Commemoration Day at Abbeystrewery Graveyard some little way outside Skibbereen. Behind us the river Ilen sparkled toward the sea. Before us a trim grassy space, about the size of a couple of Gaelic soccer fields, stretched toward the bluffs that provided a natural amphitheater for the thousands of spectators who looked down on us from a roadway girdling the hill. It was a short, dignified ceremony involving the playing of the "Last Post" by an Irish army bugler and the laying of wreaths by the ambassadors from more than a score of countries—including the United Kingdom.

A member of the Irish cabinet, Éamon de Valera's grandson Éamon O'Cuív, the chairman of the National Famine Commemoration Committee, read a short, unmemorable statement on behalf of the government. It was a moment from which trauma was excised and death and suffering sanitized.

The echoes of "Revenge for Skibbereen" were borne into history along with those from the sounding of the "Last Post" by the lapping of the gentle Ilen. I thought of the old Irish formula for dealing with delicate matters: "Whatever you say, say nothing."

We would probably not have been standing in Skibbereen and there might not have been a National Famine Commemoration Committee were it not for the efforts of a Dublin taxi driver named Michael Blanch and his wife, Betty. In 2004, the pair decided that the Famine should be commemorated annually and began walking from the site of a soup kitchen and workhouse in North Great Charles Street, near the Four Courts beside the river Liffey, to a group of sculptures by Rowan Gillespie commemorating the Famine, farther up the Liffey on Custom House Quay. In the following year they changed the route of the walk so that it began at the Garden of Remembrance in Parnell Square and went through Dublin's main thoroughfare, O'Connell Street. The ceremony was always simple: a prayer, a wreath laying. No word of anger was uttered though Michael will admit that occasionally a tear was shed.

From 2004, the indomitable pair, aided by their daughter Olivia, "the real heroine" as Michael called her, began lobbying for a National Famine Commemoration Day. They approached everyone: government, public bodies, trade unions. Initially the response was slow. Remarkably, the one person to write both speedily and sympathetically was Queen Elizabeth II of England, who in 2011 visited the Garden of Remembrance built to commemorate those who died fighting for independence from England. The Blanches' efforts triggered a series of Dáil debates, at the end of one of which, on May 21, 2008, the taoiseach of the day, Brian Cowen, somewhat precipitately after the years of delay, announced that there would be a commemoration ceremony at the Custom House that week! Following this, the National Famine Commemoration Committee was set up, and since 2009 the Irish government has officially supported annual Famine commemoration events in Ireland and throughout the world—albeit using guarded language and phraseology.

Sensitivity regarding Anglo-Irish relationships is not the only reason for Irish governmental hesitancy in initiating Famine commemorations. A sad commentary on the relationship between Catholics and Protestants in Ireland is the fact that the Famine is still viewed differently north and south of the border. There is still an element in Protestant Northern Ireland that sees the catastrophe as a product of papist fecklessness and divine displeasure; for this reason, the Dublin government, up to the time of writing, has refused to hold a Famine commemoration north of the border lest it stir old animosities to life.

If guarded language and eloquent methods of saying nothing are regarded as a trademark Irish method of dealing with awkward subjects, so too is humor. Irish humor, like Jewish humor, very often proceeds from a basis of horror. Among the gems in the priceless Famine archive in the National Folklore Collection at UCD is the following from Barnaby Workhouse in Blacklion, County Cavan. As at workhouses all over the country, death carts called each day to take away the dead. In Blacklion, there were usually several dead—often several in one bed. After the doctor had told a worker how many corpses there were for interment, and in which beds, one of the "corpses" stirred and said he was not dead. To which the worker replied, "Do you know better than the doctor?"

In all probability the subjects for such gallows levity also lay under the sod before us that day in Skibbereen. We were standing at the site of Skibbereen's mass famine grave. Did it contain the remains of eight thousand or twelve thousand victims? Both estimates have been given. What is certain is that the Famine hit Skibbereen especially hard. The union district of which Skibbereen formed a part took in a huge portion of West Cork. It stretched from Clonakilty in the east to Schull in the west. Conditions in the area may be gauged by the following letter from Schull written by an English midshipman to his parents in February 1847: "A dead woman was found lying on the road with a dead infant on her breast, the child having bitten the nipple of the mother's breast right through to derive nourishment from the wretched body. Instead of following us, beggers throw themselves on their knees before us, holding up their dead infants to our sight."

The workhouse was supposed to cater to the needs of some 104,000 people. By the end of the Famine, some 25,000 of these are reported to have died and some 8,000 to have emigrated.

The Skibbereen workhouse was designed to accommodate 800 persons. At peak, in March 1848, it held 2,500 wretched beings. The most striking exhibit in the local heritage center is a colored square set into a floor. It measures twenty-two inches square: the amount of space available to each man, woman, and child within the workhouse walls.

As can be imagined, the resultant sanitary conditions and the spread of famine fevers created horrendous death rates. But it was not simply the death toll or the dreadful conditions that gave Skibbereen its awful niche in Irish history. Such conditions were widespread. For example, Fermoy, also in Cork, recorded an average weekly death toll of twenty-five in April 1847.

What seared Skibbereen into the public consciousness was the work of three men in particular, one a doctor of divinity, the other of medicine, and the third, an artist and journalist. Dr. Daniel Donovan practiced medicine in the Skibbereen area and was a regular contributor to the leading medical journals of the time. It was he who first made the distinction that now seems quite obvious: there was a difference between deaths caused by diseases— which he recorded—and those caused by starvation.

Donovan's observations show that the early onset of acute hunger pain subsides after approximately twenty-four hours. He quotes one of his cases as telling him that feelings of acute hunger were followed by symptoms that included "a feeling of weakness and sinking and an insatiable thirst for cold water." Donovan recorded that as the wasting process proceeded, the eyes "took on a most peculiar stare. The skin began to give off an ugly odour, at the same time began to be covered by a brown, filthy looking coating." At this stage, Donovan noted, the sufferer "staggered as if drunk, spoke weakly like one suffering from cholera, whining childishly and burst into tears for no apparent reason. The physical deterioration was accompanied by profound psychological changes." Donovan described cases of people who were reduced to "a state of imbecility" and "almost complete idiocy."[6]

The divine who helped to bring it home to a wider public that such sights were commonplace in West Cork, and ipso facto elsewhere in Ireland, was Dr. Robert Traill, the vicar of Schull. James Mahoney was an artist living in Cork who was commissioned by the *Illustrated London News* to report on conditions in the Skibbereen area after Donovan and Traill had brought these to public attention by writing letters to the most influential organ of the day, *The Times* of London. Mahoney toured the famine areas of West Cork under the tutelage of Donovan and Traill.

He was powerfully affected by what he saw. His emotions translated themselves into his sketches, which contain some of the most telling images of the Famine. We are not rich in pictorial records of the catastrophe, for artists are not normally drawn to unfashionable situations that abound in horror and lethal fever and are correspondingly short of patrons who might purchase their work. Apart from Mahoney's, only one major set of depictions of famine scenes immediately comes to mind: the works of Lady Butler, whose painting *Evicted*, showing a despairing father weeping outside his tumbled cottage, now hangs in the Department of Folklore at University College Dublin (a gift from Cecil Woodham-Smith) and is one of the Famine's iconic images.

Mahoney's reports and sketches, which began appearing in the early part of 1847, had the same galvanic effect on British public opinion that the BBC reporter Michael Buerk achieved with his coverage of the famine in Ethiopia in 1984. Mahoney's reports were a causative factor in the setting up of a powerful relief committee that collected large sums of money. The British public, at that stage anyway, was far more charitably disposed to Irish famine victims than was the British government.

Like the British public, and indeed sections of the Irish public also, Mahoney had no conception of what famine was doing to the poor in the most congested districts until he arrived in Clonakilty on a coach from Cork. From Clonakilty he wrote, "For the first time the horrors of poverty became visible, in the vast number of famished who flocked around the coach to beg for alms, amongst them a woman carrying in her arms the corpse of a fine child, and making the most distressing appeal to the passengers for aid to enable her to purchase a coffin and bury her dear little baby."[7]

Mahoney and the other coach passengers had breakfast in the hotel, where they were told that the scene outside the coach was a daily occurrence. The hotel incident could be taken as a metaphor for Ireland at the beginning of 1847. Inside, for those who could afford it, there was breakfast and a degree of comfort. Outside, there was rampant starvation and death. Many people, like the woman with the corpse in her arms, came to Skibbereen and to the other workhouses at the end of their strength, reasoning that, noisome and noxious as these places were, they at least provided coffins for the dead.

The following is a report by Dr. Charles Finucane, taken from the records of Ennistymon union workhouse in County Clare and dated March 12, 1847:

> In the fever hospital and infirmary we have 129 patients in fever and 24 labouring under diarrhoea and other diseases besides those under medical treatment in the infirmary and other wards. We have had 12 deaths since Friday. . . . In fact the people are coming into the house for the sake of getting coffins . . . the state of destitution in which most of the paupers are taken in, the great number of them are all but dead and in such a state from bowel complaints that it is almost impossible to go near them and their constitutions so broken down that medical treatment is of little or no use.

In some cases this belief that coffins were provided was illusory: the coffins had hinges that allowed the dead to be tipped into mass graves and the coffins to be reused. Each day in Skibbereen the death cart went around picking up the corpses of people who had died in alleyways, doorways, or by the side of the road. Not everyone picked up by these carts was dead. Dr. Donovan recorded the case of a little girl in whom he detected signs of life as she lay in the cart that was transporting bodies to the cemetery. The child was taken to the workhouse, where she lived for some days. Another passenger to Abbeystrewery Graveyard was luckier. The gravediggers were leveling off a pile of corpses by beating them down with shovels, preparatory to shoveling earth over them, when one "corpse" that had been struck on the knee let out a cry. He was rescued, fed, and lived on into the next century.

In Skibbereen Mahoney went first to the Bridgetown district: "I saw the dying, the living, and the dead, lying indiscriminately upon the same floor without anything between them and the cold save a few miserable rags . . . to point to any particular house as a proof of this would be a waste of time, as all were in the same state, and not a single house out of 500 could boast of being free from debt and fever, though several could be pointed out with the dead lying close to the living by the space of three or four, even six days without any effort being made to remove the bodies to a last resting place."[8]

Mahoney then visited old Chapel Lane and there he "found one house, without doors or window, filled with destitute people lying on the bare floor . . . the appeals to the feelings and professional skill of my kind companion became truly heartbreaking, and so distressed Dr. Donovan, he begged me not to go into the house, and to avoid coming into contact with the people surrounding the doorway (for fear of contracting fever)."[9]

Mahoney then described similar scenes as he passed through the countryside en route to Schull. Here he had an opportunity of studying the outworkings of the Whig' policy of non-interference with the markets as propounded by Charles Trevelyan. At Schull, Mahoney encountered a case study in the effects of allowing food to be exported from the country at this time of crisis. Compounded by the inadequate payments on the work schemes, the scene to which Dr. Traill guided him could have been encountered in innumerable such villages throughout the famine-afflicted areas. Mahoney saw "three to five hundred women, with money in their hands . . . seeking to buy food, whilst a few of the government officers doled out Indian meal to them in their turn. One of the women told me that she had been standing there since daybreak, seeking to get food for the family at home.

"The food it appeared was being doled out in miserable quantities, at 'famine prices' to neighbouring poor, from stock lately arrived in a sloop, with a government steamship to protect the cargo of 50 tons whilst the population amounts to 27,000, so that you may calculate what were the feelings of the disappointed mass. Again, although sympathy between the living and the dead seems completely out of the question . . . I certainly saw from 150 to 180 funerals of victims to the want of food, all attended by not more than 50 persons, and so hardened were the men regularly employed in the removal of the dead from the workhouse, that I saw one of them, in a car driving to the churchyard, sitting up on one of the Coffins and smoking with much apparent enjoyment."[10]

One man whom Mahoney exempted from his strictures on the lack of sympathy between the living and the dead was Dr. Traill. Of him Mahoney said, "His humanity at the present moment is beyond praise." Prior to the Famine Dr. Traill had been a noted controversialist on behalf of the Protestant cause.

Traill brought Mahoney to a ten-foot-square cottage where a man named Mullins "lay dying in a corner upon a heap of straw, supplied by the relief committee." Mullins had lost his wife a little earlier. His three "wretched children crouched over a few embers of turf, as if to raise the last remaining spark of life," commented Mahoney. He sketched Traill sitting on a stool, talking to the dying Mullins. To do so he had to stand up to his ankles "in the dirt and filth upon the floor." A short time after the sketch was completed, Traill contracted a fever and died.

Unfortunately, Dr. Traill's Christianity did not reflect Protestant attitudes to the Famine in their totality. For example, the *Northern Whig*, a Protestant paper published in Belfast whose title indicates its politics, specifically argued against giving public money and aid to Skibbereen. On March 11, 1847, the paper wrote, "The sum voted will be advanced by the government and never repaid and so, jobbery and knavery meet, and scheme and luxuriate, making a benefit of the starving dead." The paper's viewpoint encapsulated Malthusian sentiment, straightforward anti-Catholic prejudice, and the view that the laws of commerce were the laws of God. As far as the paper and those for whom it spoke were concerned, the Famine presented a "favourable crisis" that provided an opportunity "for conveying the light of the Gospels to the darkened minds of the Roman Catholic peasantry."[11] Not far from Skibbereen lies the town of Fermoy, which was also hard hit by the Famine. Although the relief regulations specifically directed that Catholic clergy, who obviously knew their followers, should be included on all local committees, they were deliberately excluded. Lord Monteagle, an enlightened landlord with extensive estates in Limerick and Kerry who had served in various British cabinets, was appalled at the attitude toward the Catholic clergy, judging that without them the committees could not function properly: "Here they are labouring like tigers for us, working day and night, we could not move a stroke [without them]."[12]

In trying to assess what type of fever killed the unfortunate Dr. Traill, one can choose from a litany of maladies. "Starvation dysentery," also known as "the bloody flux" or bacillary dysentery, was widespread.[13] Dr. Jones Lamprey of Schull recorded that the floors of the cabins affected by fever were usually bespattered with mucus and blood. The dysentery struck suddenly and "within a few hours the patient would have 12 or 20 evacuations consisting of a serous bloody fluid often without a trace of mucus or faecal matter." The dysentery was accompanied by an offensive odor described by another doctor as being similar to that of "putrid flesh in harsh weather."

The word "fever" was used to describe typhus, cholera, "relapsing fever," smallpox, tuberculosis, diarrhea, pellagra, and a host of other horrors such as the eye disease xerophthalmia, brought on by an absence of vitamin A. The loss of the potato also meant a loss of vitamin C, which caused scurvy. A lack of niacin in the diet contributed to the spread of pellagra. This disease is characterized by the "four Ds": dementia, diarrhea, dermatitis, and, of course, death. Scurvy causes the gums to bleed and become spongy and the teeth to fall out. It also induces kidney and lung failure and is characterized by internal bleeding and bruise-like blotches appearing on the skin.

Typhus was another common horror during the Famine. Spread by the human body louse, it entered the skin through scratches and manifested itself in exhaustion, delirium, severe aches and pains, and an itchy rash that covered the body. This horrible disease is also accompanied by high fever and generally carried off sufferers in about two weeks; as the starving took to the roads or crowded into the workhouses, the deadly lice multiplied in the filthy rags of sufferers and so spread from one end of the country to the other. It is worth noting that Ireland was the last country in Western Europe to suffer from louse-borne typhus. As late as the 1940s, would-be emigrants to England were still hosed down with disinfectant at centers in Dublin.

"Relapsing fever" was probably the commonest form of fever. It was accompanied by heavy sweating, feelings of nausea, bleeding from the nose, and jaundice. It was called "relapsing fever" because having apparently departed after approximately a week, it returned, sometimes on a number of occasions, accompanied by agonizing joint pains.

After this mind-numbing recital of horror, readers may be forgiven for dazedly asking how a government could allow its citizens to end up housed on approximately twenty-two inches of space, every fraction of which was toxic with any number of disease-bearing bacteria. At the risk of repetition, we should here recall the premises on which the great debate was conducted.

The workhouse experiment was the first British attempt at introducing a social welfare system to Ireland. Grounded in earlier experiments in the United Kingdom, it was an English solution to an Irish problem. The harsh regime of English workhouses was designed to ensure that those who could work did so. The problem in Ireland was that there was no work available for those who sought employment. The Whately Commission, set up under the chairmanship of Anglican archbishop of Dublin Richard Whately in 1833 as part of the general investigation of the poor law system, had concluded that the English deterrent system was completely unsuited to Ireland. However, Whately's advice was disregarded. George Nicholls was sent for and, after a mere nine weeks in Ireland, he recommended that the British system be introduced there.

In England there had been some sort of social welfare system going back to Elizabethan times, but the workhouses only arrived in Ireland with the 1838 Poor Law Act. The workhouse system suffered from a disconnect with Irish society, rather than growing out of an evolving resolution that such a system was necessary. The Irish system of charity was based on individual generosity and, above all, on the churches, which, for most of the population, meant the Catholic Church.

The workhouse system neither could, nor was designed to, cope with conditions in famine-stricken Ireland. The system suffered from Trevelyan's iron determination to uphold George Nicholls's joyless philosophy of ensuring that workhouse life was made as unattractive as possible. This was, moreover, a fundamentally flawed philosophy because Nicholls had recommended it on the basis that only 1 percent of the Irish would require relief. As it turned out, a minimum of 3 million people were affected.

Workhouses were to be places of last resort for the destitute only. They were in the front line of a process designed to wean the Irish away from the potato economy and into a future of larger, more prosperous farms that

involved fewer people being engaged on the land. Where the surplus population was to be disposed of was not made clear. Another major design flaw
was the fact that workhouses specifically outlawed outdoor relief. Far from
embodying the tradition of calling at the monastery door, or at that of a large
farmer, and going home with bread, the workhouses symbolized the policy
that giving free food to the poor, even the starving poor, was "demoralizing."

While their strength held out, many people preferred to beg—in a
landscape devoid of food—rather than enter a workhouse. Once inside, the
segregation of the sexes was rigidly imposed so that families were split up.
There were areas for men, women, boys, and girls, and for those designated
as "idiots and lunatics." As the Famine took its toll, hunger forced people to
forgo their principles, and workhouse populations soared. The results were
horrific overcrowding that induced the spread of disease.

Children suffered particularly badly. Disease, bad diet, lack of education facilities, and abandonment all took their toll. Some parents brought
their children to the workhouse with them and then absconded, sometimes climbing walls thirteen feet high to get away. Others placed their
children in workhouses pretending they were orphans with the rarely realized hope of reclaiming them should emigration bring them prosperity.
A report from the medical officer of Cork workhouse, Dr. R. Stephens,
in February 1847, quoted by Joseph Robins in *The Lost Children,* one of
the most valuable pieces of research on the Famine, gives a moving account of what this must have meant for both children and parents: "It was
common practice for parents going in search of employment to get their
children admitted to the workhouse as orphans. . . . The close whispering
lest the conversation should betray them, the sobs and tears when parting,
show them to be in a closer degree of relationship. Often this was the last
meeting in this world; for the children then went out of life like bubbles
bursting on the stream."[14]

Some workhouses turned a blind eye to the practice of placing supposed orphans. Others took a harder line. During the worst of the Famine
in September 1847, the board of guardians of Mallow workhouse in County
Cork had a woman arrested just as she prepared to board ship for America
to find work, having first deposited six children in the workhouse. In

Waterford, an inspector discovered that some thirty-five persons who visited the workhouse on a Sunday afternoon were visiting not seventy orphans, as was claimed, but their own children. The inspector, one Joseph Burke, had the practice discontinued.

The official view of workhouse education, as laid down by the poor law commissioners in 1842, was that existing class structures should be preserved and that paupers should be made aware of their ordained station in life: "The only good education is that which fits and qualifies a person for the performance of his or her duties in that station of life in which it has pleased Providence to place them; such an education is not limited to reading, writing . . . or to the acquisition of what is called learning; but it likewise comprises powerful, moral and religious instruction, as well as training in habits of industry, and, for the working classes, training also in the laborious occupations of everyday life . . . the hands must be taught and accustomed to labour. . . . The girls are well trained and fitted for household work, and the boys for farming and other out-of-door employment."[15]

Educational facilities at the workhouses were appalling. Classrooms were often located in ill-ventilated rooms with barred windows, or in sheds. Surroundings were dirty and furniture was either non-existent or broken. The filthy children frequently sat on the earthen floor. Some unions did not provide books. In these horrible surroundings it was more important that the children be kept quiet than that they get an education. The Quaker group that visited Middleton workhouse on December 30, 1848, made this report: "We found about 80 boys and 60 or 70 girls in the schoolrooms but there was no paid schoolmaster or mistress and no books whatever; and a poor miserable looking man on one side and a barefooted woman on the other, each with a whip in hand, were endeavouring to keep their squalid charge in order."[16]

One can readily imagine the rates of delinquency and the speedy passage to jail that this type of "education" engendered—if the children survived. Even before the Famine, both ambience and diet were designed to produce ennui and institutionalization. In 1842, the following was the prescribed workhouse diet for children from nine to fourteen years of age:

Breakfast: 3 $^1/_2$ ounces of oatmeal and a half pint of new milk.

Dinner: two pounds of potatoes and half a pint of new milk.

Supper: 6 ounces of bread.[17]

Younger children were to receive lesser amounts, and for very young children, rice or bread was permitted instead of oatmeal or potatoes. But variations in the diet were frowned on. The board of guardians at Balrothery workhouse gave the inmates a piece of mutton for Easter Sunday of 1842. They were told by the poor law commissioners that their action was "directly opposed to sound principle."

Such were the attitudes that informed workhouse philosophy in times of what were termed "ordinary distress." As distress gave way to catastrophe and the ravages of "Black '47," this penny-pinching approach proved entirely inadequate. By 1847 and 1848 the 130 workhouses were housing some 250,000 people. The children suffered most from the overcrowding. In a Trim workhouse an inspector reported that the children were in a worse condition than were those in families whose children had died in their own homes, wretched as these were. The board of guardians was sacked in Cork workhouse after 150 boys were found to occupy a ward forty-five feet long by thirty feet wide. They had twenty-four beds between them. The inspecting doctor found that the children were "unhealthy and drooping" and said that the sewerage was so "revolting and so disgusting that I will not here enter upon it." Sixty children under the age of thirteen had died in the week before the doctor's visit.

Bad as conditions were in the Cork workhouse, Dr. Stephens found them to be even worse at Bantry. He said, "Such an appalling, awful and heart sickening condition as it presented I never witnessed or could think possible to exist in a civilised Christian community. Living and dead were lying together in the same beds, forty children had died during the previous week." A Dr. Smith who was reporting on workhouses in the North at the same time found that in Lurgan, sixty-three children had died in the first week of February. The bodies were being buried in the grounds of the workhouse near a well.

At Carrick-on-Shannon an inspector noted that "many of the children got into a condition which appears to be the effect of the irreparable injury done their constitution previous to their admission to the house . . . Sinking without any ostensible cause." Another inspector, also in the West, in County Mayo, reported from Castlebar than many children came to the workhouse "with scarcely life in them" and died within twenty-four hours of admission.

The Rev. Sydney Godolphin Osborne, an English clergyman, reported from another workhouse in Ballinasloe that "till I witnessed it I could not have believed famine could load children with all the physical appearance of old age." Tragically, not only could it load children with the appearance of age, but it could also strip adults of humanity. It was recorded in Shillelagh, County Wicklow, on the East Coast on the opposite side of the country from Ballinasloe, that a sick, starving child who had been abandoned by his parents was seen going from door to door seeking assistance. However, he was shunned as unclean because it was thought he had fever.

NINE

SOUP AND SOUPERISM

"The enemies of the faith are now endeavouring by all means to proselytise the people, have money to no end, and apostate priests and laics are the instruments selected to conduct this impious crusade. It cannot be wondered if a starving people would be perverted in shoals, especially as they go from cabin to cabin, and when they find the inmates naked and starved to death, they proffer food, money and raiment, on the express condition of becoming members of their conventicles."

—*Letter of Father William Flannelly to*
Dr. Daniel Murray, Archbishop of Dublin,
Ballinakill, Clifden, County Galway, April 6, 1849[1]

GAINST THE BACKDROP OF DISTRESS OUT-lined in previous chapters, soup kitchens began to appear in the winter of 1846. Initially they were set up on an ad hoc basis by local initiative and administered by local relief committees. Inevitably, the soup tended to vary in both quality and quantity, depending on the skill and finance available. But overall the soup kitchens undoubtedly saved lives, particularly after the Quakers began opening them in Cork in November 1846.

The Quakers' knowledge of business and their practical humanity rendered them invaluable as aid workers. But it is obvious from reading their records that even the Quakers could not hope to deal with the magnitude of the problem.[2] First, they had to gain experience, and they freely acknowledged that they made mistakes at the start. Then they had to cope with the fact that the union system was completely inadequate in areas like "the deserts of Erris" as, in a rare moment of emotion, the recorder described the horror in the district of Erris in County Mayo.

The business-oriented Quakers found it hard to adjust to a society in which most of the people who needed their assistance had no knowledge of business and subsisted by growing their own food and on an economy more based on barter than the cash register. There was no middle class; the clergy and landlords were the leaders of society, and implementing change was hard. The Quakers did their best, an almost superhuman best at times. Apart from distributing food and clothing, they also attempted imaginative schemes to improve farming, fishing, and a general self-sufficiency, but in the end their efforts were ground down between the sheer scale of the suffering and an unfeeling bureaucracy. The Quakers deserve an honored place in Irish history.

As the Irish historian T. P. O'Neill has written, the Quakers "lived up to their highest traditions of philanthropy. Their assistance was given to the poor, irrespective of religion and there was not the slightest breath of suspicion cast on the motives. They earned the gratitude of the people for the great sacrifices; for the giving of assistance on a non-sectarian basis, to the destitute in those tragic Famine years was fraught with danger of infection and death from the virulent typhus which raged through the country. Their measures of relief showed an initiative which was lacking in most of the other relief associations."[3]

The Quakers collected food and money in America as well as in England. By December 1846, the Central Committee of Friends had managed to collect some £200,000, a colossal amount for those days. Their contributions would have stood the test of best practice in modern aid agency circles. They also prompted the British government to bring into operation its most beneficial policy of the entire Famine period: the Soup Kitchen Act. Above all, often at great personal risk to those concerned, the Quakers traveled the country extensively to study firsthand the scale of suffering so that not even a Trevelyan or a Wood could discredit their findings.

The Quakers also made valiant attempts to tackle a perennial Irish problem: the fact that an island nation surrounded by some of the most fertile fishing grounds in the world failed to develop a fishing industry worth speaking about. The Quakers' efforts to develop fishing ranged from giving money to Cladagh fishermen who had pawned their nets at the outset of the Famine, to hiring trawlers to explore the seabed for likely fishing grounds. They achieved some success in setting up fishing stations and helping fishermen in Waterford, Castletownbeare in Cork, Ballinakill Bay near Clifden in Galway, and a number of places in Mayo. Overall, a lack of training, lack of investment in suitable boats, and a lack of harbors along the fertile, but ferocious coasts of the West and Southwest frustrated their efforts, but the sizeable quantities of fish that were caught probably saved many lives. There was a widespread aversion to eating fish without potatoes and little or no knowledge of fish cookery. Ireland had a somewhat arm's-length association with fish that until comparatively recent times was regarded as a penitential food to be eaten on days when the church prohibited the use of meat. All these factors combined against utilizing what to an outsider would have appeared to be an invaluable source of protein during a time of acute scarcity.

The Quakers' Cork scheme, begun on their own initiative by a group of local Friends, was an instant success and led to the establishment of the National Relief Committee, which proceeded to set up kitchens all over the country. In order to do this Quakers had to buy and distribute 290 boilers or industrial-sized cast-iron pots.

It took the government several months to follow the Quakers' example; by then, famine fevers had struck, and the efforts of the other charitable people who set up food-distribution outlets on their own initiative were outstripped by the numbers dying from disease. Nor was officialdom either prompt or generous in its assistance to those who struggled to keep local soup kitchens going.

Documents in the National Archives famine relief papers show a Major Sterne writing to Dublin Castle on behalf of the Brookeborough Relief

Committee asking for help, "anything from a postage stamp to £100." All he got in return, however, was the promise of "a formula of a soup which can be provided at a very moderate price."[4]

Nonetheless, the public-spirited major acted on his own initiative and pressed ahead with the setting up of the soup kitchen, or "soup shop" as he called it, in the following letter to the editor of the *Fermanagh Reporter* on December 7, 1846, in which he gave both the cost and the ingredients of his soup:

Dear Sir,

My soup shop is now in full operation, and any poor person can be relieved at one halfpenny per quart. Sir A. B. Brooke is, I understand, about to open one likewise, so that I trust the poor in our parish will be amply supplied, it is open to anyone to visit and witness the ingredients of which it is composed. The following is about the cost of 20 gallons, we may have occasion to vary it a little according to circumstances as we go on:

Boiler, made of best block tin, with sheet iron cover,
    iron stand, measure, ladle, etc. £1
Six pounds of meat, cow's head or otherwise three pence each.
Ten pounds of oatmeal, one shilling and sixpence.
Onions or leeks, six pence.
Turnips, cabbage and carrots, three pence.

The cost of pepper and salt and of cooking the soup came to one shilling and three pence. From this formula Major Sterne claimed to average 80 quarts of soup which was sold at a halfpenny per quart.[5]

The Quakers' operation was on a far larger scale. For example, their renowned soup kitchen in Charles Street in Dublin was capable of making 2,400 quarts a day in wooden vats and an iron boiler, all powered by steam. The soup was distributed twice a day, from half past seven until nine o'clock in the morning and from twelve to three in the afternoon. It was sold at a penny a quart with a piece of bread costing an extra halfpenny. The Quakers also used a ticket system, as did many soup kitchens throughout the country, which enabled charitable persons to buy quantities of soup according to their means and distribute the tickets free to the destitute, who could then exchange them at the kitchens for soup.

The production of this food on a large scale was no slight task, as the following description of the making of 200 gallons of soup (in a report to the Central Relief Committee of Quakers) illustrates. The recipe called for 150 pounds of beef, 70 pounds of peas, 42 pounds of oatmeal, 42 pounds of barley, 1 pound of salt, and a half pound of ground pepper and allspice. The cooking instructions were:

Fill the vessel about half full of water, when boiling put in the meat, having been previously cut into small pieces about the size of a walnut, and the bones broken small. . . . An hour after put in the peas, first dividing them into bags containing about 14lb each and tied at the top, but leaving sufficient room for the peas to swell. In about four hours afterwards, take out the bags and turn the peas into a tub; have them bruised into a paste, and put them back into the boiler along with the barley. Keep it boiling gently for four or five hours, then put in the oatmeal, which should be first blended with cold water, and fill the boiler with water to the quantity required. Put in the salt and spices an hour after the oatmeal; keep all well stirred for about half an hour, when it will be ready for delivery.[6]

The report contained a somewhat understated observation about the workings of the soup kitchen: "It is a satisfaction to the committee to observe how desirous the poor are to avail themselves of the facility it affords them to procure a good and nutritious food at a moderate price." The activities of the Quakers during the Famine were long remembered with gratitude in Ireland.

The same could not be said of the government's work schemes. Apart from their general uselessness, which is gone into in more detail elsewhere, the work frequently had to be carried out by laborers who were on the brink of death from starvation. Many in fact died either on site or on their way to or from work. By January 1847, the Famine had resulted in an increase in the price of food that placed it way beyond the reach of those who had formerly been dependent on the potato. Even had the food been available, such people had very little experience of cooking anything except potatoes. A letter written on January 4, 1847, by a good Sligo landlord, Major Charles O'Hara, to another landlord, Lady King-Tennison in Roscommon, who had sought his advice on the setting up of food shops and soup kitchens, gives a good indication of the situation. He had been in Liverpool the previous October buying a cargo of Indian corn (which by then was nearly exhausted) and, as they were known locally, "bread stuffs" (such as flour). But in the meantime "prices had risen enormously," and the cost of packaging and transport were also very high. A cargo of Indian corn that had been landed at Sligo shortly before O'Hara wrote was expected to cost £12 a ton but in fact cost £19. Nevertheless, O'Hara advocated the establishment of food shops as being "most essential."

He said, "Provisions shops are most essential: our country folk are bad cooks and know not how to turn food to the best advantage." And he went on to explain how he was attempting to meet the challenges posed by the Famine: "I am now busied in establishing four soup shops on different works so as to enable the labourers [to get] a warm meal of soup or hot porridge at a cheap rate: a halfpenny for a pint of soup or porridge, whereas the wretches were in the habit of bringing with them in the morning a little raw meal or flour and diluting it with cold water—their only food. A great point is to teach them to cook, and by the shops afford them the means of doing so at home. I sell Indian meal, oatmeal, flour, pea meal (excellent for soup), rice, American beef, and peppers and spices, onions, carrots and turnips when procurable. My working parties amount to near 1500 men daily and consume 12 tons a week of meal."[7]

The amount of relief the Quakers were able to provide was, of course, only an island in the floodtide of hunger sweeping across Ireland. Nevertheless, they provided the template for the most worthwhile of the government efforts to deal with the crisis. The activities of the Quakers' soup kitchens and the publicity the Quakers were able to generate among their powerful contacts in

England were responsible for forcing a change in British governmental policy toward providing "gratuitous assistance," as it was called. There was at least a temporary acceptance of the Quakers' argument: "When famine stares you in the face, political economy should be forgotten."[8]

Government policy was influenced by the eyewitness accounts of famine horrors by two prominent Quakers in particular, James Hack Tuke, whose accounts of evictions' aftermath we have already encountered, and James Edward Forrester. Their writing struck a chord with one of the more humane members of the cabinet, Viscount Morpeth, who had been an Irish chief secretary. He brought the Quakers' writings to the attention of Lord John Russell, who decided, as he said in a letter to the Irish viceroy,[9] Lord Bessborough, who was also a County Kilkenny landlord, that "the pressing matter at present is to keep the people alive."[10]

In view of the daily reports of the Famine's ravages that had been reaching London for several months, this could hardly be regarded as a shatteringly new concept. But it did mark a major change in Whig policy as influenced by Sir Charles Trevelyan, assistant secretary to the Treasury. As late as December 14, 1846, Trevelyan's view (as expressed in a letter to Sir Randolph Routh) was that Irish "distress" was caused not by either God or government but by a departure from "sound principle" and a failure of responsibility by individuals in Ireland. Russell's Quaker-induced policy change, however, accepted the fact that people in need of relief could have it without being expected to work for it. The change was not entirely humanitarian. It was hoped that the new scheme would prove less costly than the disastrous public works initiative.

However, moved by Morpeth rather than by Trevelyan and Wood, on January 25, 1847, Russell introduced the Temporary Relief Act in the House of Commons. It became generally known as the Soup Kitchen Act and was passed with commendable speed, becoming law on February 6. By appointing the widely respected Sir John Burgoyne, who had considerable experience of Ireland, as the chairman of the Relief Commission (which was to carry on the work of the commission originally established on the outbreak of the crisis in 1845), the government seemingly made it clear that the new commission would act with efficiency and dispatch. It was an article of faith with the Whigs that the public works scheme had been far too costly, and Routh took some of the blame for this. He was removed as chairman, although he remained a member of the commission.

Wood and Trevelyan remained in control of the Treasury and, because the demon waste had to be exorcised, Trevelyan in particular came to have even tighter control of the relief effort, whose philosophy was contained in a Treasury mission statement to the relief commissioners dated February 10, 1847: "To afford relief to the greatest number of the present really destitute population under the most economic and efficient arrangements, and with the smallest amount of abuse to encourage such principles of feeding and action as shall prospectively tend rather to improvement of the social system, consequently, of Ireland itself."

If ever an example was required of the saying that the road to hell is paved with good intentions, it could be found in that directive. This seeming concentration on relieving destitution was in fact balanced by the reference to "improvement of the social system," which meant, in effect, that the Treasury did not want to see the opportunity presented by the Famine to clear a surplus population off un-economically worked land to be frustrated by kindheartedness.

The Quakers came up against this unpleasant reality in March 1847 after the government shut down the work schemes in peremptory fashion. As a result, distress levels soared in the hardest-hit areas of Connacht, West Munster, and Donegal. The Quakers proposed to distribute relief in these districts until equal assistance as contemplated by the Soup Kitchen Act was recommended by Sir John Burgoyne, who now headed the Relief Commission. Sir John refused to make the recommendation to the Treasury. The Whigs had chosen well.

Bereft of government backing, the Quakers could not shoulder such a large-scale project unaided and had to substantially limit the scope of their activities. The Friends concentrated their efforts on helping the old and the very young. They distributed to small farmers who were prevented from receiving government assistance by the Gregory Clause. But so much came to be expected of the Quakers that they had to decline some of the burden. On paper the Soup Kitchen Act appeared to have every chance of success.

Unfortunately, there was too much paper. On April 21, 1847, the *Freeman's Journal* complained that to date all that had been produced was "14 tons of paper." It was indeed calculated by the Relief Commission that the forms and soup tickets that had to be filled in before soup could be dispensed were so voluminous that they weighed thirteen tons. No money was issued to the local relief committees until all the forms had been correctly filled in.

Filling out forms, and a bureaucratic insistence on ensuring that the Treasury instructions on economy were strictly obeyed, combined with other factors to delay the distribution of soup until June 1847. For example, a good deal of time was wasted in arguments over whether food should be distributed cooked. The prioritization of need was seriously flawed. While it might appear that the object of relief should be to bring it first to those in greatest need, this was not the case. Even widely publicized pits of human misery like Skibbereen and parts of Mayo, where people were dying like flies, did not receive soup until June 15 and 24, respectively. In his January speech to the House of Commons introducing the soup project, Russell had laid it down that the relief committees operating in the various electoral districts would be empowered to "purchase food and establish soup kitchens in the different districts."

The rates provision caused many landlords to oppose and delay the introduction of soup kitchens by any means available to them.[11] A conscientious relief official, Colonel W. Clarke, wrote to the viceroy, Lord Clarendon, on April 11 complaining that a combination of landlord apathy and form filling was preventing assistance from reaching areas where people "were literally howling with hunger."

But the worst aspect of the operation was the action that accompanied it. Acting as though the scheme were a successful countrywide fait accompli, the government began in March to progressively discharge people engaged on the works scheme. By the end of June, only some 28,000 workers from a total of over 700,000 had been retained, mainly to repair roads that had been dug up as part of the scheme. The result was that all over the country people began to find themselves with no means of earning money and no food of any kind, and an already horrendous death toll accelerated accordingly. Ironically, the soup kitchens probably contributed to the death toll because the crowds of people congregating at the soup centers led to the spread of infections.

But despite this and the delays in their introduction, the government-run soup kitchens were a remarkable success in the conditions of the time. Unlike, say, similar achievements by the Red Cross and NGOs in Africa during times of famine, there were no helicopters or motorized vehicles to assist in the food distribution. At the peak of the famine, some 3 million people were fed daily. Despite the relief commissioner's instruction that the soup was to be varied in the interests of promoting good health, the diet was often monotonous. However, monotony was preferable to starvation.

The definition of the soup was "any food cooked in a boiler, and distributed in a liquid state, thick or thin, and whether composed of meat, fish, vegetables, grain or meal." However, what often came out, according to the description by the commissioners themselves, was a "thick stirabout of meal, rice etc."

It was stipulated that the soup was to be accompanied by either a pound and a half of bread or one pound of biscuit, flour, grain, or meal. Children under nine received half a ration and there were other stipulations such as an instruction that if the soup had been made from grain only, a quarter of the flour should be issued along with the liquid. Nevertheless, this was a major humanitarian and administrative achievement as well as being a very marked departure from the Whig dogma that any form of gratuitous relief was demoralizing and left people with time and energy for that dread activity—procreation. From the outset, apart from the delay factor, a good deal of the shine was taken off the achievement by the accompanying sackings from the public works.

A simmering, discontented population with the background of Whiteboyism expressed its outrage in outbreaks of violence in parts of the country where there had been a high dependency on the money from the works. Counties Clare, Cork, Limerick, and Galway suffered in this way.

The bedrock philosophy behind soup schemes administration, as with the workhouse approach to relief generally, was that those benefiting from it had to be destitute. When the authorities found that in some parts of the country people were rejecting the cooked food and demanding that they be issued instead with uncooked food that could be prepared at home, the rejection was regarded as proof that the people were not really destitute. But as James Donnelly Jr. noted:

> The main reason for the popular resistance was plain enough. . . . The demeaning business of requiring the whole family to troop every day to the soup kitchen, each member carrying a bowl, pail, pot or can, and waiting in a long queue until one's number was called, painfully violated the popular sense of dignity.[12]

It is a matter of pride in our family folklore that my mother's birthplace, Templethouy, County Tipperary, was one of the first places to demonstrate against the manner in which the soup kitchens were operated, although, unfortunately, a woman member of the kitchen staff was one of the innocent victims of the mob's anger.

The reasoning behind the sacking of the workers described above, while primarily intended to save money, was also directed at forcing labor back to the cultivation of food for the coming winter. Unfortunately, the government did not provide enough money for the amount of seed needed. As starvation had driven people to eat their seed potatoes earlier in the year, there was no blight, but by a cruel irony, only a quarter of what would have been a normal crop was harvested in 1847.

Another disreputable aspect of the soup kitchen story that caused widespread and lasting bitterness in Ireland was the phenomenon known as "souperism." One of the worst failings of which a person could be accused was that they "took the soup." In other words, in return for soup, they had become Protestants, thereby also selling out their community in Judas-like fashion. Some Protestant Evangelical groups believed that what the starving Catholics needed was not food, but the Bible. Christine Kinealy quoted one such group as saying, "Rather than provide food, clothing and shelter, every cabin in Ireland should be provided with the word of God." "Souperism" was part of an Evangelical crusade that had been in existence for several years before the potato failed.[13] It is a phenomenon that is always associated with the Famine and has attracted widespread execration.

The Evangelical effort in turn could be seen as part of the overall British colonial project. In Seoul, South Korea, I had an experience that helps to illustrate the importance of Ireland in the eyes of other colonized people around the world. This importance would grow in the latter part of the nineteenth century and the early part of the twentieth century as actual fighting broke out between Ireland and England, and what was done in Dublin came to have heightened significance in Cairo and Delhi.

In Seoul I met with Foreign Minister Beoum-Seok Lee, one of Korea's most experienced diplomats and a trusted advisor to President Park. I was struck by his knowledge of Ireland, and I asked him if his interest had been awakened through the literature. He had indeed developed a wide knowledge of Irish culture, but he told me that as a Korean nationalist, his interest in Ireland had been awakened by an episode in the Japanese-Korean relationship. Prior to the invasion of Korea, the Japanese had sent a team of academics to study at the British Museum in London for some six months with the goal of identifying the world's most efficient colonial systems.

They settled on the British model in Ireland, which involved the extirpation of local culture, destruction of the local educational system, and cultural manifestation such as language and dress, along with a remodeling of the land system.

The Irish experience certainly justified Beoum-Seok's account, whatever the degree to which the Japanese implemented British policy. The Irish language came to be so targeted by church and state (Rome, as much as London, derived great benefit from having hordes of white English-speaking emigrants shoaling outward to take up positions in an English-speaking empire). Children were punished for speaking Irish in schools and in some cases had a notched peg hung around their necks. Parents inspected the notches, and for each time the child had been punished during the day at school for speaking Irish, a similar dose was handed out when they got home. Parents, like church strategists, wanted their children to be able to communicate with the world if, and probably when, they were forced to emigrate. Irish schoolbooks contained material such as the following:

> *I thank the goodness and the grace*
> *which on my birth has smiled,*
> *and made me in these Christian days*
> *A happy English child.*

Should the child require any further cultural reorientation, he or she could be referred to a text that said: "On the east of Ireland is England where the Queen lives; many people who live in Ireland were born in England, and we speak the same language and are called one nation."[14]

As we will see when discussing the anti-Irish press campaign in chapter 13, Irish modes of dress were caricatured and mocked, and the land system, of course, shines by its own baleful light.

Bible reading as a means of loosening the grip of Rome on Catholic children's thought processes was seen as having an important role. The Irish Society for Promoting the Education of the Native Irish through the Medium of Their Own Language was founded as far back as 1818.

In *Soupers and Jumpers,* her scholarly—and temperate—work on proselytizing, Miriam Moffitt notes that the Rev. Alexander Dallas, who founded the Irish Church Missions (ICM) in Dublin in the later part of the Famine (1849), had been eyeing the West of Ireland as a potential area of Protestant expansion before the blight arrived. Dallas had been a soldier and saw that his enemy, the Catholic Church, had left a gaping breach in its defenses. Understandably annoyed by the sort of education offered by the National Board of Education, the Archbishop of Tuam, John McHale, had nevertheless taken an unwise initiative.

He had ordered Catholic families in the sprawling Archdiocese of Tuam not to send their children to the state primary schools because he considered them a threat to both religion and nationality. As a result of his draconian edict, tens of thousands of children (possibly as many as 200,000) living

throughout Connemara and parts of Mayo in the sort of mud cabin accommodation already described, were denied an education that might have
helped them to get out of those cabins. As a result, and as Moffitt describes
and as the Protestant Rev. Dallas quickly saw, many parents, anxious for
their children's future, espoused a philosophy that if their children got an
education, no one later in life would ask them where they got it. Since 1831,
another Protestant Evangelical, Edward Nangle, a scion of a prominent
Dublin family, had been living proof of this by successfully running schools
on Achill Island off the coast of Mayo.[15] Nangle had also built a church, an
orphanage, a dispensary, and a hotel that did a good business because the
scenery of Mayo attracted visitors from all over the country. Nangle himself
attracted even more attention partly because of his attacks on Catholicism,
conducted mainly through his paper, the *Achill Herald,* which would not
be equaled in vituperation until the Rev. Ian Paisley began producing his
Protestant *Telegraph* in the 1960s.

From 1845 onward, Dallas, an Englishman, targeted the educational
void, building schools and churches and distributing money, clothing, and
food that, as the Famine worsened, helped to swell an already growing tide
of converts. Sectarian temperatures went up also. Dallas did not confine
his activities to the educational sphere. A Catholic curate, Father William
Flannelly of Clifden, County Galway, wrote to the Archbishop of Dublin,
Dr. Daniel Murray, on April 6, 1849, seeking alms for his parishioners and
described the activities of "soupers" as follows:

> Money to no end, and apostate priests and laics are the instruments se-
> lected to conduct this impious crusade. It cannot be wondered if a starv-
> ing people would be perverted in shoals, especially as they go from cabin
> to cabin, and when they find the inmates naked and starved to death,
> they proffer food, money and raiment, on the express condition of be-
> coming members of their conventicles. Scurrilous tracts are scattered in
> thousands among the poor by these emissaries of discord.[16]

Dallas espoused a particularly confrontational style of polemic, causing Archbishop McHale to refer to Protestant missionaries as "venomous

wretches." But, it has to be conceded that some good came out of the Connemara crusade.

Connemara's educational provision went up because when Dallas built a school, the Catholic Church stepped in to build a competing one. And the food that the Protestant missionaries distributed must have saved many, possibly thousands of lives when famine struck, odious though the practice of "souperism" was. Miriam Moffitt's judgment is that "As a direct result of the arrivals of the Irish Church Missions, Connemara was equipped with a more impressive educational infrastructure by the end of the 19th century than was found in many other places at a time when few educated persons lived among or interacted with the poor. Connemara's population received the attention of numerous missionary clergymen, whose arrival forced the Catholic church to increase its presence in a region they had largely ignored in the past. The ICM is said to have built 12 churches, four orphanages, and 64 mission schools."[17]

The Irish Society's purpose was to provide resources for Irish-speaking Protestant missionaries in Ireland. Protestant landlords in Ireland had a practical rather than a theological reason for furthering the cause of Protestantism. It acted as a bulwark against the threat to their position posed by a rising tide of potentially disloyal Catholic tenants.

The pious Mrs. D. P. Thompson has left us an account of one of the most significant, and certainly most controversial, attempts at proselytization. It describes the events following an outburst of souperism in Dingle, County Kerry. Thompson had the assistance of the local landlord in her effort to spread enlightenment amid the darkness of Kerry "popery." Her husband, the Rev. Thomas Thompson, was the agent for the landlord, Lord Ventry. Thompson's zeal contributed to Dingle's becoming a byword in the history of souperism. The controversy would involve Daniel O'Connell and would spark a major counter-reformation effort on the part of the Irish Catholic Church.

Both physical and theological shadows hung particularly heavily over Dingle. Mrs. Thompson's account indicates the reason and conveys something of the imperial spirit in which the Protestant Evangelicals went about their task.

Gazing at the cliffs where, at Smerwick, troops under the command of Sir Walter Raleigh had massacred some six or seven hundred Spanish and Italian troops, sent by Pope Gregory XIII, after they had surrendered, Mrs. Thompson mused on the fact that "the gallant Raleigh won golden glories of his royal mistress [Queen Elizabeth I] . . . repulsing these foreign invaders literally into dark graves of deep ocean." The symbolism of the fact that Sir Walter is also credited with introducing the potato to Ireland does not appear to have occurred to Mrs. Thompson.[18]

But she probably did know that among the "golden glories" showered on Raleigh was a gift of some 40,000 acres of land wrested from the Catholics of the area, thereby generating the triad of landlordism, rent, and religion that caused Mrs. Thompson to write her book. Mrs. Thompson's husband had a reputation for trying to get rid of Catholic tenants on the Ventry estate by charging them higher rents than Protestants. However, he was said to have lowered the Catholics' rent to Protestant levels if they changed their religion. Hundreds of Catholics are said to have been evicted because they did not "turn."

Nevertheless, for most of the 1830s Protestant and Catholic appeared to have lived together in amity in and around Dingle despite the fact that a local clergyman, the Rev. George Gubbins, vice rector of Dunuslin, had been achieving some success in furthering the aims of the mission to the Irish-speaking, a Protestant Evangelical society that specifically targeted Catholics in Irish-speaking areas. Part of his success, and the lack of sectarian tension, appears to have been due to the fact that Gubbins was clearly a good man. He worked courageously and unceasingly for the poor during an outbreak of famine and disease in 1831, even to the extent of digging graves.

Gubbins was succeeded by the Rev. Charles Gayer, who undoubtedly also had his good points but was a far more forceful character. In addition to being rector of Dunuslin, he was chaplain to Lord Ventry. With the backing of Lord and Lady Ventry, the Thompsons, and the Rev. Thomas Moriarty, a Dingle convert from Catholicism, Gayer greatly expanded the work of the mission. A coast guard unit under the command of a Lieutenant Clifford was placed at his disposal to enable him to establish a set of settlements known as "colonies" along the Dingle peninsula. These clusters of houses always included a school at which, in addition to normal subjects, the Catholic pupils were introduced to the Bible.

The teachers at these schools were chosen for their intelligence, were paid high wages, and did not have to be Protestants. A second set of scriptural teachers, whose mission it was to introduce the people to Bible reading, did not have to be Protestant either. Using these methods and, crucially, the Irish language, Gayer achieved considerable success. James H. Murphy, an authority on Dingle and souperism, judges that Gayer's teachers tapped into rural Irish piety so successfully that "in effect the Bible replaced the rosary."[19]

But there was a hidden agenda to this spreading of Bible reading. Anglican Archbishop Richard Whately, who was one of the most influential figures on the National Education Board, which was responsible for the type of schoolbooks already described, some of which he wrote himself, saw Bible reading as one of the main weapons in the war against "Romanism." He wrote a revealing letter to his friend Nassau Senior, the gentleman who thought that even if a million Irish were to die, it would still not solve the problem of getting surplus Catholic peasants off the land.

"A man," wrote Whately, "who is commanded not to think for himself, if he finds that he cannot avoid doing so, is unavoidably led to question the reasonableness of the command. And when he finds that the church, which claims a right to think for him, has preached doctrines, some of which are inconsistent and others are opposed to what he has read in the Gospels, his trust in the fallibility, the foundations on which the whole system of faith is built, is at an end.

"But such I believe to be the process by which the minds of a large portion of the Roman Catholics have been prepared, and are now being prepared, for the reception of Protestant doctrines. The education supplied by the National Board is gradually undermining the vast fabric of the Irish Roman Catholic church."[20]

Criticism of the Whately approach did not stem merely from Catholic sources. Protestant observers too were disturbed by the effort to use the wretchedness of the people to induce them to change their religion. One of the most knowledgeable observers of the Irish poor was Asenath Nicholson, an American Protestant who had been struck by the poverty and yet the cheerfulness of Irish emigrants living in the teeming Five Points slum in lower Manhattan.

After her husband died, she traveled all over Ireland, often on foot, throughout 1844 and 1845 to study the condition of the poor. She made her own contribution to relief by opening a soup kitchen in the aptly named Cook Street in Dublin's Liberties district, visiting the sick and distributing food and clothing. Like the Quakers, she did not proselytize, and like them, she lobbied English MPs regarding Irish conditions.

Her book *Ireland's Welcome to the Stranger* was one of the most insightful of the Famine period.[21] In it she expressed her dismay at the teaching in Gayer's schools. In Ventry a teacher told her geography was not taught to girls because "they are daughters of the lower orders and we do not advance them." On examination of the curriculum, Mrs. Nicholson decided that it was a force for cultural imperialism designed to perpetuate the system of landlordism that kept the peasantry in poverty by teaching them that their proper course was to accept the station in life into which they had been born.

"Converts" did not really understand the Bibles they had been given. The Protestant ethic that cleanliness is next to godliness created a superficial air of improvement in their general appearance and in their cabins. But the substantive benefits or stipends they received amounted to only eight pence a day, and upward mobility was definitely not on the agenda.

Nevertheless, between 1838 and 1845, Gayer increased the number of converts from 170 to around 800. He established a colony on the Blasket Islands, three tiny islands off the Dingle coast. A six-oared boat was provided, and Gayer appears to have been a major source of relief for the island community. As the blight took effect, Lady Ventry and a group of Protestant women began distributing what was described as "very good soup." Families who could afford it were asked to contribute a penny a week toward the cost of the soup. Those who could not pay were given the soup free. Cooked Indian meal was also distributed.

To Evangelicals like the Thompsons, the proselytizing couple mentioned above, the need to combat "popery" had become more pressing after O'Connell secured Catholic Emancipation. The feelings of such people were further inflamed when Sir Robert Peel increased the grant to the major

Catholic seminary at Maynooth. This was one of Peel's last big initiatives in government (proposed in 1845) that he hoped would improve relationships between Catholic Ireland and Protestant England. It had the opposite effect in Ireland, where there was a feeling abroad that something had to be done to prevent Protestantism from losing its position of "Ascendancy." Against this backdrop, anti-Catholicism easily embraced a belief that when the Famine did come, it was God's judgment on the workings of both pope and potato. The *Northern Whig,* the voice of Protestantism in the North of Ireland, in January 1847 also spoke for many in the South when it referred to the Famine as "the present favourable crisis" that provided an opportunity "for conveying the light of the Gospels to the darkened minds of the Roman Catholic peasantry." In the celebrated statement of Trevelyan quoted in chapter 7 where he writes of "a bright light shining in the distance through the dark cloud which at present hangs over Ireland," he saw the Famine as a work of "an all wise providence in a manner as unexpected and unthought-of as it is likely to be effectual."

As we saw, prior to the Famine, during the 1830s, one of the great sources of dissension in Ireland had been the resentment of Catholics having to pay a tithe (one-tenth) of their income toward the support of the established church.

What was known as the "tithe war" ended in 1836 with the reduction of tithes and their incorporation into payments of rent. The beneficiaries of the established church had begun to feel the power of organized Catholicism and saw (correctly) that it threatened their privileged position. Full disestablishment lay over the horizon. The move toward "Fortress Ulster" had begun. It would ultimately lead to the partition of the country, giving Protestantism six of the northeastern counties of Ulster and Catholicism the other twenty-six counties, today's Republic of Ireland.

The Dingle mission, a particular project that interested Mrs. Thompson, was part of a larger drive on the part of Protestant Evangelicals to target the Irish-speaking districts of Ireland, which, roughly speaking, lay to the west of a line drawn from Derry in the North to the point in the Southwest where the river Shannon enters the sea between the counties of Kerry and Clare. In this area, Dingle in County Kerry, Oughterrarde in County Galway, and

Achill in County Mayo became particular focal points, though there are other Irish-speaking pockets, or Gaeltachts, in various parts of the country.

In their zeal to take advantage of Providence, the proselytizers did not take sufficient account of the effect of their activities on observers, to say nothing of the effect on their target audience, the Irish Catholics. Here is how the activities of the Achill Island mission impacted on an English Protestant couple, Mr. and Mrs. S. C. Hall, who were touring Ireland at the time and later wrote a lengthy and widely popular account of their travels that included the following description of what they saw in Achill:

> It was impossible not to appreciate the magnanimity of the poor, miserable, utterly destitute and absolutely starving inhabitants of Achill at the time of our visit enduring privations at which humanity shudders. And to know that by walking a couple of miles and professing to change their religion they would have been instantly supplied with food, clothes and lodging. Yet these hungry thousands—it would scarcely be an exaggeration to say that 9/10 of the population of this islet, in the month of July last, were entirely without food—preferred patiently to endure their suffering, rather than submit to what they considered a degradation. . . . But we have deemed it our duty to submit the case fully to our readers, with a view, particularly, to invite consideration of the subscribers to "The Mission."[22]

The extraordinary docility of the people of Achill was not replicated in Dingle, where the Catholic Church mounted a vigorous counterattack against the Evangelicals that, as we shall see, was later successfully extended to other parts of the country. Mrs. Thompson gives a partisan account, based apparently on the word of someone who claims to have been in the church at the time when a priest deployed anathema—bell, book, and candle—an excommunication ceremony against a woman who had sent her children to a Protestant school. According to Mrs. Thompson's account, a priest "'cursed' every inch of her carcass . . . Her eyes, ears, her legs . . . Every bit of her. The congregation were warned not to speak to her, deal with her, have anything to do with her. . . . The woman was pregnant at the time and the priest is alleged to have 'cursed everything that would spring from her.'"[23]

Mrs. Thompson claimed that the priest "threw off his clothes and put on a black dress!" The windows were shuttered and all the candles extinguished. The priest is said to have concluded the performance by crashing shut a huge book, saying that "the gates of heaven were shut upon her that day." Unsurprisingly also, the woman and her child were shunned by Dingle's Catholics thereafter. However, when her child was born, despite the fact that he had pronounced anathema on her and cursed the child, the priest stood sponsor for the infant and baptized it. But in the eyes of the local Catholics, the woman remained accursed, shopkeepers refused to serve her, and former friends crossed the road rather than speak to her.

That particular controversy seems to have ended with the priest ensuring a supply of food for the woman—lack of food being the reason she had sent her children to scriptural school in the first place—and the children returning to Catholic schools.

It can be imagined how the sectarian tensions incited by the foregoing warfare heightened when it was announced that a local curate, the Maynooth-educated Father Denis Lynne Brasbie, was turning Protestant!

Brasbie was subsequently awarded £25 as a result of a successful libel action he took against the president of Maynooth, Dr. Laurence F. Renehan. Renehan, who was unpopular with the Maynooth seminarians and known as "Raddle" because of his red hair, which resembled sheep dye, had written a letter to the bishop of Worcester saying that Brasbie had been dismissed from the priesthood. As a result of the letter, Brasbie lost his post as a minister in the Worcester diocese. Renehan later corrected the false impression he had created—that Brasbie had been expelled from the church rather than leaving of his own accord—but Brasbie seems to have received only temporary positions subsequently.

When the Dingle controversy was at its height, Brasbie had feared for his life to such an extent that he refused an offer from the Catholic Church to set him up in America because he feared that Irish emigrants would kill him, either en route or on landing. The parish where I was born,

Monkstown, County Dublin, on the East Coast, was chosen as the most Protestant and safest place for him to marry.

In the inflammation of the moment, Robert Byrne, the editor of the *Kerry Examiner*, launched an attack on Gayer that led to a highly publicized libel suit being launched against the *Examiner* and Gayer's being awarded compensation of £40 at the Recorder's Court, Tralee, on March 20, 1845. He won another case the following year, this time securing an ejectment order against tenants of one of his colonies who had reconverted to Catholicism. Gayer successfully pleaded that having rejoined Rome, the tenants were now presumably acceptable to their neighbors and no longer required the shelter of his houses, which were needed for other converts who had remained Protestant and consequently did require protection.

The favorable verdicts appeared at first to be a remarkable triumph for Gayer. Mrs. Thompson cited the libel suit's outcome in her book as evidence of an extraordinary new spirit in Dingle—the jury had been composed of equal numbers of Catholics and Protestants. However, the legal successes were to prove pyrrhic victories for the Dingle mission. The two Catholic lawyers involved in the case, David Piggot and James Byrne, owed their qualifications to the emancipation secured by Daniel O'Connell, and they successfully lobbied the aged liberator for assistance in furthering a plan they devised to counter Gayer's mission: the Vincentian Fathers should be invited to Kerry to conduct a Catholic mission to Dingle.

The Vincentians were strongly imbued with the spirit of the Council of Trent (1545–1563), one of whose principal objectives had been to combat the spread of Protestantism. As James H. Murphy has pointed out, a blitzkrieg-like method of attack was the chosen method of warfare. Murphy's authoritative article deserves to be read not merely for its account of what happened in Dingle but as a microcosm of how the Catholic Church won power and influence in Ireland from the mid-nineteenth century onward.

It was a method that was not confined to Dingle but that spread to other dioceses also. In the Archdiocese of Tuam, where, as we have seen, Protestant missionaries were particularly active, the Vincentians were joined by teams of Rosminians and Redemptorists. Their sermons were tactfully described by Father Kieran Waldron as being "very dramatic and fiery. . . .

Penitents who recanted their apostasy were publicly reconciled with the Church."[24] Readers who have studied Mrs. Thompson's account of a missionary in action will appreciate Father Waldron's delicate use of language.

When a team of Vincentians descended on a congregation, their modus operandi was to attack with equal force Protestantism and the presence of "folk religion" in Irish Catholicism. The Vincentians were extremely ultramontane (meaning literally "beyond the mountains," in effect taking the teachings of Rome beyond the Roman hills) in their approach, seeking to ensure that Irish Catholicism took on a distinctly Roman character and that customs such as saying Mass, or conducting wakes, in homes should be discontinued in favor of church-centered ceremonies. The small, badly maintained churches of an impoverished people were to be replaced by bigger and more numerous churches. Thus, triumphantly, by the use of brick and mortar would the church on the hill proclaim the benefits of emancipation and those that derived from the piety of the Irish who survived the Famine.

However, neither the local clergy nor Cornelius Egan, bishop of Kerry, initially favored the introduction of emissaries from the head office into local affairs. There was considerable opposition to the Vincentians until O'Connell persuaded the bishop to allow them to conduct a mission in Dingle.

This was a decisive event. The Vincentians succeeded in arousing an almost unbelievable enthusiasm. For some six weeks in August and September 1846, six priests conducted a program of saying Mass, hearing confessions, and delivering nightly sermons. Confirmations had been held in Dingle before the missioners' arrival, but their invocations led to another thousand confirmations being held, mostly among adults. The Vincentians' visit led to the establishment of a Christian Brothers School and of societies for the male laity known as confraternities. After all that had gone on—landlordism, dispossession, hunger, and more lately, the cultural and religious tensions and uncertainties generated by Gayer, the Irish mission, and souperism—a Catholic enthusiasm amounting to hysteria hung over Dingle. Confession tickets had to be issued in order to cope with the disorderly queues that gathered to make their confessions. The distributors of the tickets had to be issued with horsewhips for their own safety. The following is a description, by Father Thomas McNamara, the leader of the six-man Vincentian team, of what happened at the close of the mission:

> The people pressed forward and the confraternity men [acting as stewards] pressed them back until, unable to resist by any other means, they had actually to use sticks and clubs in the struggle and what can scarcely be believed blood flowed copiously from the blows inflicted, the confraternity men feeling they had a duty to perform even to so terrible an extremity and we who attended the Bishop right and left had to witness with his Lordship of the poor people for the way to come forward. Such a scene is only to be imagined among the poor rude people urged onwards by their religious enthusiasm to offer, as one might say, violence to heaven.[25]

Hysteria perhaps, but it worked. The emotions released in Dingle illustrate the tensions the Irish Catholic peasantry lived under and the significance of the church to their lives. The priest was the arbiter and inspiration, the dominant, but also the only sympathetic, authority figure in their lives. From the earliest days of the crisis the value of the contribution of the Catholic clergy to the relief effort was recognized by the more knowledgeable and less blinkered English decision-makers. We know from the papers of a former chancellor of the English Exchequer, Lord Monteagle, that when Trevelyan attempted to exclude the Catholic clergy from relief committees in 1846, Monteagle had the attempt quashed. He wrote to Chief Secretary Lord Bessborough, pointing out that the curates were "working like tigers for us" and that without them nothing would be accomplished.

Priests and nuns paid with their lives for ministering to their people in reeking, fever-infested cabins. As the "soupers war" raged in Dingle, several nuns from convents throughout Kerry contracted famine fever while visiting the sick and died. Mortality amongst nuns and priests is a frequently overlooked aspect of the Great Hunger.

After the Vincentians departed, by boat because the roads were clogged with well-wishers, the Dingle mission went into decline. Gayer contracted famine fever and died, and his ostracized converts had to be spirited out of Dingle to other parts of Ireland. Dingle marked a turning point in Irish Catholicism.

The skirmishing activities of the Vincentians coincided with the arrival in Ireland of the able and ultramontane Archbishop Paul Cullen, who was determined to bring about a "devotional revolution" in Irish Catholicism; the blitzkrieg-like tactics fit in perfectly with Cullen's plans. The Vincentians successfully attacked another flourishing Protestant mission field at Oughterard in County Galway, deliberately using ostracism as a tactic.

The theological shoot-out in Dingle between Gayer and the Vincentians was an important precipitating engagement in the war—carried out on a broad front by other orders and by diocesan clergy—to install a type of Catholicism in Ireland that could be said to have maintained its grip until the Vatican Councils of the 1960s. In that war one of the Catholic clergy's most potent propaganda weapons was the widespread use of the term "souperism." Thus, ironically, the "soupers" strengthened rather than hindered the growth of the Irish Catholic Church. Out of this growth there came the extraordinary numbers of Irish nuns and priests who built schools, hospitals, and churches all over the world, at the same time distributing food to the needy. The Irish generally refer to this development with admiration and an understandable pride. The word "proselytizing" is never used. "Missionary" is the approved term.

But without disparaging the selflessness, and often the heroism, of what Catholic missionaries, and very often Protestant ones too, have contributed to the Third World, one can't help wishing that the soil of Ireland in which this growth was propagated could have been tilled in the Quaker spirit of disinterested philanthropy rather than with the sectarian partisanship displayed by Irish Christianity in the nineteenth century.

Before leaving the subject, fairness demands that two points be made: first, that the clergy and nuns who risked their lives in visiting reeking cabins, infested with fever, to bring solace to the dying should never be forgotten. The second is to note the strengthening of the impulse of the Irish public toward helping the Third World, an impulse that has persisted to the present day in the form of both donations and aid work.

TEN

THE POOR LAW COMETH

"Neither ancient nor modern history can furnish a parallel to the fact that upwards of 3 millions of persons were fed every day in the neighbourhood of their homes, by administrative arrangements emanating from and controlled by one central office."[1]

—Charles Trevelyan

THE FOREGOING WAS THE GLOWING PRAISE that Charles Trevelyan bestowed on the operation of the Soup Kitchen Act, much of which he had diligently overseen and for which he felt entitled to take credit. What he did not state was that he had subsequently moved on to play a leading role in the operation of the Irish Poor Law Extension Act of 1847, which effectively undid much of the benefit of the soup kitchens and brought an incalculable amount of suffering and death upon the starving.

The Poor Law Extension Act was the spawn of two conflicting ideological parents: one maintained that Irish property should pay for Irish poverty; the other that, for both ideological and economic reasons, relief should not be given outside the workhouse walls. To provide outdoor relief, according to the moralizing political economists, would be both "demoralizing" and ruinous, given the numbers involved. These doctrines were so rigorously adhered to that in some cases they even led to the ending of food distribution *within* the workhouses.

The workhouse in Cashel, County Tipperary, was suffering from "frightful overcrowding" as Christmas 1846 approached and they had to turn away five hundred people who were eligible for admission but for whom there was no room. Because of their eligibility, the workhouse authorities, as was done elsewhere, gave the five hundred one meal a day inside the workhouse, arguing that this could not be considered outdoor relief because the food was eaten inside the workhouse. Officialdom would not accept this plea and said the practice had to stop.

However, back in London realization had set in that the work scheme had been a disaster and that something fresh had to be attempted. Barely a month after Cashel was forced to deny the starving five hundred, Lord John Russell announced a policy reversal. It made way for an expansion of the poor law to allow for the introduction of outdoor relief later in the year.

This legislation depended first on an impossibility and second on a cruelty. The impossibility lay in the principal assumption underlying the poor law extension, namely that it would be paid for out of the rates (local taxes) collected in Ireland. The doctrine on which this decision was based, that Irish property should pay for Irish poverty, would have been better phrased "Irish poverty must support Irish property."

The ruinous state of the country generally and that of the landlord class in particular has already been described. Even *before* the failure of the potato, in 1844, the Conservatives, who were never in any danger of being accused of excessive tenderheartedness where the collection of Irish taxes was concerned, had taken part in a spectacular demonstration of the difficulties of extracting blood from a stone. In Mayo only one-quarter of the rates nominally due were collected even after the rate collectors had been provided with the following backup: two companies drawn from the Sixtyninth Regiment, one troop from the Tenth Huzzars, fifty police, police inspectors, and two magistrates—backed up by two revenue cutters and a major warship, the *Stromboli*. This was not an isolated case. In the same year it had taken the deployment of seven hundred troops to collect the rates of neighboring Galway.

This use of the army and the navy to collect rates had been debated in the House of Commons. The Whigs were fully aware of the difficulty of rate collection and the general situation regarding destitution in Ireland. What Trevelyan knew, chancellor of the exchequer Charles Wood knew. It would be an absurdity to suggest that the pair somehow managed to keep the prime minister and their cabinet colleagues in the dark over Ireland. Trevelyan, whatever his other faults, could not be accused of laziness. Every detail concerning relief had to be brought to his attention. In order to deal with a mountain of paperwork and the decision making this necessitated, he moved into a flat away from his wife and family so that he could work undisturbed, even over Christmas. He censured Sir Randolph Routh for wanting to take holidays at Christmas so that he could attend the vice-regal festivities, pointing out the "impropriety of appearing in public when the lives of such multitudes of persons depend on your unremitting exertions."[2] Events were to prove, however, that Trevelyan's concern on that occasion was based not so much on sympathy with the "multitudes" as on public relations considerations.

For, as that grisly year of 1847 wore on, Trevelyan decided that the situation had improved so much that he could now take a well-earned holiday and in mid-August took his family off to France. Before going, in preparation for the coming into effect of the Poor Law Extension Act, which had become law on June 8, he oversaw the closing down of the soup kitchens and ordered the ending of the sale of meal from government depots. The instruction to these depots was clear: "Ship off all, close your depot and come away."[3] Any meal remaining in the depot at the time of closure was either sold at market prices or, if unsold, removed in a government ship.

Trevelyan's view was that government relief had made the people worse, not better, and that the time had come to "try what independent exertion will do." By the beginning of October, the last soup kitchen and food depots in even the most distressed areas had ceased operations. Trevelyan described the cessation as follows: "The multitude was again gradually and peacefully thrown on its own resources at the season of harvest, when new and abundant supplies of food became available, and the demand for labour was at its highest amount."[4]

He wrote to Sir John Burgoyne, "This year is not merely a cessation but a transfer. . . . The responsibilities and duties which we lay down have been imposed by the legislature on the poor law commissioners and the boards of guardians."[5]

Trevelyan then headed for the Loire Valley. Not until the closing days of World War II when Hitler was issuing directions to non-existent armies would Europe see policies so irrelevant to reality put into effect.

Ireland was struck by a further application of Murphy's Law. England was hit by a financial crisis in 1847; ironically, much of it was caused by unwise speculation in the wheat trade.

By the end of the summer, wheat that had been bought forward earlier in the year was selling at less than half the purchase price. This, coupled with similar collapses in railway shares, triggered a financial crisis in which over one hundred firms perished, eleven of them banks. The crisis only began to ease in late October after the government agreed to indemnify the Bank of England when it began to print money over and above the amount of gold reserves it held in backing for the British currency. Writing to the Irish viceroy, Lord Clarendon, in the midst of this financial carnage, Lord John Russell spelled out the implications for Ireland: "I fear you have a most troublesome winter ahead of you. . . . Here we have no money."[6]

Some historians have denied that Trevelyan should be regarded as "a Victorian Cromwell," pointing out that he was only a civil servant. However, he was the civil servant who controlled Charles Wood, the chancellor of the exchequer, and the man who controlled the purse strings. As the Famine reached ever more frightful proportions, Clarendon complained to Russell that Trevelyan was openly declaring that his core philosophy on the solution to the crisis was "the operation of natural causes." This cold and cruel dogma meant in practice that people who were deprived of food or shelter and exposed to disease and starvation would naturally die off.

We have already encountered the philanthropic Quaker James Hack Tuke's description of the aftermath of eviction in bad weather. Here is another account by him of the closing down of the Clifden workhouse, which went bankrupt through lack of support from local ratepayers and the government's unwillingness to make up the deficiency. Hack Tuke describes how he saw people who "had taken up their abode in some holes or cavities in the hillside, where gravel appeared to have been dug."[7] Their physical condition at that stage may be judged from the appearance of a boy of fourteen who asked Hack Tuke for "a little meal to keep the life in me."[8] Tuke said that the boy was "a living skeleton, wasted with hunger and sores." That was in the autumn; one can readily imagine what the onset of winter and Trevelyan's "natural causes" did to that boy and to the gravel dwellers. Such was the aftermath of "Humanity Dick" Martin's bankruptcy and an illustration of why the auctioneers could assure would-be purchasers of the estate that the tenants who were present on the estate in 1847 "will not now be found on the Lands."[9]

By November the situation in many workhouses was exemplified by the sale of the furniture of the Scariff workhouse in County Clare, which was auctioned to pay some of the costs of writs served on it by traders whose bills had not been paid. T. N. Redington, the undersecretary to the lord lieutenant, mindful of the consequences of this action, appealed to the Treasury to do something for Scariff and the many situations like it. However, Trevelyan's response may be gleaned from an instruction he issued to Edward Twisleton, the poor law commissioner, who eventually resigned. He wrote, "The principle of the Poor Law as you very well know is that rate after rate should be levied for the purpose of preserving life, until the Landlord and farmer either enable the people to support themselves by honest industry, or dispose of their estates to those who can perform this indispensable duty."[10]

What was to befall the paupers in the winter of 1847 while "new ownership" was found he did not say. What did emanate from the Treasury, however, was a very forcible edict from Charles Wood on the subject of rates. These were to be collected come what may. "Arrest, remand, do anything you can," he wrote to Clarendon on November 22: "Send horse, foot and dragoons, all the world will applaud you, and I should not be at all squeamish as to what I did, to the verge of the law, and a little beyond."[11]

The ringing declaration on rates was in part make-believe, in part a fig leaf for the true Treasury policy of getting rid of surplus population to make way for that longed-for "new ownership" that would create larger farms and would substitute cattle for potatoes. The real situation throughout much of Ireland where rates were concerned was eloquently, if despairingly, described by Colonel George Vaughan Jackson, a good resident Mayo landlord who was doing his best to maintain both his estate and his tenants in appalling circumstances. He wrote, "No men are more ill-fated or greater victims than we resident proprietors, we are consumed by the hives of human beings that exist on the properties of the absentees. On my right and my left are properties such as I allude to. I am overwhelmed and ruined by them. These proprietors will do nothing. All the burden of relief and employment falls on me."[12]

The following month, on December 16, 1847, Lord Sligo, another landlord, wrote to *The Times* explaining what the poor law meant in practice: "On the express condition that they should make no provision for the future. . . . There are now therefore, at this moment, in obedience to the law, 26,000 people in Westport who are destitute of food, fuel and clothing. . . . The long account of money spent will not feed the crowds of destitute, the rates cannot do it, and if the union be left to that fund alone, these myriads must perish by famine."[13]

The government had a most precise and up-to-date awareness of the truth of the situation described by Lord Sligo and Colonel Vaughan Jackson. Lord Clarendon himself bore out the truth of their observations, telling Sir George Grey, the home secretary, that unless financial aid was forthcoming, "I dread some calamity . . . some hundreds dying all at once of starvation, which would not only be shocking but bring disgrace on the Government."[14]

However, he received nothing but contempt in response to his appeal. Grey replied, "It may be that if numerous deaths should occur the Government would be blamed . . . but there is such an indisposition to spend more money on Ireland, that the Government will assuredly and severely be blamed if they advance money to pay debts."

That "indisposition" was greatly furthered by a public opinion–molding campaign (see chapter 13) in which Clarendon himself, but in particular

Trevelyan and Wood, had taken part. In vain did Clarendon reply angrily to Grey that "it meant wholesale deaths from starvation and disease, and John Bull won't like that, however cross he may be at paying."

Clarendon's remonstrance, however, produced nothing. Chancellor Wood affected to believe that Clarendon was exaggerating the situation in Ireland. He wrote that "there had been exaggeration last year and there was probably exaggeration now."

Clarendon realized that the hand in the puppeteer's glove controlling Treasury policy was that of Charles Trevelyan. He wrote bitterly to a colleague, the influential Charles Greville, clerk of the privy council, complaining about Trevelyan's influence. Greville noted that "Clarendon attributes a great part of the obstacles he meets with to Charles Wood, who is entirely governed by Trevelyan; and C.W. is to the last degree obstinate and tenacious of the opinions which his Secretary puts into him."[15]

Despite Clarendon's pleas, the situation was left to the mercy of "natural causes," and the calamity that he predicted duly ensued.[16] Wood struck a note of real hostility toward Ireland in his communications with Clarendon as he sounded the constant refrain of "no money." As the ending of the soup kitchens and the beginning of the implementation of the Poor Law Extension Act approached, Trevelyan was adamant that the new law would have to be financed from Ireland. All the chancellor was prepared to do was to forgive the £4.5 million that had been expended on the road schemes and soup kitchens and that, in theory, should have been repaid by the various relief committees. This was a large sum of money at the time. But, realistically speaking, in view of the necessity to involve the army and the navy in rates collection described earlier in this chapter, there was no hope of collecting it anyhow.

Wood was also prepared to support a minor measure whereby property owners could borrow money to improve their estates at 3.5 percent. He and Trevelyan were *ad idem* on the subject. Wood told Clarendon that he and Trevelyan "had the most perfect understanding of this subject." His view was that "our rations" had afforded the Irish a "safe and comfortable existence." However, he added that "they have hardly been decent while they have found their bellies full of our corn and their pockets of our money."[17]

At this stage there were, of course, comparatively few full bellies in Ireland, but there were many overly full graveyards, and fever was adding massively to their contents on a daily basis. But the financial crisis, donor fatigue, and a growing belief among Protestants that the Famine was God's method of punishing the Irish for their own fecklessness had begun to affect England.

Like Trevelyan and Clarendon, Wood was in constant touch with John Thadeus Delane, the editor of *The Times*. To underline both the financial situation and the state of Protestant opinion, Wood passed on to Clarendon a snippet of information Delane had given him; the previous Sunday (October 17, 1847) special prayers had been offered all over England in thanksgiving for the unusually fine harvest. At these services a letter from the queen was read appealing for aid for Ireland. Wood informed Clarendon that the editor had told him that in one post alone he had received sixty-two letters from clergymen objecting to collecting the aid funds. For good measure, he added that at the service he had himself attended in Whitehall the clergyman had taken the opportunity of condemning "the ingratitude of the Irish."

Further cause for "ingratitude" lay around the corner. The new poor law was supposed to come into operation on October 1, 1847, and, unlike all that had gone before, was also supposed to be planned and controlled from Dublin by a new Irish Poor Law Board. But the new board consisted of an old cast of characters, including Edward Twisleton, who had considerable experience with the earlier relief commissions. It was he who was supposed to plan for the administration of the new law. But he looked into the future and decided it would not work. In light of his experience, combined with the fact that fever and famine were raging all around him, and that there was to be no money from London, Twisleton could not visualize how the new law could possibly work; he avoided the responsibility of being blamed for its failure by simply neglecting to produce a plan.

Trevelyan, however, had no compunction about stepping into the breach; he drew up a plan that he said was "also the opinion of the Chancellor." Events would prove that he was all too correct in making this claim. For the plan rested on a provision that, viewed through the arches of the years, appears to turn normality upside down. The aged and the infirm, the widow and the orphan were to be *expelled* from the workhouses and given outside relief solely in the form of cooked food. Only the *able-bodied* were to be given relief inside the workhouses. And, in order to ensure that the new scheme was not inundated by able-bodied men, plans carried the familiar stipulation that entrance to the workhouses was to be made as difficult and as unattractive as possible.

Trevelyan wrote that his plan called for drawing "the broadest and most impassable line between those unions which, with exertion, could support their own poor and those which never could."[18]

Twenty-two unions in the West and Southwest fell on the poor side of the line and were to receive some assistance under "special and powerful control." The other 108 were supposed to fend for themselves via the rates and whatever charitable funds they could lay hands on.

Then, early in October, Trevelyan gave a demonstration of his preeminent role in Irish relief by visiting Dublin with a view to overhauling the Board of Works accounts, confronting Twisleton, and discussing with Sir John Burgoyne how his new plan should work. His second visit to Dublin mirrored the first. He again created controversy by writing to a newspaper without consulting anyone. Apparently discovering that Burgoyne was writing to *The Times* making the case for renewed assistance for Ireland because of the widespread destitution, he also wrote to the paper (on October 12) giving details of the new poor law and making it crystal clear that he was concerned not with the alleviation of famine but with changing the structure of Irish agriculture. He wrote that "the change from an idle, barbarous, isolated potato cultivation, to corn cultivation, which enforces industry, binds together employer and employed in mutually beneficial relations, and requiring capital and skill for its successful prosecution, supposes the existence of a class of substantial yeomanry who have an interest in preserving the good order of society, is proceeding as fast as can reasonably be expected under the circumstances."

Clarendon was outraged. In a protest to Wood he wrote, "There never was such an invention as a Secretary of the Treasury coming over here and writing a State paper to *The Times* from his hotel without any communication with the Government here or with his official superiors."[19]

The protest elicited neither satisfaction for Clarendon nor censure for Trevelyan. In a separate complaint to Lord John Russell, Clarendon made a telling admission. He said he was "surprised and annoyed to read in *The Times* two letters signed by Burgoyne and Trevelyan about the distress and the necessity for relieving it. *Very true* but . . . these official statements will increase my difficulty in *resisting applications for relief.*"[20]

Clarendon, who as lord lieutenant was the man who was allegedly directly responsible for alleviating the situation, could play only a minimalist role, one as much concerned with the refusal of aid as with its disbursement. Clarendon was not a cruel man and was under no illusion as to what his position was—and what London's view was. He had not sought the Irish posting. It had been offered to him by Russell "in his most cold, short, abrupt, indifferent manner—much as if he was disposing of a tide-waiters place to an applicant."[21]

Russell had led Clarendon to believe that his stay in Dublin would be a relatively short one, approximately three years, and that his main task would be to become the last Irish viceroy. Russell had plans to abolish the post, replacing it with a secretary of state, thus making Ireland less of a colony and more a proper member of the Union on the same footing as Scotland and Wales. That aspiration went out the window with the onset of famine. The realization that Ireland was not seen in the same light as Scotland and Wales was soon borne in on Ireland; there was a rare coming together of orange and green. At a meeting in Fermanagh described as one of the largest public gatherings seen in the country since the days of O'Connell's "monster" meetings, it was resolved that if Ireland was indeed part of the Union, then it was the duty of the imperial exchequer to contribute to that union. However, the sound of the orange drum beating alongside the piping of the green produced no echo of sympathy from London.

As the 1847 grain harvest ripened, many landlords began seizing their tenants' corn in lieu of rent. When rate collectors arrived in distressed areas like Connemara, they found no crops to seize and instead took any article of value that might be found, including clothing. "Look sharp about the rates," Wood advised Trevelyan on being told of the landlords' behavior. There was to be no relief until a rate of 15 shillings in the pound had been levied, Russell informed Clarendon. Levied on whom was the question.

For some time Clarendon had been wrestling with the problem of extracting blood from a stone. As early as September 20 he had written to Russell asking what was to be done about areas where there was no one to levy rates on. He said, "There are whole districts in Mayo and Donegal and parts of Kerry where the people swarm and are even now starving and where there is no landed proprietor to levy on. He is absent or in Chancery and the estate subdivided into infinitely small lots. . . . What is to be done with these hordes? Improve them off the face of the earth you will say, let them die. . . . But there is a certain amount of responsibility attaching to it."[22] There was indeed a "certain amount" of responsibility, a very large amount, but Clarendon must have known in his heart of hearts that he was only writing for the record.

There was not a snowball's chance in hell of securing a meaningful humane response to the Irish Famine from the English cabinet. Trevelyan's plan had been largely for the optics. To operate successfully, the new poor law would have needed to have collected £14 million in rates. As the bill passed through the House of Lords, it was pointed out by Lord Mountcashel that Irish landlords were in debt to such an extent that repayments on their borrowings came to some £10.5 million per annum and that their actual annual income would only have been somewhere around £3.5 million a year. This inconvenient truth was ignored.

The noble record of the Quakers in dealing with the Famine has already been described. No greater condemnation of Trevelyan's scheme could be made than to simply record that when the details of his plan became known, the Quakers refused to operate it. They pointed out the impossibility of it succeeding in parts of the country where one could go for thirty or forty miles without encountering a workhouse. The man who had refused to furnish his own fig-leaf plan, Poor Law Commissioner Twisleton, did what he could for approximately a year and a half to make Trevelyan's allegedly realistic blueprint work, but eventually resigned in angry disgust in March 1849. The Quakers also resigned from their humanitarian efforts in

1849, writing to Russell on June 5 that despite all their efforts matters had not improved and that the situation could only be dealt with by government action, not philanthropy. Reform of the land system was essential. The decision of the efficient and humanitarian Quakers to pull out of Ireland in the teeth of raging famine, albeit cloaked in the politest of terms in their letter to Russell, may be seen as an appalling indictment of government policy which in its own right deserves to be read alongside Mitchell's more forthright "God sent the blight but the British sent the famine." Clarendon described the reasons for his resignation to Russell as follows: "He thinks that the destitution here is so horrible, and the indifference of the House of Commons is so manifest, that he is an unfit agent of a policy which must be one of extermination. . . . Twisleton feels that as Chief Commissioner he is placed in a position . . . which no man of honour and humanity can endure."

But the policy of "extermination" was to continue. A number of circumstances assisted the Liberals in following this path. Ironically, one of the most important was the effect of the Famine itself, which gave rise to widespread lawlessness and the shooting of landlords. Famine conditions also served to bring to the boil simmering divisions in Daniel O'Connell's party, leading to the Young Irelanders' bloodless insurrection. While it never had the remotest possibility of succeeding, it proved a godsend for government propaganda.

For example, as the reappearance of the potato blight cast an ominous light on the government's grossly inadequate relief plans, the influential London *Times* published an editorial on August 30, 1848, that could have been—and, as we shall see later, quite possibly was—written in the offices of either Trevelyan or Wood. It referred explicitly to the bad effect on public opinion of the failed insurrection and went on to claim: "In no other country have men talked treason until they are forced, and then gone about begging for sympathy from their oppressors. In no other country have the people been so liberally and more unthriftily (sic) helped by the nation they denounced and defied, and in none have they repeated more humble and piteous supplications to those whom they have previously repaid with monstrous ingratitude. As a matter of state economy, some relief would be given to Ireland, in case she needs it, but we warn that such relief will not be carried to the extent, or dealt forth, after the measure of former years."

The policy of *The Times* consistently opposed repeal of the Act of Union but, as in other influential circles when it came to spending money on Ireland, was clearly regarded as *partibus infidelium.*[23]

The insurrection and the attacks on landlords will shortly be discussed in detail. For the moment it is sufficient to say that ancestral prejudice, incited by the government's use of the press, the financial crisis, and the effect of the political economists—coupled with Russell's inability, or perhaps disinclination, to override the Trevelyan/Wood axis, whose policies clearly had the sympathy of powerful members of the cabinet—ensured that the governmental strategy for Ireland was based on what was, in effect, a blueprint for depopulation drawn up by Trevelyan.

By April 1848 Russell had recognized that some of the innocent should be spared the lash of Trevelyan and Wood and promised that 200,000 children who had hitherto been fed by the British Relief Association, whose funds were now nearing exhaustion, should be sustained from the public purse. He committed himself to this objective in writing, saying, "The government will take up the charge when the British Association lays it down."[24]

However, the government did not take up the charge. As the November chill gripped Ireland, Trevelyan, neither checked nor hindered by Russell, also put it in writing that the feeding of the children was to stop.[25] Tiny Treasury grants that had been allowed to the more distressed unions were also terminated. Trevelyan cited lack of money as the reason for these barbarous actions, but a better insight into his reasoning, and that of his ally Wood, may be gleaned from a memo to Twisleton in which he refused a repetition of an act of charity of the previous year—the issue of substandard ordnance clothing to the destitute. Trevelyan wrote, "It is a great object not to revive the habit of dependence on Government aid."[26]

The soullessness of this approach may be partially assessed when one considers the appalling fact that by now the country was reeling from the blow of the potato blight's having struck yet again. But even saying this does not convey a true picture of the seething horror that was the Irish countryside in 1848. It was a year of hatred vying with optimism. The former was directed principally at the landlords by their tenants and, to a lesser degree, at the British government. The optimism at the prospects of a hugely improved harvest of potatoes lasted almost to the end of July. Encouraged by the good results from the small percentage of seed potatoes sown in 1847, the already impoverished people pawned or sold everything they still possessed—clothes, bedding, furniture—in order to plant potatoes in every conceivable scrap of land. All over the country people planted many times the amount of seed that had been set the previous year. Very few green crops were sown. Reliance on the potato was greater than ever before. The corresponding distress caused by the reappearance of the blight was also proportionately greater.

Among those who had high hopes of better times following the increase in the acreage of potatoes were the landlords. Tenants would be able to pay their rents, and creditors could be paid off. Instead, the opposite proved to be the case. The reappearance of the blight meant that arrears soared and, with them, evictions. Now it was not merely merciless landlords like Lord Lucan, who objected to paying paupers lest they become priests, or Walshe of Belmullet, who evicted young and old during a Christmas gale, but humane figures like Lord Sligo who found themselves under pressure to become evictors.

Sligo's estates on paper brought in an income of £7,200 a year. But debts, largely inherited, came to approximately £6,000 a year. He had had no rents for some three years but had managed on at least two occasions to keep Westport workhouse open for the destitute at his own expense by curtailing his lifestyle even to the unheard-of extent of not keeping a carriage. However, the failure of the potato led him to write to Lord Monteagle on October 8, 1848, saying that he was under the necessity "of ejecting or being ejected."[27]

Other landlords invoked many different compulsions. Lord Clanricarde, one of the most brutal absentee landlords on record, who had joined in Lord Palmerston's brutally frank assessment of the need to clear the surplus peasantry from the land, claimed to Clarendon that "the landlords are prevented from aiding or tolerating poor tenants. They are compelled to hunt out all such, to save the property from the £4 clause."[28]

As an example of how Pontius Pilate washed his hands, this could hardly be bettered. What Clanricarde carefully did not say is that he was a senior member of the government doing the "preventing." The result of the hunting may be gauged by two descriptions of evictions from different parts of the country during the earlier and latter parts of the year. The first is from County Clare at a time (March) when some of the doomed potato crop was still being sown. Sir Arthur Kennedy, then a poor law inspector, was describing the aftermath of the destruction of some one thousand cabins in the space of three months. He said that the "wretched, helpless, homeless" wander the countryside "scattering disease, destitution and dismay in all directions. . . . The most awful cases of destitution and suffering ever seen. When the houses are torn down, people live in banks and ditches like animals, until starvation or weather drive them to the workhouse. Three cart loads, who could not walk, were brought in yesterday."[29]

The condition of such evictees was worsened when the weather turned foul. Colonel Jones of the Board of Works has left a report describing how the conditions favored the spread of blight: "Throughout August: rain fell in one continuous cataract . . . , incessantly." Hay was "actually floating." Conditions were "as bad as 1846."[30] They were to get worse. Tens of thousands of desperate, starving peasants were torn from their homes and left at the mercy of the elements.

A searing account of what this meant in practice comes from an eyewitness, one Sir William Butler, describing an eviction he witnessed as a boy in Tipperary: "The sheriff, a strong force of police, and above all the crowbar brigade, and, a body composed of the lowest and most debauched ruffians, were present. At a signal from the sheriff the work began. The miserable inmates of the cabins were dragged out . . . the thatched roofs were torn down and the earthen walls battered by crowbars (practice had made these scoundrels experts in their trade); the screaming women, the half-naked children, the paralysed grandmother and the tottering grandfather were hauled out. It was a sight I have never forgotten. I was 12 years old at the time, and I think if a loaded gun had been put into my hand I would have fired into the crowd as they plied their horrible trade. . . . The winter of 1848—lingers in my memory as one long night of sorrow."[31]

Sir William's reactions were shared by Kennedy. Years later at a fashionable English dinner table, the subject of the Famine came up. Kennedy turned to his host, Lord Carnarvon, and said, "I can tell you, my lord, that there were days . . . when I came back from some scene of eviction, so saddened by the sights of hunger and misery I had seen in the days' work, that I felt disposed to take the gun from behind my door and shoot the first landlords I met."[32]

Neither Butler nor Kennedy did take up a gun, but inevitably, outside the ranks of the Ascendancy, there were those who did. Whiteboyism had not gone away but had been given added impetus by the Famine. Throughout 1847 a series of murders or murderous attacks took place in which some sixteen landowners were killed. Given the state of misery in the country and the number of famine deaths, the toll of shootings may not seem large, but it was sufficient to arouse enormous fear and anger. In the poverty-stricken counties of Leitrim and Sligo alone, the police were aware of the names of at least ten landlords whose lives were said to be not worth a piece of paper. There were reports of landlords leaving the country, and it was said of those who remained that "the personal insecurity of *all* property owners is so hideous that the impression is of being in an enemy country."[33]

In the next chapter, we shall see what this meant in practice.

ELEVEN

LANDLORDS TARGETED

"It is quite true that landlords in England would not bear to be shot like hares and partridges . . . but neither does any landlord in England turn out fifty persons at one go and burn their houses over their heads, giving them no provision for the future."

—*Lord John Russell to Clarendon*[1]

G IVEN THE FEARS AND SUSPICION TOWARD the natives, it is not surprising that the Famine created a heightened sense of danger and insecurity. Tensions rose so high that the viceroy, Lord Clarendon, sent his children out of the country.

Clarendon feared a general insurrection, a forecast in which he was to be proved spectacularly (or farcically) wrong. What I term the "equally hard bullets" syndrome added fuel to the authority's imaginings. The many incidents by which the syndrome was formed probably began occurring at the time of the Anglo-Norman invasion and continued during the subsequent tangled years of British-Irish relationships. My definition was created by an angry resident of the Republic of Ireland who was stopped and searched by a British foot patrol in Belfast during "the Troubles."

A member of the patrol tried to be friendly, telling him, "I'm from the Republic too." The angry driver replied, "Your bullets are just as hard."

The most notable landlord victim of the "equally hard bullets" syndrome was Major Denis Mahon of Strokestown, County Roscommon, who had inherited a classically mismanaged estate from a mad relation. During his relative's illness, rents on the Mahon estate had accumulated some £30,000 in arrears. Rates were not paid for several years and the land had become hopelessly divided and subdivided to a point where, when the potato failed, the man's holding was completely overcrowded and unproductive.

Mahon tried to meet the situation by offering work and free passage to Canada to any tenant who voluntarily quit his holding. Some eight hundred tenants accepted the offer. Thereupon, Mahon, a humane and generally well-spoken-of personality, spent £14,000 to charter two ships and provision them generously in the spring of 1847. The ships were not in particularly bad condition according to the standards of the time, but standards of hygiene during such voyages were atrocious, and typhus spread rapidly among the passengers. On top of this, one of the ships got into difficulties and had to return to Ireland for repairs before continuing on to Canada.

Rumors spread that both vessels were "coffin ships" that foundered because they were unsuitable for the Atlantic crossing. Both ships did, in fact, eventually make port in Québec, but typhus had taken a terrible toll during the protracted voyage. One ship was said to have lost over 260 passengers.

Back on the Strokestown estate, the departure of 810 tenants did little to alleviate the crisis on the land, so Mahon set about evicting the remaining 3,000 tenants who, in a popular phrase, could neither "pay nor go." Inevitably, these clearances affected the elderly, widows, and defenseless children. An intense resentment built up and Mahon, an ex-cavalry major, fell out with the parish priest of Strokestown, Father McDermot, who was later alleged to have denounced him from the altar, saying that Mahon was "worse than Cromwell—and yet he lives."[2]

On November 2, 1847, Mahon was shot dead as he returned in his open carriage from a meeting at which he had been working on plans to keep the local workhouse open. It is said that earlier in the day, at another meeting, his tenants had cheered him. However, as the news of his assassination spread, bonfires blazed on the hills around Strokestown. Appropriately enough, the Mahon estate is now a Famine museum.

Such a development would have seemed impossible in the weeks following Mahon's murder. The killing served as a sort of lightning rod for all the passions generated by the widespread evictions and consequent assassinations. Lord Farnham set the heather blazing in the House of Lords a month after Mahon's murder, claiming that Father McDermot had indeed spoken the words quoted above. A leading English Catholic, the Earl of Shrewsbury, then proceeded to demonstrate all the traditional upper-crust English Catholic disdain of the Irish version of that religion, coupled with the equally traditional obtuseness of the aristocracy, by launching into print to endorse and enhance Farnham's claims in the *Morning Chronicle* on January 4, 1848.

In fact, McDermot had never denounced Mahon and was able to prove as much, but Shrewsbury claimed that the statements attributed to the priest were true and that he should be punished for incitement to murder. He went on to denounce the Irish Catholic Church as being "a conniver at injustice, an accessory to crime . . . a pestilent sore in the commonwealth."[3] This brought both *The Nation*, published by Young Ireland, and Archbishop John McHale of Tuam into the fray. The paper defended the Irish clergy against the charges of inciting murder and said that the British press was generating a climate in which the solution to the Irish situation was to "hang a priest or two and all will be right."

As might be expected, Archbishop McHale also vigorously defended the Irish clergy for standing up for their people. In an open letter to Shrewsbury, he delivered a telling shaft at Russell's government: "How un-grateful of the Catholics of Ireland not to pour forth canticles of gratitude to the ministers, who promised that none of them should perish and then suffered a million to starve."[4] This was a more telling point than it might at first appear. Although made in the context of the Major Mahon/Father McDermot controversy, it did point the finger of blame for the Famine at those most responsible—the British government.

Enough has been said about the role of the Irish landlords to make it quite clear that a proportion of the guilt, and a high one at that, has to be laid at their door. But an even higher segment of blame has to be apportioned to the British government, which had both the power of initiative and the resources to greatly alleviate the suffering caused by the potato failure and did not do so. After the horrors of 1847, we can imagine the shock and terror that spread over Ireland as reports once more spread from all over the country that overnight, as if by the wave of a demon's wand, apparently healthy potatoes seemed to have been "sprinkled with vitriol."

The government was neither shaken nor stirred into action. Nothing that could befall the Irish peasantry was going to intimidate Whitehall. Sir Charles Trevelyan was clearly articulating cabinet thinking when he wrote on July 19, "The matter is awfully serious, but we are in the hands of Providence with no possibility of averting the catastrophe, if it is to happen we can only await the result."[5]

As previously stated, the realpolitik of government policy was composed of laissez-faire and the teachings of their favorite political economists, backed up by a public relations campaign invoking Providence and a distaste for both the Irish and the Irish landlords, all mixed with a generous dose of hypocrisy. The objective sought, and *achieved* at the end, was an ending of the overpopulation of Irish land, the introduction of efficient farming methods, and an abundant supply of cheap agricultural products on the imperial power's doorstep, rather than a drain on the exchequer. As it turned out, the policy was so successfully and surreptitiously pursued that, despite securing independence, the economy of the Republic of Ireland was to remain largely geared toward supplying cheap food to England until both expansion and diversification occurred when Ireland joined the EEC in 1973.

Lord John Russell himself led the chorus of Irish landlord culpability for the Famine in the key Irish debate, which, conveniently for the government, succeeded in centering on the evils of Irish landlords and bypassed the sufferings of the Irish tenantry who were facing starvation. England washed her hands of responsibility for famine relief through the Irish Poor Law Extension Act. Russell said, "I must say that though great numbers of the resident gentry have done their utmost, have exerted their best energies and being contented in some instances to forego their usual mode of living . . . yet I do not think that, taken as all—as a body residents and absentee . . . the exertion of property for the relief of distress have not been what they ought to be. . . . Sir, I would not go further into this part of the subject. I felt bound to state what I have stated, for I felt it pressing on my mind."[6]

It pressed on the minds of other contributors to the debate also. There were references to Irish landlords as slaveholders with white slaves who had "done nothing but sit down and howl for English money." Irish landlords "had so mischievously employed the great Powers entrusted to them by law as to have worked themselves to the brink of ruin and the whole people to the brink of starvation. Landlords had not done their duty . . . England was doing everything."[7]

Absentee landlords were castigated for having given not one shilling for relief but having instead sent their agents for their rent. Later in the year, Russell repeated his criticism of Irish landlords to Lord Clarendon when turning down the latter's request for extra troops and more coercive powers to deal with unrest in the maddened country. He said, "I am not ready to bring in any restrictive law without, at the same time, restraining power of the landlord. . . . It is quite true that landlords in England would not like to be shot like hares and partridges. . . . But neither does any landlord in England turn out 50 persons at once and burn their houses overhead, giving them no provision for the future."[8]

Lord Russell did not mention the fact that sitting with him at the cabinet table were a number of Irish landlords. Three of these in particular, Clanricarde, Lansdowne, and Palmerston, were, as we shall see, responsible for turning out considerably more than "50 persons at once"—and turning them out in particularly bad circumstances at that. Many Irish landlords were cruel, extravagant, and inefficient. But many were merely what was in the main a horde of indigent chinless wonders, debt-strangled financially by their own and their ancestors' follies and an accretion of middlemen as they cowered behind crumbling high walls in Ireland or lived in debt abroad, held solely responsible for the plight of a country suffering from some of the worst aspects of England's colonial project.

But, as the skies darkened over Ireland, there occurred an event that gave both an air of credibility to governmental propaganda and an opportunity to heighten anti-Irish sentiment generally. This was what became known as the Young Ireland rebellion in 1848. The Young Irelanders were the cadre of O'Connell's followers whom Trevelyan had referred to as the young intellectuals in the *Morning Chronicle* article that had displeased Peel.

In military terms the use of the word "rebellion" considerably overstates what actually occurred; "episode" would be a more apposite description. But politically, the Young Irelanders' protest had a lasting effect. The newspaper the Young Irelanders produced was called *The Nation*. As the title suggests, it preached nationality and was opposed to the Union. But it also sought to promote harmony between Catholic and Protestant and maintained a high literary standard, printing criticism and poetry along with political articles.

The paper cost sixpence, which in those days was often a day's pay for a peasant, and illiteracy was widespread among the audience it aimed at. These difficulties were partly overcome, particularly in rural areas, by people clubbing together to produce the sixpence and then gathering in an appointed house, sometimes over several nights, to hear the contents of the paper read by a literate person who was officially designated as "The Reader." Long after *The Nation* ceased publication, I found myself in Belfast interviewing Hugh McAteer, who had been chief of staff of the IRA in the 1940s. I asked him what influences had led him to join the IRA. In his reply he cited, with considerable pride, the fact that one of his ancestors had been "A Reader." After the Troubles broke out, Hugh's son Aidan became a prominent Republican and at the time of writing is one of Sinn Fein's most important strategists.

The leading figures in the Young Ireland Group were the writer Thomas Davis, the landowner and member of parliament William Smith O'Brien, Thomas Meagher, and Charles Gavan Duffy. John Mitchel took a more independent and revolutionary line than the rest of the group and was one of *The Nation*'s most controversial contributors. James Fintan Lalor was not interested in repeal but preached that Ireland's salvation lay in a solution to the land problem. Some indication of the caliber of Lalor and his family may be gauged from the fact that his brother Peter Lalor was one of the principal leaders of the Australian gold miners' historic Eureka Stockade uprising, which was the most significant uprising in Australian colonial history. The miners, many of them Irish, revolted against government taxation and a variety of other governmental injustices. Lalor and his descendants subsequently became important figures in the Australian gold-mining industry.

This is not the place for going into a detailed digression on the Young Irelanders, their policies, and their differences with O'Connell, which eventually led them along the road to insurrection. The Young Ireland leaders were men of ability and character; in a properly run country where justice prevailed, it would have been difficult to imagine any of them stoking the fires of revolution. One among them was John Mitchel, the son of an Ulster Presbyterian minister and a passionate advocate of physical force. His journalistic prowess and Swiftian indignation made him one of the great Irish polemical writers of the nineteenth century.

For a time, 1848 appeared to be the year of opportunity for the Young Irelanders. Governments were toppling like ninepins all over Europe. And in France, the darling of many of the fiery young Irish intellectuals, the Young Ireland leader John Blake Dillon visited Alphonse de Lamartine in Paris to seek military support. Instead he was given a flag whose colors still fly over the Irish Republic: green for the Catholic and nationalist tradition, orange for the Protestant one, and white for peace between them. The flag encapsulated the ideals of the Young Irelanders, but the gift left them short of guns with which to back them up. Prior to Blake Dillon's visit, the British ambassador had warned Lamartine that assisting the Irishmen would lead to a rupture in Franco/British relationships.

The French had provided one lesson in realpolitik, and the Irish peasantry were about to supply another dose of reality. After all the sunburst oratory and the fiery articles, the high heroics of the Young Irelanders' attempts to raise Ireland militarily and morally collapsed in a widow's cabbage garden in Ballingarry, County Tipperary, on July 29, 1848. Their previous few days had been spent journeying around the South of Ireland, principally in the counties of Kilkenny and Tipperary, with William Smith O'Brien at their head trying to rouse the populace, ultimately without success. Initially, this did not appear to be the likely outcome. On paper the movement was strong and well organized throughout the country. Everywhere the Young Irelanders' leadership went, cheering crowds assembled. The British responded with equal measures of alarm and outrage. Dublin Castle poured forth cascades of arrest warrants. In London, the Duke of Wellington breathed fire and urged a large-scale military response. It appeared that Clarendon's fears had been vindicated. But appearances were deceptive. As soon as the rebels finished speaking at a public meeting, Catholic clergy would appear, and earlier incitements to rebellion such as dark references to having their three days were forgotten. One reason for the amnesia was the fact that in an uprising against the monarchy in Paris, Archbishop Denis-Auguste Affre had been shot dead a short time earlier. The Irish Church didn't want that sort of thing spreading to Ireland. The priests told the people to go home, and the people obeyed the clergy.

Smith O'Brien was a brave and principled man but hardly a military leader. Although short of resources, he refused to allow banks to be robbed because such robberies would spoil the character of the movement. A landowner himself, he also shrank from ordering the one course of action that probably would have guaranteed him mass support—urging the fearful but starving peasantry to attack the landlords and seize their crops. To Smith O'Brien, property was inviolable.

At Mullinahone, in Tipperary, he and a few of his colleagues walked up to the local police barracks and told the five-man party to surrender their weapons. However, the sergeant in charge told Smith O'Brien that if he and his men handed over their guns to a small group, they would all be dismissed. Then, with famine raging, what would happen to their families? The sergeant suggested that instead Smith O'Brien should come back with, say, thirty men, which would allow the police to safely hand over their guns with the excuse of overwhelming odds. But when Smith O'Brien came back with the larger force, he found that the police had decamped, taking with them their precious weapons.

At Balingarry he also lost the chance of securing badly needed arms. He allowed a British cavalry officer and his troop to pass safely through a barricade after the officer had given his word not to attempt to arrest the rebels. Smith O'Brien's men had the British surrounded at the time and could easily have killed or captured the troops, their arms, and their horses. It was also at Balingarry that the insurrection finally petered out.

A group of police were pursued from the village by the rebels and surrounded at a farmhouse they commandeered. The house was owned by a widow called McCormick, who was away at the time, but her children were inside. Smith O'Brien called on them to surrender, telling them that he wouldn't harm them as they were Irishmen. They refused, although a number of them shook hands with Smith O'Brien through the windows. While he was parleying, most of his men took refuge behind a stone wall in front of the house. Oblivious to their leader's safety, some of them foolishly began throwing stones at the house. A number of police fired their rifles in response, and two of the rebels were fatally injured. Smith O'Brien remained in an extraordinarily dangerous position, exposed to fire from both inside and outside the house, but he courageously stayed on, trying to bring about a peaceful outcome.

Hearing the shooting, the widow returned, hysterical at the danger to her children. Under fire, some of the rebels courageously escorted her to the house so that she could see through a window that her seven children (all under the age of ten) were safe. The presence of the children caused Smith O'Brien to order that an attempt to fire the house be abandoned. The fire from the police intensified, and O'Brien, the last man to do so, was eventually persuaded to withdraw. The curtain came down on the attack when two priests arrived and persuaded the men to disperse despite Smith O'Brien's entreaties.

That was the end of the shooting portion of the Young Irelander saga. The leaders were arrested, tried, and sentenced to death but had their sentences commuted to transportation to Van Diemen's Land, from whence they subsequently escaped and went to America. To follow their later careers in any detail would take us too far from the famine story. Suffice it to say that most of them eventually made successful careers for themselves and secured an enduring place in Irish legend. However, in the immediate aftermath of the "revolution," they were accorded a similar high standing in the canon of English execration, as indeed were the Irish generally (the subsequent damaging but effective Whig press campaign is described in chapter 13).

TWELVE

EMIGRATION: ESCAPE BY COFFIN SHIP

"In Westport a ship is said to have foundered, with the loss of all on board, within sight of land, watched with horror by the relatives to whom the emigrants had just said farewell. . . . Ships sailed that were overcrowded, not provided with the legal quotas of provisions and water, and dangerously antique in construction: these were the vessels that were given the name of 'coffin ships.'"

—Cecil Woodham-Smith in The Great Hunger[1]

W HEN A TIDE, EVEN A TIDE OF MISERY, builds up sufficient force, it will burst a dam. Throughout 1847 and 1848 such a tide built up in Ireland; it manifested itself not in revolution, as the Young Irelanders had found to their cost, but in emigration as a frantic people sought to flee their accursed land. There was something akin to frenzy hanging in the air, as the reaction of the Dingle population to the Vincentians indicates, and this inflammation manifested itself in a rush to emigrate. Children were sometimes left to die of fever as their parents took ship. In one such case, it only came to light years afterward when a Protestant clergyman heard the story from his maid and made it public. The only member of a family to arrive safely in Canada was the mother, who found work in the service of the clergyman and confided her horrific story to him. Her story is told in greater detail later in the chapter. As a class, the Catholic peasantry had traditionally never strayed more than a few miles from their cabins, but now under the duress of hunger, traditional patterns were broken. People began locking up their homes and moving around the country on journeys of up to a hundred miles, seeking work or food. Then, as disruption and death from disease and starvation began to spread, eyes turned to places across the sea—Canada, America, and, because it was nearer, England.

As Black '47 turned bleaker and more deadly, the better-off among the smaller farmer class of tenants began to leave. They went in whole families, usually with sufficient funds and above all sufficient farming skills, to find a better life in the New World. Then, as a national panic began to set in, 1848 saw a terrified hemorrhaging of the peasantry, prepared to risk the Atlantic crossing in horrific conditions and in the depths of winter rather than face near-certain death from starvation in their own country. This emigration had both long- and short-term consequences. The long-term consequences lay in the fact that, particularly in America, the Irish eventually helped to shape world history, but in the short term emigration also helped to strip away any vestiges of justification from the naked reality of British government policy.

When Lord Monteagle, a humanitarian landlord and a member of the cabinet (but without a fraction of the influence of the other Irish landholding members, Palmerston, Clanricarde, and Lansdowne), wrote to Sir Charles Wood, the chancellor of the exchequer, warning that "substantial farmers" necessary for the future of the economy were shoaling out of the country, he received an answer remarkable for its candor and brutality: "I am not at all appalled by your tenantry going . . . that seems to me to be a necessary part of the process."[2]

As Wood saw it, Ireland needed larger holdings, and for holdings to grow in size, the number of holdings had to fall. Sir Charles Trevelyan was even more explicit: "I do not know how farms are to be consolidated if small farmers do not emigrate. . . . By acting for the purpose of keeping them at home, we should be defeating our own object. *We must not complain of what we really want to obtain.* If small farmers go, and then landlords are induced to sell portions of their estates to persons who will invest capital, we shall at last arrive at something like a satisfactory settlement of the country."[3]

"Acting for the purpose of keeping them at home" would, of course, have required feeding the starving. The results of not doing so, apart from the hardships inflicted on a fleeing, terrified population, meant that one could drive for a day in parts of Connacht and Munster without either seeing a man at work in the fields or hearing the lowing of a cow. The large empty tracts of land bespattered with roofless cottages were frequently compared to the aftermath of war.

Prior to the Famine, Monteagle had been one of the relatively small group of responsible landlords who had helped tenants to emigrate by giving them money and paying for the cost of their passages. He was responsible for setting up a House of Lords committee on emigration, the Select Committee of the House of Lords on Colonisation. Monteagle's approach, and that of a number of other landlords, meant that after the first potato failure occurred in 1846, some one thousand tenants of different landlords had arrived in Québec and other cities in sufficiently good health to be able to find work. They would have received inducements like those provided by Mr. Spaight of Limerick, who, through his interest in the shipping trade, offered free passage and provision to those willing to emigrate. On top of this, each tenant received £2 on disembarkation provided they had pulled down their cabins. This offer applied only to entire families, and Spaight said of it that he had "got rid of crime and distress for £3.10s a head."[4]

Emigration saved the landlords money. A pauper could be shipped out at about half what it cost to maintain him in the workhouse for a year. Once shipped off, he almost inevitably never came back.

The advantages of this system became only too obvious to landlords in January 1847 when the government transferred its responsibilities toward the destitute by making landlords responsible for them under the poor law through the payment of increased rates. Emigration was seen as a better option than eviction. Sir Robert Gore Booth articulated the landlords' defense of emigration after being criticized by an immigration agent in St. Johns,

New Brunswick, for "exporting and shovelling out the helpless and infirm to the detriment of the colony."[5] Sir Robert said, agreeing with Wood, that emigration was the only method of putting properties in Ireland on a satisfactory footing. He pointed to the very evident fact that the country was overpopulated and said that it was not right to evict people and to turn them out into the world. To compel them to emigrate was the only solution.

Viewed in the light of abstract analysis, Sir Robert's argument carries a certain validity. Yet it is shocking that sympathy for it has to be colored by knowledge of the clearances for which he was responsible on his Lissadell estate even before the famine began. In 1839 he launched an infamous set of evictions in which huge numbers of tenants who had paid their rents were evicted and very brutally "turned out into the world." Subsequently hundreds of these evictees were shipped to America aboard a coffin ship, the *Pomano,* which sank with great loss of life.[6] Later the Gore Booths prohibited the singing of a ballad about the episode, "The Sinking of the *Pomano,*" by tenants of their estate on pain of eviction. However, though Gore Booth was an evictor, looking at the Lissadell affair and the Irish exodus of 1847–1848, one's judgment has to be that a large portion of the responsibility for the famine evictions, and much else that befell Ireland, can be traced to the cabinet table and the policies of influential men who crafted and supported the clearance drives.

No one in high places disagreed with him or pointed out that there were humane ways of dealing with the Irish land problem. Did no one in government say that it was cruel and inhumane to subject old women and children with no adult to support them to the rigors of an Atlantic crossing in a coffin ship, followed by disembarkation in the snows of Canada, the stews of New York, or, possibly worst of all, the slums of Liverpool? Did no one say that many of these people would die aboard ship and be buried at sea? Or that when they landed in a filthy, emaciated state, unskilled in anything but the lowest laboring work, for which disease had in any case unfitted most of them, they would be received in their new situations with fear and execration?

The answer is that of course they did. Humane observers like the Quakers, officials like Edward Twistleton, correspondents like Father

Theobald Matthew, and even the hardened politician Lord Clarendon continually protested government policy, but to no avail. Not only were Trevelyan and Wood aided in the cabinet by out-and-out doctrinaire Whigs like Sir Edward Grey, but they also had the passive and powerful support of what the Irish call "sneaking regarders" in the government.

In his excellent book on the Famine Peter Gray drew up a table showing the opinions of the cabinet.[7] In one category were the "Foxites," those who followed in the footsteps of Charles Fox, the classical Liberal Whig. In another were the "Moralists," basically those who prated about Providence, among whom he included Wood, Trevelyan (a measure of his influence since he was not a member of the cabinet), and Grey. The third group was the "Moderates," including Monteagle and also the three large Irish landlords, the Marquess of Clanricarde, the Marquess of Lansdowne, and Viscount Lord Palmerston.

Lord Clanricarde's initial reaction to unrest in Ireland following the spread of blight was to initiate a Coercion Bill in the House of Lords on February 12, 1846. The bill allowed the authorities to impose a curfew on Ireland between sunset and sunrise, which in the wintertime made for long stretches of time. Select districts were placed under martial law. Homes could be entered at will in search of firearms, the possession of which merited seven years' transportation. Even suspicion of possessing a firearm became a criminal offense. Lord Clanricarde carried out wholesale evictions among his Irish tenants, using the £4 valuation clause as a justification. He wrote to Clarendon, saying solemnly: "The landlords are *prevented* from aiding or tolerating poor tenants. They are compelled to hunt out all such to save their property from the £4 clause."[8] It was the eighteenth Coercion Bill introduced in Ireland since the Act of Union, yet another telling indication of that act's harmfulness. It accurately represented Clanricarde's view of what famine-threatened Ireland required—more soldiers, not more food— and gives some indication of the mind-set of what the term "Moderate" could mean in British governmental circles of the time.

Lord Palmerston's views on emigration caused a far more widespread shuddering than did his contribution on land clearances at the cabinet table. He became the subject of very public international controversy when he was

attacked along with Major Mahon, who, as we saw earlier, was murdered
for perception of his emigration policies. In an open letter to Earl Grey, the
British colonial secretary, Adam Ferrie, a member of Canada's Legislative
Council, condemned the dumping on Canadian soil of half-naked paupers,
the aged, the infirm, beggars, and vagrants "without regard to humanity or
even common decency."[9] Ferrie itemized the crimes committed against the
emigrants. They had been promised clothes, food, and money—up to £5 for
a family—when they arrived in Québec on a ship carrying twice the number
of passengers for which it had been built in conditions that were "as bad as
the Slave Trade."[10] Ferrie's complaint gives some indication of where the
power lay in the British cabinet concerning famine policy. It can be safely
assumed that Earl Grey would not have approved of Palmerston's treatment
of his tenantry, but Palmerston was clearly free to act as he did without having to consider let or hindrance from his cabinet colleague.

None of the promised food or clothing was forthcoming. Palmerston's
tenants had formed part of a sizeable flotilla of nine ships that picked up
his tenants in Sligo and Liverpool. Some of the ships, including the *Eliza
Liddell,* the first to arrive at St. John, New Brunswick, brought only the aged,
the decrepit, and widows with young children. No one had the skills necessary in a fledgling colony. Another ship, the *Lord Ashburton,* which arrived in
Québec just before the winter ice closed in on October 30, 1847, carried 477
passengers. This overcrowding would in itself have made the passage a hell-
ish experience, but in addition to the overcrowding, fever had broken out,
and 107 passengers had been buried at sea. Nearly half the survivors were
described as being almost naked to an extent that eighty-seven of them had
to be clothed before they could be allowed ashore. One woman is recorded
as having come ashore completely naked. The crew were in such a bad state
that the ship had to be sailed from the mouth of the St. Lawrence by five
passengers.

On entering New York harbor at Ellis Island, Dr. Griscom of Public
Health Medicine noted that he found "Emaciated half nude figures, many
with the petechial eruptions still disfiguring their faces, crouching in their
berths. . . . Some were just rising from their berths for the first time since
leaving Liverpool, having been suffered to lie there all the voyage wallowing

in their own filth."[11] How much filth there was may be gauged in the fact that 115 cases of typhus were found aboard the ship.

Even worse than the *Ashburton* was the case of the *Aeolus*, which arrived at St. John on November 2. Winter had begun, but the captain of the *Aeolus* was forced to pay £250 in bonds before he could land his cargo of 240 passengers at St. John. The surgeon at St. John found that 99 percent of the emigrants immediately had to become a charge on the public. The men were "riddled with disease," and the women, widows with young children and decrepit old women, were, like the men, in a state of near nudity.

The story of what became the tenants of a third cabinet member's Irish estate, those of Lord Lansdowne, could be taken as a microcosm of the sufferings undergone by emigrants to America generally. Lansdowne and his history could also be taken as symbols of the process of the dispossession of the Irish of their land by predators such as Henry VIII and Oliver Cromwell. Lansdowne's ancestor Sir William Petty came to Ireland with Cromwell and conducted a national land survey. Those who carried out the survey, like those who had subscribed money to pay for Cromwell's adventures in Ireland, were paid in land. Petty, who was already a rich man, acquired a great deal of this land by offering cash to those who wanted to return to England. He thus acquired vast estates, and by the time of the Famine his descendant the Marquis of Lansdowne was popularly said to own so much land in Ireland that it would be possible to walk from Dublin to Kerry on his holdings. This is surely an exaggeration. But it is true that Lansdowne's west Kerry estates alone comprised 95,000 acres. The careers of Petty and Lansdowne accurately illustrate how the acquisition of land in Ireland led not merely to wealth but also to political power in England.

The Lansdowne saga has prompted two of the more remarkable works on the operation of landlordism in Ireland. One is Gerard J. Lyne's massive two-volume study of the Lansdowne estate and its agent William Steuart Trench.[12] Lyne became known and respected by students of Irish history all over the world in his role as a custodian of manuscripts in the National Library of Ireland. His ancestors had been tenants on the Lansdowne estate, and the Lansdowne papers were deposited in the National Library, which gave Lyne a double incentive not only to produce his important book but to appear later in a well-received accompanying television documentary on Ireland's national broadcasting station, RTE, following its publication in 2001. The second work is an authoritative article by Tyler Anbinder detailing the handiwork of Steuart and his aristocratic master in inducing Lansdowne's tenants to cross the Atlantic to settle in the Five Points slums in New York.

Despite his vast inheritance Lansdowne acquired the unenviable distinction of being responsible for sending the most wretched emigrants hitherto seen in New York. The Catholic archdeacon of Kenmare, John O'Sullivan, went further and said that even before the Famine began, laborers on the Lansdowne estate "were the most wretched people upon the face of the globe."[13]

By February 1849 gruesome reports of starvation again began emanating from Kenmare. "I was shocked in Skibbereen, Dunmanway [and] Bantry," wrote a visitor to Kenmare who had just come from those infamously destitute West Cork towns, "but they were nothing to what was now before. . . . Bad as the Bantry paupers were they were 'pampered rogues' in comparison to those poor creatures. . . . Spectres from the grave could not present a more ghastly, unearthly appearance. . . . The very thought of them to this moment sickens me." The emaciated once again crowded into Kenmare, "dying by the dozens in the streets." According to Archdeacon O'Sullivan, "theft and robbery and plunder became . . . universal"[14] as others used any available means to stave off starvation. But as Tyler Anbinder pointed out, "However obtained, food alone did not necessarily ensure survival." The cholera epidemic sweeping Europe and North America in the spring of 1849 also struck Kenmare, and due to the overcrowding in the workhouse, its inmates were particularly susceptible. Dysentery afflicted many as well, observed O'Sullivan, its victims so thirsty that they would barter their weekly one pound of relief ration of cornmeal "for a noggin of new milk to try and quench the burning thirst which invariably follows them."[15] Despite government declarations that the Famine was over, the death toll in southwest Kerry climbed steadily higher in 1849. By the end of that year, after the blight again destroyed the 1849 crop at least 1,000 (and perhaps as many as 1,700) of Lansdowne's 12,000 tenants had succumbed to the Famine and the diseases spread in its wake.

It is hardly necessary to point out that neither Lansdowne nor his ancestors would ever have tolerated these conditions on his English estates. Different approaches and standards applied to the management of estates in England and in Ireland, and Lansdowne's relationship with his tenants was not dissimilar to that of a man who owns shares in a potentially valuable mine in another country. Lansdowne was not a bad man, and his rents were regarded as fair. His concern was with dividends, not the condition of the workers. As the Famine progressed, Lansdowne decided that something would have to be done with his Irish inheritance. Abstract economic discussions at his English estate, Bowood, in Wiltshire were increasingly irrelevant to the progress of starvation in Kerry.

In 1850 Lansdowne hired the celebrated estate manager William Steuart Trench and was easily persuaded by Trench that the mathematics of emigration were far more attractive than those of maintaining paupers in the poorhouse. After listening to a dissertation from Trench on the savings to be made, Lansdowne immediately wrote a check for £8,000 sterling, estimated to be worth around $800,000 in today's values. Trench's account of what happened subsequently states that the tenants were overjoyed when they learned of the possibility of assisted emigration, and the offer was eagerly taken up.

Instead, expenditures on aid were cut back, and even those who did receive assistance did not get enough. By February 1847, deaths from starvation were common. "This neighbourhood is becoming depopulated with railway speed," wrote one relief official from Kenmare.[16]

Eyewitness accounts from the district spoke of an average of three people a day dying out of a road gang of three hundred. The bodies were buried in adjoining fields "without noise or sign of grief." People were described as being discolored by dropsy, suffering from dysentery, or "mad with fever." A relief official wrote, "I daily witness the most terrible spectacles on the works people—driven there by the terrible necessity of trying to get as much as would purchase a meal. . . . With most of these working is a mockery; they can scarcely walk to and from the roads, and how can they work. . . . When a respectable person passes the houses of these poor people, the saddest sights present themselves; women, children, and old men crawling out on all fours, perhaps from beside a corpse, to crave a morsel of any kind of food."[17]

Given the situation that the Lansdowne emigrants left behind them, it is not surprising that they arrived in a shocking state. It wasn't long before New York began to take notice and the press began to comment on both the condition of the emigrants and the fact that they had come from Lansdowne's estate. The *New York Tribune* described emigrants wandering the streets ragged and half starved. There was much critical newspaper comment. Anbinder quotes an editorial in the *Herald:*

IRISH EMIGRANTS—It is really lamentable to see the vast number of unfortunate creatures that are almost daily cast on our shores, penniless and without physical energy to earn a day's living. Yesterday, groups of these hapless beings were to be seen congregated about the [City Hall] Park and in Broadway, looking the very picture of despair, misery, disease and want. On enquiry, we ascertained that they had arrived here by the ship Sir Robert Peel, and that they had been, for the most part, tenants of the Marquis of Lansdowne, on his county Kerry estate—ejected without mercy by him, and "shipped" for America in this wholesale way. Among them were grey haired and aged men and women, who had spent the heyday of their life as tillers of their native soil, and are now sent to this country to find a grave. This is too bad—it is inhuman; and yet it is an act of indiscriminate and wholesale expatriation committed by the "liberal" President of the council of her Majesty Queen Victoria's "liberal" ministry.[18]

The press coverage forced Trench to defend himself. He claimed that the emigrants had been given new clothes but that they had hidden them so as to make themselves more ragged-looking and hence more liable to get charity. However, it was established that not only had many tenants not received clothes; they had not gotten food either. The ship's allowance on which they were forced to live consisted of 1 pound of bread, or meal or biscuits or even flour, and 13 ounces of water. By contrast, although Palmerston's emigrants were the cause of severe criticism of His Lordship, they did at least receive some rations as part of their agreement to leave his estates: on top of the ship's allowance, they were given 6 pounds of biscuits, 3 $1/2$ pounds of flour,

1 pound of pork or beef, 1 pound of sugar, 1 pound of rice, 8 ounces of treacle, 4 ounces of coffee, and 2 ounces of tea. As a result of the negative publicity, Trench was forced to see to it that subsequent emigrants were decently clothed and received a payment of a few shillings each. The amount spent on each tenant rose from nine pence to seventeen shillings. However, from the landlords' point of view, the emigration scheme was an unqualified economic success. In 1850 the Kenmare workhouse contained 2,500 paupers whom Lansdowne had to maintain in however wretched a condition, but by 1853 the workhouse population had shrunk so that Lansdowne was responsible for only fourteen paupers from his estates. In New York most of the Lansdowne emigrants headed for what was universally regarded as the worst slum in New York, the Five Points in lower Manhattan, where they formed a ninth of the total inhabitants. Many readers will probably have seen for themselves Martin Scorsese's re-creation of the slum in his 2002 film *The Gangs of New York*. Charles Dickens described it as being the home of everything "loathsome, drooping and decayed."[19]

The "American letter" began to be a feature of Irish life. The following is an example, from a dutiful daughter to her family in Cork:

My dear Father and Mother,
I remit to you in this letter 20 dollars, that is four pounds, thinking
it might be some acquisition to you until you might be clearing away
from that place altogether and the sooner the better, for believe me
I could not express how great would be my joy at our seeing you all
here together where you would never want to be at a loss for a good
breakfast and dinner.

Your ever dear and loving child
Margaret McCarthy[20]

That "American letter" and many thousands like it were made possible by the initiative of the Irish Emigrant Society, one of whose initiatives was to stem the flow of misery created by famine emigration, and the foundation of the Emigrant Industrial Savings Bank in 1850. Marion Casey has described how one Five Points resident successfully used the bank to combat the conditions in the Five Points. Mary O'Connor borrowed $2,000 in 1855 to buy a three-story house. She paid $120 in interest each year and paid off the mortgage on December 8, 1880. By then, her house had appreciated in value to $12,000. The Emigrant Savings Bank supported many Mary O'Connors and Margaret McCarthys.[21]

Readers may decide for themselves how much credit Messrs. Trench and Lansdowne deserve for these achievements, or if indeed they deserve any credit at all.

EMIGRANTS IN AMERICA

Standing on reclaimed land at the very tip of Wall Street there lies one of the most tasteful and evocative memorials to the Famine in the world. The Irish Hunger Memorial at Battery Park City consists of a roofless salmon cottage brought over from Mayo and re-erected stone by stone at the behest of Governor George Pataki in the year 2001 to commemorate the Great Famine. Around the cottage is a tiny field, approximately the size of a potato patch in the Famine years. The grass is a luxuriant green, set off here and there by yellow irises. A stone from every one of Ireland's thirty-two counties forms part of the memorial, the only blemish of which to an Irish eye is the fact that, being a Mayo field, the grass does not contain some weeds! However, the peace of the memorial and its evocative design should be regarded not merely as a fitting tribute to the millions affected by the Famine but as the very antithesis of the experience of famine victims when first they landed in New York.

New York was the main entry port for the Irish into America, and it was not a welcoming place. The first reaction of the American Congress toward emigrants from the Famine was to try to keep them out. Far from validating a subsequent inscription on the Statue of Liberty, which welcomed the poor and huddled masses of the world, Congress passed Navigation Acts in the early part of 1847 that tightened up embarkation laws in various ways. Captains either had to enter a bond that no passenger would become a burden on the city or pay a "commutation fee," as it was known, of $10 per passenger. Boston went further and placed a levy of $1,200 on aged or infirm persons. Ships with fever aboard were refused landing rights. This meant that passengers who had suffered the horrors of the Atlantic voyage were then driven away from New York and Boston and sent to British ports such as those in British Canada. This resulted in cases of dreadful hardship and of riots breaking out when passengers attempted to land and were forcibly restrained, sometimes at the point of cutlasses.

Initially, these measures worked, diverting the flow of refugees from American ports to Canada. But the determination of the emigrants was such that, having landed in Canada, they proceeded to pour back across the American border on foot to such an extent that yet another barrier was added to their hopes of gaining prosperity. The fear of fever and general raggedness and evidences of bad character such as begging was now added to labor antagonism. As the following contemporary quotation illustrates, "The Yankee hod-carrier, or Yankee wood-sawyer, looks down with ineffable contempt upon his brother Irish hod-carrier or Irish wood-sawyer. In his estimation, 'Paddy' hardly belongs to the human family. Add to this that the influx of foreign labourers, chiefly Irish, increases the supply of labour, and therefore apparently lessens relatively the demand, and consequently the wages of labour, and you have the elements of a wide, deep, and inveterate hostility on the part of your Yankee labourer against your Irish labourer, which manifests itself naturally in your Native American Party."[22]

The antagonisms and tensions encountered by the Irish triggered another unpleasant reality: anti-black feelings on the part of the Irish. As the Irish started to find their feet, they began to rail at the fact that black labor was undercutting their wages, and anti-black riots became part of the Irish American experience. Black versus Green antagonisms were not the only problems the Irish would encounter. The WASPs who controlled America and nativist groups such as the "Know Nothings" were also antagonistic to the hordes of ragged, starving Irish Catholics. A convent had been burned in Boston, and there was fierce rioting in Philadelphia and in New York between Catholic and Protestant mobs. But the most immediate challenges to the Irish were the conditions they lived in while getting purchase in American society.

As indicated in the descriptions of Lansdowne's tenants in the Five Points, slum conditions were appalling, but when one considers the backdrop from which many of the Irish emigrants came, such as the heaps of filth outside Mayo cottages, slum conditions in New York and elsewhere at least had the advantage of not having to be endured along with slow starvation; if emigrants leaving Mayo, for example, were not inured to hardship, the Atlantic passage certainly prepared them for it.

New York in those days was a wild and woolly place. Not only were the Irish accused of living like pigs; they also owned them. The *New York Sun* estimated in August 1847 that there were ten thousand pigs roaming the streets of the city. The pigs were meant to be kept in "hog lots," pens erected on vacant spaces, but the pigs were allowed to roam the streets freely, eating up all the garbage and refuse they could find. When public outcry led to a police crackdown on the keeping of pigs, the Irish put up such a stern resistance to police efforts to commandeer their animals that eventually they were left to continue with their piggeries. Packs of stray dogs also roamed the streets at risk of being rounded up and having their brains bashed out with cudgels by men who received a bounty for this work. It was said that the dogs eventually grew so streetwise that they learned to anticipate the hours at which dog killers roamed the street and stayed indoors until they had left.

In 1847, the area where the Irish Hunger Memorial now stands was a heavily congested district. The Wall Street area attracted emigrants because it was near the harbor, and Manhattan, being an island, could not in those days expand to the east or west. Therefore, the Irish, like other poor emigrants, could not undertake long walks to the north for employment and worked as near to home as they could.

Slum accommodation was created principally in two ways: one was the old "Knickerbocker houses" once owned by the wealthy who got out as the emigrants started to come in. These soon turned into the sort of tenements one met with in Dublin after the Act of Union when once-fine old houses fell destitute as their owners left for London. The second type of slum accommodation was deliberately constructed. The flimsy, jerry-built "barracks," as they were known, were let out to emigrants by the room and very soon became overcrowded. The houses were so dangerous that in some cases they fell down during the course of construction, and generally were only supported by being built in rows that leaned against each other. All these habitations had one thing in common: dirt and lack of sanitation.

The barracks were generally built behind existing buildings and therefore had to be reached through narrow, noxious alleys in which dirt of all sorts soon accumulated. Ten years after the Black '47 emigrant influx had begun, a Committee on Tenement Accommodation reported that "to reach these tumbling and squalid rookeries the visitor must sometimes penetrate a labyrinth of alleys behind horse stables, blacksmiths forges and inevitably beside cheap groggeries." Rubbish collection was unheard of, pigsties abounded, and there were piles of what was described as "decaying matter" giving off awful smells. The buildings were surrounded by moats of sewerage that were "pools of standing water."[23]

Pride of place for horror was given to a three-story building erected on top of a stable where the Express Company kept its horses. The "particularly horrible building" was described as being unsafe. Rickety walls were mildewed, and some of the walls were breaking off. The building was so leaky that in winter the top story was flooded. All the tenants in this building were Irish. Needless to say, such buildings were fire hazards. One, at 39 Cherry Street, was described as having a staircase barely twenty inches wide. Another, at 410 Water Street, was cited as having a similar staircase and only one exit for four hundred tenants. The staircases in both houses were unlit.

Given their poverty and numbers, it was inevitable in the early decades of Irish mass emigration to North America that the words "slum" and "Irish" became synonymous.

Boston, the other great point of Irish immigration in America, was surrounded by water. To get out of the waterfront areas, the Irish would have had to cross bridges and pay tolls for which they did not have the money, so they congregated in what became known as "the Eighth Ward," an area known today as the affluent Back Bay district—and spreading out occasionally, as in New York with the Knickerbocker houses, to the homes of wealthy Boston citizens in the North End.

These old houses had large gardens that rapidly became covered in cabins reminiscent of those the immigrants had left behind. Even the alleyways were built over.

A committee on public health visited Ann, Hamilton, and Oliver Streets and reported during August 1847 that "each room from garret to cellar is filled with a family consisting of several persons and sometimes two or three more families."[24]

In addition, the spaces between the houses and sometimes the houses themselves "had within them stores, shops and places where fruit, vegetables and refreshments were sold."

"Refreshments" was a euphemism for strong spirits, frequently home brewed, with which the Irish sometimes alleviated and more often worsened their conditions. One figure they did not succeed in leaving behind them in Ireland was the landlord. These rooms cost between $1 and $1.50 each, and immediate eviction followed failure to pay.

Inevitably, these horrific conditions posed a threat to Bostonian society on almost every front one could think of: crime, the environment, public health. Most of Boston's water supply in the mid-1840s came from wells and collected well water, and it was estimated that of the city's ten thousand wells, approximately six thousand were unfit to drink. The Board of Aldermen reported in 1849: "The Back Bay at this hour is nothing less than a great cesspool, into which is daily deposited all the filth of a large and constantly increasing population. . . . A greenish scum, many yards wide stretches along the shore and the basin, while the surface of the water beyond is seen bubbling like a cauldron with the noxious gases that are escaping from the corrupting mass below."[25]

Houses in the area were reported to be "flooded with every tide," yet the Irish packed into the cellars of such houses. These cellars had low ceilings, in one case only five feet high, but it held eighteen people, the same number as the width of the cellar. Crime flourished in these conditions. The Boston Police Court Return for the year 1848 recorded the increase in crime over a five-year period that the dramatic increase in immigration had brought about. It was estimated that three-quarters of this immigration was Irish, and the statistics were as follows:

- Complaints for capital offenses had increased by 266 percent.
- Attempts to kill had increased by 1,700 percent.
- Assaults on police officers had increased by 400 percent.
- Aggravated assaults committed with knives, dirks, pistols, slingshot, razors, pokers, hot irons, clubs, hot iron weights, flat irons, bricks, and stones had increased by 465 percent.[26]

Inevitably, these conditions weighed most heavily on the children, whose major outdoor activity was not playing football or childish games but begging. It was reckoned that there were some 1,500 children engaged in this occupation throughout the city. Given the Boston weather, they would not have been involved in such an activity for very long. Mortality among Irish Catholics was estimated between 1841 and 1845 as having decimated the children: 61.5 percent died under the age of five. Lemuel Shattuck, a health official who analyzed the census, wrote that Irish children were apparently "literally born to die." The average age of persons buried during the period he studied was 13.43 years.[27]

The exclamation mark in the litany of horror that punctuated the emigrants' flight from their accursed land was a picturesque island at the mouth of the St. Lawrence River. Grosse Île was one of the quarantine stations that passed into Irish folk memory because of what happened there and because of the importance of the St. Lawrence entry point for North American emigration by the Irish. The St. Lawrence was the main artery through which the Irish flowed into the towns of Québec, Montreal, Kingston, Toronto, the Ottawa Valley, and the rest of Canada. Many subsequently made their way into the United States.

CANADA

Despite the tough laws introduced by the United States to keep out the pauperized and fever-ridden emigrants, a steady tide of the destitute breached the legal barriers simply by walking through Canada, often in the dead of winter, until they slipped across the American border. Though many died in the attempt to reach America, these pedestrian emigrants were in the main the healthy ones. Grosse Île was where the unhealthy landed, sometimes dead, sometimes in a dying condition, but always in danger of contracting fever either through the conditions aboard the coffin ships, or on the island itself.

A conscientious member of the Limerick landlord family of De Vere courageously undertook passage on one of these ships and wrote a harrowing account of what he saw: "Before the emigrant has been a week at sea, he is an altered man. How can it be otherwise? Hundreds of poor people, men women and children of all ages, from the drivelling idiot to the babe just born, huddled together without light, without air, wallowing in filth and breathing a foetid atmosphere, sick in body, dispirited in heart, and fevered patients lying between the sound, in sleeping places so narrow as almost to deny them the power of indulging by a change of position, the natural restlessness of the disease, by their agonizing ravings disturbing those around."[28]

Grosse Île had a horrific reputation even before the events of Black '47. In 1832, the coffin ships—designed not as passenger vessels but as ships to carry timber from North America—were filled with Irish people as farepaying ballast for the return journey. These ships were instrumental in bringing cholera to Canada from Ireland and the flophouses of Liverpool. Some 25,000 people had died in an epidemic that devastated Ireland in 1832, and in trying to get away from the outbreak, many people contracted cholera in the appallingly insanitary conditions of the filthy, overcrowded vessels.

It is thought that about one thousand victims were buried in mass graves in Grosse Île's so-called Valley of Death, the only place where the soil was deep enough, but the death toll is an estimated one. Many people are known to have drowned in the shallows, too weak to struggle ashore from the boats. In fact, Grosse Île may have greatly contributed to the spread of the epidemic because it brought the sick and the well into close proximity, and thus thousands of seemingly healthy emigrants left the island carrying the infection and spread the disease farther up the St. Lawrence into Québec, Montreal, and the smaller towns and villages.

It didn't have to be like that. In February 1847, months before any of the coffin ships arrived, Dr. Douglas, the medical officer on Grosse Île, warned the Legislative Assembly that the summer would bring greatly increased numbers of immigrants to Canadian shores because the American ports were closed to the plague-ridden Irish. Knowing something of Irish conditions, he forecast that the closures would "augment the number of poor and destitute who will flock to our shores," thereby bringing with them "a greater amount of sickness and mortality."[29] He asked for £3,000 to increase the quarantine facilities. The Assembly gave him £300—enough to buy fifty extra beds.

The doctor was to use his own money to commemorate the dead. These included four doctors, four priests, two Anglican ministers, and more than thirty nurses, orderlies, and other helpers. Douglas himself only partially survived the horrors of Grosse Île. He lived through "the Irish Summer" healthy in body, but fell prey to depression and, having saved the lives of thousands of emigrants, took his own life at the age of fifty-five. The plaque on the cross he erected reads: "In this secluded spot lie the mortal remains of five thousand, four hundred and twenty-five persons who, flying from pestilence and famine in the year 1847, found in North America but a grave."

Dr. Douglas was not alone in his display of humanity. The Canadian response to the Irish influx was as generous as it was courageous and is accurately summed up in a quotation from a history of the famine period: "If buildings and fences can be obliterated, not so with memories: they abound with tales of horror and heroism; of the *Soeurs Grises* and the *Soeurs de Charite* who with a spirit of unbounded love devoted themselves to the forsaken, caring for them, and dying with them; of John Mills who, as mayor of Montreal and Chairman of the Emigrant Commission, 'in a time of great confusion' acted effectively to protect the interests of citizens and sick alike, and who, as an ordinary person with a mission, ministered to the needs of the sick in the 'sheds' and died, as they did, of typhus."[30]

The mayor's wife constantly entreated with him not to visit the fever sheds, but he was so appalled by the sufferings of the Irish that he insisted on visiting them every day, inevitably catching the disease and dying from it.

The St. Lawrence was also memorable for two contrasting acts of great cowardice and great heroism and skill involving healthy emigrants whom fate struck down as they neared what they had hoped was to be the final stage of their journey to a new and better life, the mouth of the St. Lawrence. On April 29, 1849, the brig *Hannah*, carrying emigrants from Newry, County Down, struck ice at 4:00 A.M. and sank in less than an hour. Captain Shaw of the *Hannah* and many of his crew fled the sinking vessel in a longboat, leaving a small number of his crew to deal with the desperate situation and a large number of passengers. Somehow, in the darkness a large number of the terrified, traumatized passengers managed to get off the sinking vessel and onto the ice floe.

They spent some fourteen hours in freezing conditions before Captain Marshall of the bark *Nicaragua*, from Gloucester, who was obviously made of finer stuff than the fleeing Captain Shaw, saw a distress flag on the ice and began rescue operations. He sailed into the ice, lowered ice fenders, and initially managed to take off about fifty-two passengers. Then, using one of the *Hannah*'s longboats that he found on the ice, he succeeded in rescuing a total of 129 passengers and 6 crew members.

As with the *Titanic*, there were several individual horror stories. For example, John Murphy and his wife, Bridget, who had already lost a child in a house fire before boarding the *Hannah*, lost their two eldest children. John dived into the freezing water in a vain effort to save them. He held a rope in his mouth and as a result lost all of his teeth in the severe cold. Their three-year-old daughter, who also fell into the water, was so badly traumatized that she did not speak for three years. Their two-year-old son was pulled out of the water by a woman who mistakenly thought she was rescuing her own child.[31]

Captain Marshall's subsequent report said, "No pen can describe the pitiable situation and destitution of those passengers, parents with loss of children, children with loss of parents, and they themselves all but naked, and the greater part of them frostbitten."[32]

LIVERPOOL

Mention has been made of the flophouses of Liverpool. The story of Grosse Île gives an indication of what befell some of those who escaped such places, but overall the emigrants to Canada fared better than many of those who landed in Liverpool, the principal port of entry for England. England, being closer to Ireland than North America, was naturally the cheapest and shortest journey for the fleeing paupers, and the number of ferries and packets serving Liverpool made it the principal port of entry for the emigrants. The huge numbers and the conditions they lived in are part of the reason that tens of thousands of Liverpool supporters today sing a variation of "The Fields of Athenry" called "The Fields of Anfield," based on the name of the grounds of the famous football club.

Liverpool in the 1840s was a huge bustling Moloch of a city. Vast wealth derived from the trade of empire, including slavery, had created both mansion and slum, the latter being probably among the worst in Europe. A feature of the city was the number of the poor who lived in cellars or in "courts," streets of houses built facing each other that were often separated by roadways only nine feet wide. The filth and stench of these areas were almost indescribable, with sewage and surface water being carried off through open, and often clogged, drains.

An account by one of Trevelyan's correspondents gives us an idea of the conditions that the influx of Irish inflicted on the already hideous state of the Liverpool slums: "The peasantry are coming over here by regiments, particularly the women and children to beg." The correspondent went on to record what he had been told by a local magistrate, a man apparently noted for his kindness: "He told me today he was fairly beat. He did not know what to do with the mass of human misery that came before him . . . when returning to my office an Irish Steamer having just come in, there was a stream of these poor creatures coming up from the boat to live, if they can, upon English charity. We believe that in some parts of Ireland they are paying their passage over to England to get rid of them, and they will not return at the expense of this parish, preferring to go to gaol, but what is the good of committing them when . . . gaol is a comparative Paradise to them?"[33]

Even today, the result of this type of scene replicated all over Liverpool appears incredible. In 1841 the population of Liverpool was 250,000, according to the census returns. Between December 1846 and the following June, the population had increased to 300,000 by pauperized Irish. Their numbers and condition presented a threat to the city and to themselves, but the only official relief provided was a distribution of tents and the provision of two floating hulks on the river Mersey as hospital ships for fever victims.

The police reports show that landlords in Ireland were giving the emigrants a shilling or two to encourage them to emigrate and that the lucky ones received a similar sum from their priests to help keep them alive both while traveling and on landing.

Dislocation, anxiety, hunger, and want created such mental stress among the Irish emigrants to Liverpool that insanity reached incredibly high levels in all Lancashire asylums of the day. A joint study conducted by University College Dublin and the University of Warwick in 2011 found that by the late 1950s, 50 percent of the inmates of Rainhill Asylum were Irish emigrants. Anecdotal evidence suggests that the percentages in the early stages of emigration to centers such as Boston and New York reached similar levels and that mental illness among Irish emigrants exceeded that of West Indians, the next highest category in England, as late as the 1990s.[34]

The Irish emigrants generally saw themselves as exiles rather than emigrants, for they had no history of travel from their native place, no folk memory of it, and no idea of the society they were traveling to. There were particularly sorrowful decades of the rosary of Irish emigration that do stand out even in the pre-Famine story of emigration when the Irish encountered the ever-present nemesis of the Catholic peasantry, racial prejudice and poverty. The story of Duffy's Cut in Pennsylvania and that of the building of the Pontchartrain Canal, New Orleans' New Basin, epitomize much of what the flood of famine emigration created for the fleeing emigrants.

Duffy's Cut is a portion of railroad in Pennsylvania, not far from Philadelphia, where several Irish workers (estimates vary as to how many) were murdered by nativist vigilantes because they had cholera in 1832. A few years later, during the building of the New Basin Canal at New Orleans, tens of thousands of Irish died of one of the multiplicity of fevers attendant on swamp work. They were buried in the mud they died in, their dreadful working lives contributing to a pattern that continued for decades, thereby generating much hostility toward the Irish—they worked for lower wages than anyone else and in more dangerous conditions. Slave owners, for example, would not allow their slaves to work on the New Orleans Canal because they possessed a commercial value that the Irish did not. The Irish exodus during the Famine, following in the footsteps of the workers who had died building the canal, made New Orleans the second-biggest port of entry to the United States after New York during the Famine.

It would be impossible to properly chronicle the frenzy and despair that impelled the Irish out of Ireland during the Famine years. It was a time when able-bodied, law-abiding men actively courted transportation to Van Diemen's Land, anywhere to get out of Ireland. Death lay all around, touching every individual and every family. One family tragedy may be taken as epitomizing what befell generally. In 1847 the Willis family, John and Mary Willis and their five children, left Limerick for Canada. Before embarking, one of their children contracted typhus, which would have rendered the entire family ineligible for sailing. So, in a decision outweighing even that which faced the heroine of *Sophie's Choice*, who had to decide which of her two children was to be killed by the Nazis, the Willises left a little boy to die friendless and alone from the fever. On the journey, four more of the children died, and when they landed in Canada, John followed his family to the grave. Mary survived, and her story was recorded by the Protestant clergyman for whom she worked. The difference between what befell John and Mary Willis and countless other emigrant families was one of degree rather than of kind.

THIRTEEN

THE PROPAGANDA OF FAMINE

"The English are very well aware that Ireland is a trouble, a vexation, and an expense to this country. We must pay to feed it, and pay to keep it in order . . . we do not hesitate to say that every hard-working man in this country carries a whole Irish family on his shoulders. He does not receive what he ought to receive for his labor, and the difference goes to maintain the said Irish family, which is doing nothing but sitting idle at home, basking in the sun, telling stories, going to fairs, plotting, rebelling, wishing death to the Saxon, and laying everything that happens at the Saxon's door. . . . The Irish, whom we have admitted to free competition with the English labourer, and whom we have welcomed to all the comforts of old England, are to reward our hospitality by burning our warehouses and ships and sacking our towns."

—The Times, *July 26, 1848*

"It is ridiculous to say that there is no capital in Ireland where there is labour and land. A country which exports the means of millions can of course pay for its own improvement."

—The Times, *August 19, 1846*

"The Irishman is destitute, so is the Scotchman, and so is the Englishman. . . . It appears to us to be of the very first importance to all classes of Irish society to impress on them that there is nothing so peculiar, so exceptional, in the condition which they look on as the pit of utter despair. . . . Why is that so terrible in Ireland which in England does not create perplexity and hardly moves compassion?"

—The Times, *September 8, 1846*

THE PRESS WAS INDEED A BATTLEFIELD FOR the British public's opinion of Irish famine. It is certainly fair to ask whether the policies of Sir Charles Wood, the chancellor of the exchequer, and Sir Charles Trevelyan, the assistant secretary to the Treasury, would have achieved their horrific results without the Whigs' manipulation of the press. At first, the public was prepared to allow Peel, as prime minister from 1841 to 1846, sufficient latitude in his efforts to avert famine. Initially also, the public's response to the Relief Commission's appeal was generous, and this saved many lives.

The reaction of the Society of Friends, the Quakers, on the early public reaction to the Famine was that money "on a gigantic scale [was] made available by parliament. Local and Central Relief Associations distributed alms which could not have fallen far short of a million and a half."[1] The Quakers' report also referred to the enormous generosity of the Irish themselves, both at home and abroad, and rather touchingly expressed the hope that the outpouring of generosity by the British public might lay the foundations for better relations between the two countries in the future.

However, as the Famine progressed, opinion turned (or, it might be argued, was turned) completely in the opposite direction. If one takes the response to the queen's second appeal in late 1847 as an indicator of the shift in public opinion, one has to concede that the second response was wretched, and this at a stage, during Black '47, when one would have legitimately expected that the widespread evidences of suffering would have produced the opposite effect. The amount raised throughout the empire by the first letter was £171,000. The second realized less than a sixth of this, £30,000.

As we have seen, one can cite many contributory factors for this sea change: donor fatigue, anti-landlord sentiment, and a recrudescence of traditional anti-Irish prejudice that was heightened by the appearance of hordes of Irish famine victims fleeing to English soil. Even though Trevelyan, in his famous self-justificatory book *The Irish Crisis,* which he published in 1848, established the fiction that the crisis ended that year and subsequently stuck to this line, evidence to the contrary could be seen daily on the streets of England in the form of poverty-stricken Irish emigrants.[2] Official attitudes to these were reflected in *The Times,* which, despite the clear evidence of Irish emigrants still pouring into England, chose to bolster the government's generally anti-Irish propaganda line. Three years after Trevelyan declared the Famine over, *The Times* was still depicting Irish paupers in hues of hatred rather than sympathy. It said that England was being "positively invaded, overrun, devoured, infected, poisoned, and desolated by Irish Pauperdom."[3]

To this must be added a "we told you so" attitude on the part of Protestants who had opposed Catholic Emancipation and the grant to the Catholic seminary at Maynooth and who, through the distorting lens of "providentialism," viewed the Famine as divine retribution for the Irish crime of "popery." And one must accord a certain understanding of the feelings of patriotic, law-abiding British citizens toward seemingly inexplicable events such as agrarian crime or the Young Irelanders' rebellion.

But, knitting all these different strands of opinion together was the oft-repeated theme that the Famine was the result of a flaw in the Irish character—the fecklessness and laziness that produced the potato economy also produced the other ills that afflicted the unhappy country. Far from doing too little, England had been too generous, but its efforts and expenditures came to nothing because of Irish ingratitude. The Famine was not a curse, but a blessing sent by Providence to cleanse Ireland of its many blemishes.

The three principal conductors of this orchestra were Wood, Lord Clarendon, and Trevelyan. Lord Palmerston at different times in his career also used Secret Service monies to get corrupt journalists, and others, to play the tunes he favored. Palmerston was particularly notorious for the manner in which he manipulated both the *Morning Chronicle* and the *Morning Post* to work as mouthpieces in furtherance of his policies. He made a practice of seeming to agree with his cabinet colleagues over the issues of the day, notably during the latter stages of the Crimean War (1853–1856), and then arranging for pieces to appear in the *Morning Post* that were diametrically opposed to what had been agreed.[4] Clarendon did not depend solely on *The Times*. When he first came to Ireland, in the summer of 1847, his initial public-opinion target was the starving tenantry themselves. Using the cover of the Royal Agricultural Society and government money, he sent "agricultural instructors" to the worst-affected areas to hold public gatherings at which those present were reassured of the government's benignity, urged to till their holdings—cease looking for salvation in public works and relief.

The instructors' experiment, however, foundered on the rocks of physical and psychological reality, and the report on their activities, which was published the following April, was something of a public relations disaster. In Mayo, for example, where the ravages of poverty and eviction have already been described, the problem for the instructor Thomas Martin lay in the difficulty of finding any living tenants to whom he could preach benignity. He wrote: "It was almost impossible to produce any impression in this wasted and neglected district . . . from Bangor to Crossmolina, all was desolate and waste. . . . Driving with a Protestant clergyman, the Rev Mr Stark, in his gig he pointed out to me a number of farmhouses in the Mullet, all deserted and the land too. Nothing possibly could be done there, for the tenants were all gone."[5]

As Lord Clarendon might have realized earlier, eviction and famine do tend to produce such an effect.

Another instructor, one Fitzgerald, reported from Connemara of finding whole villages of roofless houses and commented in exasperation that the people always seemed to have "one excuse or the other"—for example, that they had no seed and, even if they had, that they had no strength to till the land and nothing to live on while waiting for crops to mature. Instructor Goode reported from Connacht that he met with widespread despondency and the universal argument that there was no point in attempting cultivation because the tenants expected to be ejected from their homes in the coming spring.

Mr. Goode failed to lift the clouds of despondency by telling the starving people that evictions were not a matter for him but that he had been "sent amongst them by a kind, intelligent gentleman, merely to tell them what course to pursue." In Dublin, the "kind, intelligent gentleman" had realized earlier that this was not the way to win friends and influence people, and certainly not the way to counter the growing influence of the Young Irelanders. Instead, he turned to a man called James Birch, who earned his living from blackmail and gutter press journalism. Despite, or possibly because of, the fact that Birch had been convicted of blackmailing offenses, Clarendon gave him what were at the time substantial payments of Secret Service monies to attack the Young Irelanders and generally to advance government policies in Birch's paper, *The World*, which deserves to be remembered in the annals of journalism as the precursor of Rupert Murdoch's infamous *News of the World*.[6]

The public only became aware of Clarendon's manipulations long after the Young Irelanders' leaders had been tried and transported. Birch himself brought the matter to light by suing Clarendon for money he claimed was owed him. Clarendon first tried to pass the matter off lightly by saying that the transaction had made little impression on him, but that he thought he had promised Birch £100 for his services. He then admitted to £350 and to other regular payments to Birch, who finally received a £2,000 settlement on giving a promise that all incriminating documents would be handed over to Clarendon. Despite, or possibly because of, these revelations, Birch was subsequently employed by Lord Palmerston, whose biographer described him as "probably knowing more about press intrigues than most."[7]

While *The Times* may legitimately be regarded as the most formidable engine driving anti-Irish political sentiment in nineteenth-century England, it is literally true to say that the most graphic examples of such prejudice were those created by the magazine *Punch*. Under the editorship of Mayhew and Lemon the journal created an ideal image of the "typical" Irishman in the popular mind. Irishmen appeared as "monkeys in a menagerie."[8]

Punch cartoons constantly portrayed "Paddy" as a simian in a tailcoat and a derby, engaged in plotting murder, battening on the labor of the English workingman, and generally living a life of indolent treason. This concept of the Irishman was implanted in the popular mind as a given, not merely throughout the Famine but during the Fenian movement that grew out of the Famine and the home-rule campaign some forty years later.

Punch did not rely merely on its cartoons for its simian imagery and an allied anti-black prejudice. It could also write things like the following:

> A creature manifestly between the Gorilla and the Negro is to be met with in some of the lowest districts of London and Liverpool by adventurous explorers. It comes to Ireland, whence it has contrived to migrate; it belongs in fact to a tribe of Irish savages; the lowest species of the Irish Yahoo. When conversing with its kind it talks a sort of gibberish. It is moreover, a climbing animal and may sometimes be seen ascending a ladder with a hod of bricks. The Irish Yahoo generally confines itself within the limits of its own colony, except when it goes out of them to get its living. Sometimes, however, it sallies forth in states of excitement, and attacks civilized human beings that have provoked its fury. The somewhat superior ability of the Irish Yahoo to utter articulate sounds, may suffice to prove that it is a development, and not, as some imagine, a degeneration of the Gorilla.[9]

While the simian motif was not confined to *Punch*, the journal should be regarded as the principal procreant cradle of the species.

A point to be noted about the foregoing type of writing is that many of the *Punch* contributors were Irish, their contributions to the magazine validating the old axiom that whenever the British needed a stage Irishman for a West End part, they could always be certain of getting an Irishman to portray him. When M. A. Busteed and R. I. Hodgson spoke of "multi-layered Irish demonology" to describe the continuing strain of anti-Irish prejudice in influential English circles, they spoke truly.[10] Where the era of the Famine is concerned, a particularly virulent strain of anti-Irish prejudice may be traced throughout the nineteenth century from the first failing of the potato in 1845 to the end of the century, when the ugly growth of prejudice could be seen flourishing in the unlikely setting of the writings of Sidney and Beatrice Webb, influential socialist economists and co-founders of the London School of Economics and Political Science. "Multi-layered" accurately describes this strain, for it was not merely anti-Irish, but contemptuous of blacks, Catholicism, and Celts as well.

The historian James Anthony Froude bolstered the *Punch* image by writing in 1845 that the people in Catholic Ireland were "more like tribes of squalid apes than human beings."[11]

Such theories were given a pseudo-scientific patina of respectability by the writings of people like Robert Knox, a Scottish anatomist and zoologist and a popular lecturer about race, who wrote, "The Celtic race does not, and never could be made to comprehend the meaning of the word liberty. . . . I appeal to the Saxon men of all countries whether I am right or not in my estimate of the Celtic character. Furious fanaticism; a love of war and disorder; a hatred for order and patient industry; no accumulative habits; restless; treacherous; uncertain; look at Ireland."[12]

Charles Kingsley, an Anglican clergyman, historian, and novelist who is best remembered today as a writer of children's fiction including *Hereward the Wake* and *The Water Babies,* wrote after a visit to Ireland, "I am daunted by the human chimpanzees I saw along that hundred miles of horrible country. I don't believe they are our fault. I believe that there are not only many more of them than of old, but that they are happier, better and more comfortably fed and lodged under our rules than they ever were. But to see white chimpanzees is dreadful; if they were black, one would not feel it so much, but their skins, except where tanned by exposure, are as white as ours."[13]

Thomas Carlyle chose a lower place in the animal kingdom to describe the Irish. He wrote, "Ireland is a starved rat that crosses the path of an elephant: what is the elephant to do? Squelch it, by heaven! Squelch it!"

Apparently not convinced that the squelching process would be sufficient, Carlyle also suggested that the best course for England in dealing with the Irish was to "lead them and put them over with the niggers."

Carlyle's rat reference and his repellent anti-black sentiments could be dismissed as vulgar abuse, but his description of the workhouses and of outdoor works were more damaging and played straight into the hands of people like Trevelyan and Wood, who were looking for ways to stop spending money on Ireland and increase the clearances from the land. Carlyle first visited Ireland for four days in 1846, during which he saw the blackened potato fields and met with the Young Ireland leader Charles Gavan Duffy, who introduced him to John Mitchel. Carlyle made a comprehensive tour of Ireland in 1849 during which he visited a Westport workhouse. After witnessing the conditions, he wrote, "Human Swinery has here reached its acme, happily; 30,000 paupers in this union, population supposed to be 60,000. Workhouses proper (I suppose) cannot hold 3 or 4,000 of them, subsidiary workhouses, and outdoor relief the others. Abomination of desolation; what can you make of it! Outdoor quasi-work; 3 or 400 big hulks of fellows tumbling about with shares, picks and barrows, 'levelling' the end of their workhouse hill; at first glance you would think them all working; look nearer in each shovel there is some ounce or two of mould, and it is all make believe; 5 or 600 boys and lads, pretending to break stones. Can it be charity to keep men alive on these terms? In face of all the twaddle on the earth, shoot a man rather than train him (with a heavy expense to his neighbour) to be a deceptive human swine."

There is no disputing the efforts that the contemporary opinion makers, the Whig spin doctors, exerted in making the Famine seem not so bad. Their propaganda took quite extraordinary forms. In one humiliating tableau designed to show that the government was taking active steps to improve the diet of the starving in April 1847, Alexis Soyer, the French chef at the Reform Club in London, which at the time was the Liberals' own bastion, was brought over to Ireland to add luster to the opening of a soup kitchen in Dublin. Soyer was regarded as one of Europe's leading chefs, and he had garnered considerable publicity in London for devising a soup for the poor that he averred was sufficient to sustain a healthy diet when consumed with a biscuit. The ingredients were "$1/4$ lb of leg of beef; costing 1d, to 2 gallons of water, the other ingredients being 2 oz. of dripping $1/2$ d; 2 onions and other vegetables 2d; $1/2$ lbs of flour, seconds; $1/4$ d; $1/2$ lb of pearl barley; 1 $1/2$ d; 3 oz. salt and $1/2$ oz. brown sugar; total cost 1s.4d. 100 gallons could be made for under £1 including an allowance for fuel."[14]

There was subsequent controversy as to the nutritional value of Soyer's soup. Critics pointed out that it ran through the recipients almost immediately and thus provided little lasting energy, but the most telling criticism of the Soyer performance came from Sir John Burgoyne, who commented on the methodology employed by the authorities in staging the Soyer demonstration. Bowls affixed to chains were provided in the wooden structure erected for this piece of dietary theater. A bell rang and a hundred starving persons were admitted at a time, drank their soup, received a piece of bread, and left the building. Then the bowls were rinsed, a bell rang again, and another hundred of the destitute shuffled forward. Sir John complained that this was treating the poor like "wild animals."[15]

Various medical experts contested Soyer's estimate of the value of the soup, which, as Mr. Dobree of Sligo wrote, "was no working food for people accustomed to 14lbs. of potatoes daily."[16] A liquid diet in itself could not provide all the essential nutrients required to maintain a healthy body. Experts in Skibbereen who had all too much firsthand acquaintanceship with starvation wrote that the soup "passed through people dangerously quickly and in fact gave rise to dysentery." However, as we have seen in the chapter on souperism and soup kitchens, soup based on more nutritious foundations than Soyer's, when accompanied by bread, did keep people alive, and the use of the chef by the government provided a gala public relations exercise in Dublin, at which members of high society were quoted as finding Soyer's recipe tasty and sustaining.

But the most extraordinary coup was a royal visit paid by Queen Victoria in August 1849. The visit highlighted the nearly incomprehensible, but continuing, popularity of the British Royal Family (evidenced yet again by the visit of Queen Elizabeth to Ireland in 2011) in a nation upon whom such suffering had been heaped in the name of that same crown. Queen Victoria was welcomed in Cork by displays of loyalty that included coating the waterfront buildings in sumptuous red cloth. The leitmotif of her visit was symbolized by the banners that greeted her saying, "Hail Victoria, Ireland's hope and England's Glory." Her route was carefully stage-managed. She saw Cork but nothing of the famine-stricken West of the county wherein lay Skibbereen, and she traveled by sea to Kingstown (now Dun Laoghaire) in County Dublin without seeing any other afflicted part of the country. Her drives through Dublin lay through the imposing main squares, and she saw nothing of slums although she perceptively recorded in her diary that she saw more ragged people in Dublin than anywhere else. But, overall, the queen was struck by the beauty of the women and the huge welcome evidenced everywhere by cheering crowds and triumphal arches. At Kingstown an old woman shouted, "Ah, Queen dear, make one of them Prince Patrick and Ireland will die for you."[17]

Needless to say, all this provided endless opportunities for gushing reports in the press depicting an "Ireland of the Welcomes" in which famine did not occur and there were glamor and merriment on a scale not seen in Ireland since the days when she had her own parliament.

John Mitchel has left us a vivid description of another form taken by the influencing of public opinion—straightforward intimidation at election time, when voters who wished to vote against a landlord candidate had to run the gauntlet of bailiff, policemen, soldier, and, if they persisted in disobeying their orders, eviction, with fatal results to themselves and their families:

When we arrived, the city (Galway) besides its usual garrison, was occupied by parties of cavalry and all the rural police from the country around; they were to suppress rioters of the O'Flaherty's party, and help those of Monahan's, cover their retreat, or follow up their charge. The landlords and gentry, Catholic and Protestant, were almost unanimous for Monahan, and highly indignant at strangers coming from Dublin to interfere with the election. Accordingly, in the Courthouse on the day of nomination, a young gentleman of spirit insulted O'Gorman who forthwith went out and sent him a challenge. This was beginning a Galway election in regular form. The meeting, however, was interrupted by some relative of the aggressor who discovered the challenge; and they were both arrested. There was no further disposition to insult any of us. The tenantry of the rural district of the borough (which happened to be unusually large), were well watched by the agents and bailiffs; who, in fact, had possession of all their certificates of registry; and when the poor creatures came up to give their reluctant vote for the famine candidate, it was in gangs guarded by bailiffs. A bailiff produced the certificates of the gangs which were under his care, in a sheaf and stood ready to put forward each in his turn. If the voter dared to say, *O'Flaherty*, the agent scowled on him and in that scowl he read his fate; but he was sure to be greeted with a roaring cheer that shook the Courthouse and was repeated by the multitudes outside. Magistrates and police inspectors, pale with ferocious excitement, stood ready eagerly watching for some excuse to precipitate the troops upon the people; and when the multitudes swayed and surged, as they bore upon their shoulders some poor farmer who had given the right vote, the ranks of infantry clashed the butts of their muskets on the pavement with a menacing clang, and the dragoons gathered up their bridles and made hoofs clatter, and spurs and scabbards jingle, as if preparing for a charge.

I took charge of one of the polling booths as O'Flaherty's agent. A gang of peasants came up, led or driven by the bailiffs. One man, when the oath was administered to him, spoke only Gaelic, and the oath was repeated, sentence by sentence, by an interpreter. He affected to be deaf, to be stupid, began the oath, and as often failed to have it correctly repeated after him.

The unfortunate creature looked round wildly as if famishing little ones at home still restrained him. Large drops broke out on his forehead; and it was not stupidity that was in his eye, but mortal horror. Mr Monahan himself happened to be in that booth at the time, and he stood close by his solicitor, still urging him to attempt once more to get the oath out of the voter. Murmurs began to arise, and at last I said to Mr Monahan: "You cannot, and you dare not, take that man's vote. You know, or your solicitor knows that the man was bribed. I want you to give up this vote and turn the man out." In reply he shrugged his shoulders and went out himself. The vote was rejected and with a savage whisper the bailiff who had marshalled him to the poll turned the poor fellow away. I have no doubt that man is long since dead, he and all his children.[18]

The scene at the Galway polling booth may be taken as an example of the obvious use of force in maintaining the status quo in Ireland. Had Clarendon had his way, there would have been a less obvious method employed—he wanted Russell to take a leaf out of the book of William Pitt the Younger in provoking rebellion before the Irish were properly organized. In December 1847 Russell made a concession to Clarendon's alarm at the prospects for what he termed a "servile war," a "revolt of slaves," which he felt had been set in train by the shooting of landlords and the receipt of numerous death threats. He threatened to resign, but Russell calmed his fears by dispatching five thousand men to the towns of Arklow in County Wicklow, Clonmel in turbulent Tipperary, and Limerick City. However, Lord John Russell refused to attempt general disarmament: "the government did not have enough force at their disposal." Significantly, and to his credit, neither was Russell prepared to accept another course urged upon him, the precedent set by Pitt prior to the 1798 rebellion. We are told that he was not "ready to adopt like Pitt 'ripening' measures to force on a rebellion."[19]

The most effective weapon in the hands of the Whig government for managing the Irish debate was not the army, but *The Times*, which controlled not merely pockets of disaffection in remote, incomprehensible Ireland but the vastly more important domestic British public opinion. In the history of mass communication no newspaper has ever outshone *The Times* as far as influence was concerned. In pre-television, pre-radio nineteenth-century England, *The Times* set the agenda. Richard Cobden, the political economist and an influential Whig opponent of government spending in the Irish crisis, described the paper as being "the most powerful vehicle of public opinion in the world."[20]

More pertinently, where Ireland was concerned, Clarendon said of the paper: "I don't care a straw what any other paper thinks or says they are all regarded on the Continent as representing persons, cliques, but *The Times* is considered to be the exponent of what English opinion is or will be. It is thought that whatever public opinion determines with us the government ultimately does. An extraordinary and universal importance attaches to the views of *The Times*."[21]

Clarendon wrote this in a letter to John Delane, the editor of *The Times*, whose dictum was: "The Press lives by disclosures." Clarendon saw to it that Delane was made the recipient of disclosures of all sorts. His relationship with the editor was such that it was said that Russell, who disliked Clarendon, only gave him the post of Irish viceroy in the hope that it would stem the flow of leaks to *The Times*. But Russell himself was so much in fief to *The Times* that he deserves to be regarded as a senior, if silent, partner in the exchange of news for influence that characterized the Whig government's relationship with the paper.

Russell had taken power at a time when the controversy over Peel's Corn Laws policy had eroded party discipline in both the Conservative and Liberal camps. Russell's control in all areas of government was further weakened by the results of the 1847 election, which returned political economy-minded radicals like Richard Cobden to the already powerful segment of Liberal members who felt there should be less rather than more state intervention in the Irish crisis. Even before 1847 Russell had presided over an arrangement brokered by Clarendon that was described by Prince Albert as meaning that "Russell got *The Times* over by giving it exclusive information."[22]

As it turned out, the arrangement resulted in Clarendon's "becoming the member of the Cabinet with the most influence over *The Times*."[23] But other cabinet members also acquired a powerful "in" with the paper. Delane evidently felt sufficiently sure of his ground that he approached Wood for support at the end of 1848 for the candidature of his brother-in-law George Webbe Dasent as Regius Professor of Modern History and Modern Languages at Oxford.

In at least one instance, Wood was able to persuade Delane to accept an editorial from him in preference to one requested by Clarendon, who had sought to strike a more merciful note. Wood was opposed to a grant of £50,000 sanctioned by Russell to alleviate situations like that described by a Protestant clergyman in Louisburgh, County Mayo, who spoke of being "hourly beset with crawling skeletons begging for food."

The editorial in question was that quoted in chapter 11: "It is the last straw that breaks the camel's back, etc. And it must be confessed that this fresh grant of £50,000 to Ireland has almost broken the back of English benevolence. . . . We believe the real reason to be the total absence not merely of gratitude, not merely of respectful acknowledgements, but of the barest 'receipt' for all these favours."[24]

The foregoing appeared at a time when it was reported from the western unions that "deaths are now so frequent as almost to escape observation."

Irish ingratitude had been the theme from the time of the earliest days of the crisis. In several editorials between November 1845 and March 1846 the prospect of increased aid for Irish "distress" was constantly bracketed with the need to compensate British taxpayers for the sufferings they endured in providing Irish aid.

The Devon Commission has already been mentioned. Unsurprisingly it found that the Irish peasantry were probably the worst off of all the peasants in Europe. Landlord insolvency was blamed for this state of affairs, as was the over-subdivision of land by middlemen. The bad state of relationships between landlord and tenant was also noted, but the Devon Commission relied on public opinion to check abuses by property owners. On the grounds for this optimism, the commission was silent, but it advocated a remedy for the chaos in the Irish agricultural system, in which public opinion was doomed to prove an ineffectual safety catch: it advocated as an imperative the increase in farm holding size while at the same time recommending that the inevitable clearances/evictions should be balanced by schemes of wasteland reclamations and subsidized emigration.

The Devon Commission report was inevitably controversial, as any proposals affecting property rights or government expenditure were bound to be; the approach of *The Times* to the report provided a telling indication of the paper's power. Before there could be any formal government response, the paper sent Thomas Campbell Foster, a writer who had earlier reported on conditions in Scotland and Wales, to tour Ireland as a "Times Commissioner" in August 1845. His articles on the "condition of the people of Ireland," which appeared throughout August and September, were far more widely read than the findings of the Devon Commission and were subsequently reprinted in book form.

Foster found a number of ills. For example, he blamed the lack of capital on the lack of proper rewards for labor and the consequent grinding down of tenants to subterranean levels of existence by landlordism. He also criticized the fact that profits from Irish produce were not used to reinvest in Irish agriculture but were spent elsewhere. He also pointed to the lack of skill on the part of Irish laborers.

All of this, of course, had been glaringly obvious for decades. However, Foster also found that one of the root causes of the economic situation was that it proceeded from Irish morality, or the lack thereof. He said, "When Irishmen as a nation, learn that true spirit of independence which looks for help to no man, and which does not lie in blustering but in the quiet evidence of self-supporting strength, then, and not till then, they and their concerns will demand respect and will have every attention."[25]

The Times was capable of flashes of both humanity and real understanding of the Irish situation. For example, after the March 1846 Galway evictions by Mrs. Gerrard, the paper wrote that there should be "penal consequences to the ejector," asking, "How long shall the rights of property in Ireland continue to be the wrongs of poverty and the advancement of the rich be the destruction of the poor?"[26] However it could also revert unblushingly to the Trevelyan text that it was the hand of God guiding the Irish Famine. For example, it had written before the evictions temporarily swung the pendulum of public opinion toward the Irish and against the landlords: "The Irish peasant starves because his whole existence depends on his own patch of ground, and that failing he had nothing to offer in exchange for the necessities of life elsewhere. . . . In England, on the contrary, the laws of commerce operating fairly . . . will preserve us from this horrible affliction. . . . It is not in breaking the laws of commerce, which are the laws of nature and consequently the laws of God, that we are to place our hope of softening the Divine displeasure to remove any calamity under which we now suffer or which hangs over us."[27]

Trevelyan's central belief was that the people had to be taught to help themselves and that the blight was Providence's answer to the corruption of

Irish society. His 1848 book *The Irish Crisis*, in which he claimed that the crisis was over, set forward his thesis as a justification for his Irish policy: "The only hope for those who lived upon potatoes was in some great visitation of providence to bring back the potato to its original use and intention as an adjunct, and not as the principal article of national food and by compelling the people of Ireland to recur to other more nutritious means of aliment, to restore the energy and the vast industrial capabilities of that country."[28]

This viewpoint had already found its expression in one of *The Times*'s more notorious editorials on the Famine as panic was spreading through Ireland at the realization that the blight was striking again: "For our part, we regard the potato blight as a blessing. When the Celts once cease to be potatophagi, they must become carnivorous. With the taste for meats will grow the appetite for them; with the appetite, the readiness to earn them. With this will come steadiness, regularity, and perseverance; unless, indeed, the growth of these qualities be impeded by the blindness of Irish patriotism, the short-sighted indifference of petty landlords, or the random recklessness of Government benevolence."[29]

Readers are invited to compare this editorial with Trevelyan's comment to Lord Monteagle mentioned in his letter in chapter 6.

Bolstering the argument, Sir Charles Wood told the House of Commons, "No exertion of a Government, or, I will add, of private charity, can supply a complete remedy for the existing calamity. It is a national visitation, sent by providence." This sentence provides a distillation of the effects of the political economists' debate and the Treasury's justification for allowing the Irish to starve.

The relevance of this exchange of high-sounding economic rhetoric among themselves by English theoreticians who, generally speaking, knew so little about Ireland that they could have found their way to Dublin's Sackville Street only with great difficulty, was that it provided an ominous bank of ideas for Trevelyan and others to draw upon when it came to combating—or not combating—the famine.

As the Famine worsened, Trevelyan would thunder, and I quote for a second time, "every system of poor relief must contain a penal and repulsive element, in order to prevent its leading to the disorganisation of society if the system is such as to be agreeable either to those who relieve or to those who are relieved, and still more if it is agreeable to both, all tests of destitution must be at an end."[30] The task of the Treasury subsequently would be to insist more strictly on "sound principle."[31]

The teachings of Adam Smith took on a literally fatal hue when they moved out of the smoking rooms of London clubs and became the principles on which the giving or withholding of food was to be based. Every commissariat officer and clerk dealing with the Famine was issued with a special edition of Adam Smith's "Digression Concerning the Corn Trade and Corn Laws" from his 1776 *An Inquiry into the Nature and Causes of the Wealth of Nations*. The point Trevelyan wanted driven home was that price control—that is, providing cheap food—would produce "instead of the hardships of a dearth, the dreadful horrors of a famine." Staff dealing with relief were also urged along the non-intervention path by being given extracts from Edmund Burke's "Thoughts and Details on Scarcity."

When these utterances fell on what was to Trevelyan "the stony ground of humanitarian objection," he had the offending officials removed. Throughout the crisis he harried dissenting officials like Edward Twiselton with memoranda concerning their performances, seeking better account keeping, more minute reports, and so forth. In short, the armory of the Treasury was deployed to ensure that the dictates of political economy and reform of the Irish land system took precedence over the relief of starvation.

While the foregoing ideas clearly found a strong echo in British famine policy initiatives, *The Times* wrote complacently in 1848, "A Celt will soon be as rare on the banks of the Shannon as the red man on the banks of Manhattan."

And so, to sum up, what was the purpose behind all this manipulation of public opinion? Could it be argued that the Whig policy toward Ireland in the Famine years was merely a bungled attempt at relief, that the policies followed had a genocidal outcome but not a genocidal intent? The verdict that should have emerged from these pages by now is an unequivocal no! John Mitchel's stark analysis that God sent the blight but the English created the Famine rings true.

Trevelyan's reliance on "natural causes" and Wood's admission to Monteagle as to what the cabinet really wanted to achieve are only two tiny tips of an iceberg. Whig policy was directed at getting the peasants off the land, and if it took mass death to achieve that objective, so be it.

Behind the rhetoric of *The Times* editorials and the utilization of economic jargon and extreme Protestant prejudice to stem the flow of relief, even for the feeding of children or the provision of clothing for the naked, the underlying thrust of Whig policy had the aim of clearing man from the fields and replacing him with the bullock. Defenders of the Whigs have argued that Trevelyan and Woods could not be accused of a deliberate attempt to commit genocide because they were men of conscience and after the Famine, their consciences did not trouble them. Trevelyan, his defenders would argue, was not a Cromwell, only a civil servant carrying out government policy.

The conscience argument is absurd. The Irish peasants, if they were considered at all, rated no higher than *Untermenschen*. Cromwell regarded the slaughter of Catholics not as a matter to trouble the conscience but as an act for the glory of God. Trevelyan was not a mere civil servant; he was the architect and executor of government policy, a policy that sheltered behind the economic dogma that the laws of business were the laws of God.

Article 2 of the UN Convention on Genocide defines genocide as meaning "acts committed with intent to destroy, in whole or in part, a national, ethical, racial or religious group," by means that include the following:[32]

- Causing serious bodily or mental harm to the members of the group.
- Deliberately inflicting on the group conditions calculated to bring about its destruction in whole or in part.
- Imposing measures intended to prevent births within the group.
- Forcibly transferring children of the group to another group.

Article 3 includes under "Punishable Acts":

- "Direct and public incitement to commit genocide" and "complicity in genocide."

Certainly in the years 1846–1851 responsible Whig decision makers were complicit in genocide and did direct public incitement, as the columns of *The Times* sadly confirm only too well, toward furthering that end. Just as there are those who still attempt to deny man's role in global warming, there are those who would still attempt to defend the Whigs' role on the grounds that the UN Convention on Genocide stems from 1948, not 1848. To them I end by saying there is another, even older command on which the UN declaration draws, and it is not disputed: *Thou shalt not kill.*

EPILOGUE

A ND SO, WHAT WERE THE LASTING EFFECTS of the Famine? Echoing Charles Trevelyan's declaration that he could see a bright light beginning to break over Ireland despite the fact that thousands were dying in agony, the archetypal agent William Steuart Trench wrote in his memoir that the Famine "had produced a social revolution in Ireland. It hurried on the introduction of free trade. It indirectly brought about the arterial drainage of many of the main rivers of Ireland. It created the Land Improvement Act. It brought into existence the Encumbered Estates Court, one of the most important Acts ever passed in Ireland. It drove some millions of people to the other side of the Atlantic, and sent many thousands to an untimely grave. It broke up to a great extent the small farms of Ireland. It relieved the plethora of the labour market. It removed the needy country gentlemen, and forced them to sell their estates into the hands of capitalists. It unlocked the millions of capital since then laid out on the improved cultivation of the land. It brought over hundreds of Scotchmen and Englishmen who have fare on an extended and more scientific system than had been the practice in Ireland, and in short, it has produced a revolution in the country that has lasted ever since."[1]

Trench's description of the effects of the Famine as seen through the eyes of a Whig spin doctor conveys a seriously flawed picture of the economic and psychological effects of the great disaster.

True, there are many carpetbaggers who, as Trench indicates, did well buying up the land of dead cottiers. But overall, the land issue was far from settled. The latter part of the century saw a bitter struggle in what was known as "the land war," in which agrarian reformers like Michael Davitt

and the Irish political leader Charles Stuart Parnell fought to give substance to James Fintan Lalor's vision of "the land of Ireland for the people of
Ireland" at the head of the Land League. Ultimately, their efforts produced
a series of land acts that had the effect of creating a peasant proprietorship
as the British government issued bonds to buy out the landlords who were
in turn recompensed by a system of annual land annuities. In the often angry but largely peaceful struggle, the Irish used tactics that passed into the
English language in the term "boycotting." Captain Charles Boycott was a
landlord who was first singled out for the deployment of the process known
as "boycotting" wherein no one would associate with him, supply him with
goods, or perform any work for him. No one resisted the Land League more
bitterly or more continuously than Lord Clanricarde, who clung to his estates for several decades.

The political impact of the Famine was seen most clearly in the creation
of a massive Irish diaspora, particularly in America, which I have chronicled
in my book *Wherever Green Is Worn*. Irish Americans then supported the
move for Irish independence and proved to be hugely influential in forging
the conclusion of the Good Friday Agreement of 1998.

Despite the docility implicit in Trench's account of the aftermath of the
Famine, the strain of physical force in Irish self-assertion continued where
the Whiteboys had left off. The post-Famine Fenian movement, founded
by the Irish Republican Brotherhood in the 1860s, derived enormous support from the American emigrants and was in effect motivated by revenge
for Skibbereen and many places like it. From America also would come
the support for this tradition that led to the 1916 Easter Rising, and the
subsequent foundation of the IRA and the Anglo-Irish war of 1919–1921.
The Famine is still a touchy subject in the six-county state of northeastern
Ireland. The efforts in Dublin to have a national Famine commemoration
have foundered on a continuing feeling that the Famine was a self-inflicted
Catholic wound. While annual commemorations can be held in a respectful
atmosphere in the twenty-six southern counties, it is felt among the government departments that deal with the North, chiefly the Department of
Foreign Affairs, that the time is not yet right for such commemorations
across the border, as indicated earlier. The Good Friday Agreement will be

seen to have its final success, not only North and South, but also Ireland and England will be definitively seen to be at peace when the day comes that such Famine commemorations can be held.

Psychologically, the Famine accentuated some unlovely Irish character-istics, and the peasant cunning that coined the saying "whatever you say, say nothing" was deepened and enshrined in Irish life. The condition of learned helplessness manifested itself in a revulsion against the early marriages that had contributed to the Famine, and in rural Ireland, particularly west of the Shannon, bachelordom, spinsterhood, loneliness, and alcoholism took a toll in mental illness and high rates of schizophrenia.

Poverty and emigration remained continuing themes in Ireland. Joining the European Economic Community and the coming of television helped to raise educational and living standards. A more enlightened Ireland has found in recent years that its defenses were too fragile to cope with long-standing Irish vices such as clientism and corruption. The learned helpless-ness syndrome has meant that on all sides, as this is being written, one hears anger that no one has gone to jail over the banking scandals, but the anger is almost inevitably accompanied by a helpless "and they won't either."

However, it is not unreasonable to hope that a country that could weather the trauma described in these pages can also emerge with some strength from its current difficulties. A land that could survive the Famine can survive almost anything.

APPENDIX 1

TREVELYAN LETTER, OCTOBER 11, 1843

PART ONE

To the EDITOR of the MORNING CHRONICLE.

Sir—As English travellers have been as rarely seen in Ireland this year as white men at Timbuctoo, some of your readers may be glad to have an authentic account of the actual position of affairs in that country, from one who for six weeks past has seen, read, thought, inquired, and spoken nothing but Ireland. Up to the last day of September, in last year, the boatmen on the lakes of Killarney obtained 74 days hire. Up to the same date, in this year, they had obtained only 25; the difference being owing to the falling off in the number of English tourists, of whom only eight or ten parties had visited the Lakes this year.

Having crossed the south of Ireland in a variety of directions, and conversed with people of every description from the nobleman to the peasant, I feel that I am not guilty of presumption in enabling my countrymen to participate in the result of my observations. One peculiarity of the present extraordinary state of the public mind in Ireland is that everybody speaks out. The Roman Catholic peasantry appear to be so confident in their numbers and unanimity, as to consider any concealment of their plans and intentions quite an unnecessary precaution; and as I was merely an English tourist, of whom they had been accustomed to see many hundreds in the course of every year, they opened their minds to me with greater freedom than they would have done to any of the official or military persons resident in Ireland. On my part, finding that I had visited the country at a crisis of no ordinary importance, I regarded romantic scenery and other usual objects of a traveller's attention as of minor importance, and applied myself carefully to the study of the popular mind.

Before I left England I took great pains to form a just opinion as to the real nature of the popular movement in progress in Ireland, and the conclusion I came to was the same which has, I believe, been arrived at by the best informed persons in this country. The whole affair appeared to me to be a gigantic piece of blarney on O'Connell's part. I believed it to have its root in the vulgar, but, nevertheless, very powerful motive of saving himself from pecuniary ruin. Besides this, every demagogue is, from the necessity of his position obliged to go forward. He is by progression a fisher in troubled waters. The demagogue sinks into insignificance just in proportion as public affairs settle down into tranquillity.

O'Connell, no doubt, also aimed at upsetting the present Government, and getting some instalments for Ireland; but that a shrewd person like O'Connell, who has attended Parliament year after year, and who knows the power and resources of the British nation, and the fixed determination of the great majority, in numbers, wealth, and intelligence, not to submit to a dismemberment of the empire, should seriously believe in the possibility of Repeal, is so unlikely as to be really incredible.

It soon became apparent to me, after my arrival in Ireland, that although this view of the case was perfectly correct as far as O'Connell was concerned, the matter had taken much deeper root. Other leaders besides O'Connell either appeared on the stage, or skulked behind the scenes; and, above all, it was evident that the great mass of the Roman Catholic peasantry had thoroughly taken the matter to heart. The people were bursting with repeal. It was not in the least necessary to put searching questions to them, in order to get at their sentiments. You could not make the commonest inquiry without bringing on a repeal discussion. If you asked the price of pork or fish in the streets, the old women were sure to say something of this sort after they had answered your question: "Well, sir, when are we to have our rights? When will our Parliament sit in College-green?"

The people, in short, were determined to have repeal—by fair means, if possible—but, at any rate, repeal. They had, moreover, fully made up their minds to the sacrifices consequent upon a popular rising, and had familiarized themselves to all the contingencies of an insurrection in an extraordinary degree. There was not a single important point connected with the subject on which they were not prepared with a good military answer; and in whatever part of the country the question might be asked, you were sure of receiving the same answer in substance, and generally speaking, in nearly the same words. This last-mentioned circumstance proves to demonstrate that the plans of operation with which the heads of peasantry were tilled did not originate with themselves, but that they had emanated from some common source, and were, in fact, the instructions of superior minds, which had been carefully prepared to suit the exigency of the case, and had been afterwards disseminated by means of some established organization among the people.

If the Rebellion of 1798 were spoken of, the remark invariably made was to this effect: "Those, sir, were the days of drinking whisky. Our people lay drunk in the ditches, and the troops obtained an easy victory. But now we are sober, temperate, and religious people." If I heard this remark made once, I heard it fifty times.

If the superiority of disciplined over undisciplined troops were adverted to, the answer was always of this kind: "Oh, sir! You don't suppose we shall give you the advantage of fighting a pitched battle with us. We shall rise in our counties and baronies, and do all we want (which means, making a clean sweep of the Protestants), and when the troops arrive, they will find the people quietly at plough, and we shall be doing our work elsewhere." Reference was also constantly made to cutting off convoys and detached parties, by lining the hedges with pikemen and closing upon them, in the way that was practiced with some success during the rebellion of 1798, and subsequently, on the occasion of several well-known conflicts with the police.

Workmen were employed in boring loopholes in the walls of the first barrack which I happened to pass. A person who was with me pointed with his thumbe to the people so employed, and said, "Pretty nonsense that, sir. When the boys rise, they will pull the soldiers out by their shoulders." I asked him to explain himself, and he went on to say that the walls of the barracks would be scaled in every direction by night, and that the people would tumble in over by thousands, and squeeze the troops to death, if they did not take them out and throw them into the river. I believe this to be a perfectly correct military idea. The contour of many of the barracks is very extensive. The walls are low; there is no ditch; and if the people had tumbled in over by hundreds at night, when the raking fire from the bastions would have less effect, it is possible that before our preparations were so complete as they now are, the assailants might have carried some of the barracks. I afterwards found that this plan of attacking the barracks was generally diffused among the people.

There is another horrible prevailing idea, which really startled me the first time I heard it. I was waiting for my car early in the morning in the street of a small, sulky, ill-conditioned town, when seeing a farmers' wife setting up a potato stall, I asked her the price of her potatoes. She gave me a civil answer; but two men were standing by, one of whom said, without my having previously addressed him, or having made any remark calculated to encourage the observation, "We shall eat *wheaten bread* next year, sir." I was really unable to make out his drift, and told him good-humouredly, that I was very glad to hear it but begged to know how the change would be brought about. "There will be fewer of us, sir," was the reply. I then began to understand his meaning, and, as I encouraged him to speak out, he proceeded to say that there were eight millions of them, that one or two million might be spared with advantage, and that the country would be for the survivors. I afterward heard the same idea, either in whole or in part, in a variety of poems, but the burden of the song always was, that the land was not able to bear them, "Protestant and Catholic will freely fall, and the land will be for the survivors."

Their commissariat also was arranged. Every man was to bring so many days potatoes, and butter and bacon, if he could afford it.

Amidst all this warlike preparation, I was surprised to hear nothing of drilling, or of the manufacture of arms, and I made various inquiries upon the subject. It appeared from the result, that it formed no part of the plan of the popular leaders to drill the people in an ostensible military manner in that stage of their operations. The tactics they had resolved upon, which are mainly those of a guerrilla warfare, did not require a high state of discipline, and to have assembled large bodies of men for the purpose of training them would have led to a premature explosion. With regard to arms, the answer I always received was, that there was no want of arms already in the country, and that as the people were all of one mind, when they rose, they would convert everything into weapons of war.

Their reliance seemed to be on the stock of firearms constantly concealed in the country; on their national weapon, the pike, which may be manufactured by any common blacksmith, in large numbers in the course of a single day, and on the pitchfork (scarcely less formidable than the pike), which is in every cabin. But their main reliance was in their numbers and unanimity. The people of Zurich effected their Strauss revolution with their red umbrellas, and the people of the south of Ireland seem to fancy that if they once rose as one man, every body must quail before them.

If you spoke to them of the army, the remark commonly made was, "But, sir, you forget that three-fourths of the army are Irishmen, and every Irishman is a repealer."

If you spoke of the Protestants of the north, the answer was, "The Presbyterian tenants will not stand by their landlords. Lord Roden called a great meeting on the subject, and he was obliged to give it up, because the tenantry were prepared to come forward with a demand for fixity of tenure as the price of their adherence." It is remarkable that on no one occasion did I hear it stated by the Roman Catholic peasants that they could *beat* the Protestants of the North. What they always said was, that the Protestants would not turn out at the call of their nobility and gentry.

Reference was also constantly made to assistance which they expect from foreign powers, and from Wales, Scotland, and the manufacturing districts, and the remark invariably made was, that although the affair might commence in Ireland, it would not end there.

Yet after the people had been talking in this strain, if you said that you were sorry to find them in such a temper of mind, the answer always returned was, "Sir! We have no intention of going to war." "Not going to war!" was the natural rejoinder—"Why, you have been talking nothing but treason and rebellion for the last hour, and now you say that you do not intend to go to war. What do you mean?" "No, sir," was the regular reply, "We do not mean to go to war with the government, but if the government goes to war with us, then all the boys will rise." This again required explanation, and on inquiry it always turned out that their real meaning was as follows:—They have unlimited faith in O'Connell's practical talents and in his knowledge of the law. They are persuaded that he will not take any step which will be contrary to law. They looked forward to the assembly of the three hundred as the crisis on which the whole question depended. If the government interfered with the meeting of the three hundred, they considered that the first aggression would then decidedly be on the part of the government, and that was to be the signal for their rising. It has been carefully impressed upon them that they are not themselves to take the initiative, but that they are to leave the government to put itself in the wrong by making the first attack. It may also be observed that they never speak of their rising as an insurrection or rebellion, but that the term always used by them is "going to war." The genius of the Irish is decidedly military.

It is due to the people to say that, while they have rebellion and massacre on their lips, they are, nevertheless, decidedly advancing in sobriety, industry, and, except in the case of the horrible Tipperary murders, in good order, and respect for the laws. Faction fights have ceased to exist, and shillelaghs are rarely seen except in the police offices, where they are used as firewood. Repeal has been for some time past their master passion, and everything else, even what are generally considered the milder virtues, has been pressed into the service. The motto which is put most prominently forward at their repeal meetings is "He who commits a crime gives strength to the enemy." Although the organization of the Temperance Societies preceded the Repeal movement, that organization has been adopted into it. The congregation of each Roman Catholic chapel generally forms a temperance society. The repeal wardens are the officers; the temperance band, the members of which are dressed in uniform, are the rallying point; and when it is determined to show the strength of the country, the male members of the Temperance Societies are marshaled under their respective bands and colours, and march out to the monster meetings. The people appear to take a pride in displaying their fixity of purpose and the supposed moral excellence of their cause, by an obvious abandonment of their previously habitual vices. They feel ashamed when a drunken man appears reeling in the streets, and I have seen them rebuke mendicants whom they have observed in the act of importuning a stranger. Intoxication is now rarely seen in Ireland. I visited three crowded fairs, and did not see a single instance of it; and I did not observe more than six or seven drunken people all the time I was in Ireland.

There is nothing new under the sun. The same unwonted quiet preceded the breaking out of the last rebellion. The following well-known passage is almost as applicable to the present crisis as it was to that of 1798: "I apprehend we shall have a rough winter again, though we have had so still a summer. The people about us are too hush and too prudent; it is not their natures; there's something contriving among them; they don't break one another's heads at fairs as they used to do; they keep from whiskey; there must be some strong motive working this change upon them—good or bad, 'tis hard to say which." God forbid that I should undervalue the existing symptoms of an improved morality; but nobody will deny that it will be an advantage if we can have the morality without the rebellion.

I am also bound to say that although the people talked to me of blood and murder as familiarly as young ladies talk of puppy-dogs and kittens, I did not meet with a single instance of incivility. I was told more than once, that if the boys were to rise, my life would not be worth a bad pound note; and certainly, at two or three places, the people were in such a gloomy frame of mind, that, after one or two trials, I did not venture to ask them any questions on any subject. The only privation I suffered was the absence of the free flow of genuine Irish humour with which travellers in Ireland in better times have been delighted. The people were, as a general rule, in too serious a mood to indulge in jokes; nevertheless, the fun which every Irishman possesses would occasionally ooze out. If you asked them what they would do if they did not get Repeal, they generally looked glum, and talked rebelliously; but some would say, after a little consideration, "Why, sir, I suppose we should do without it," or "I suppose we should do as we did before." Not to get Repeal, always seemed to be quite a new idea to them; and when the impossibility of it was pointed out, it seemed to have the same effect upon their minds as a violent shock might have been expected to have upon their bodies.

Hitherto I have been speaking only of the Roman Catholic peasantry of the south of Ireland. They are naturally an amiable, good humoured, and contented people, but they are very ignorant and very excitable, and they have been systematically plied with misrepresentations to a degree which was, perhaps, never practiced before. I never saw a poor people in such a miserable state of delusion.

The Roman Catholics of the middle class, both in town and country, have also generally given in to the movement. The popular torrent was running too strong for them to withstand, and they have, one by one, been carried away by it. Some are influenced by mistaken patriotic motives, but the generality have merely yielded to the necessity of their situation.

The case is very different with some few of the gentry, both Protestant and Catholic, who have given their sanction to the movement. Their independent fortunes place them in a situation which enables them to speak out when all others are obliged to be silent. Their liberal education, and the general information possessed by them, must have convinced them that the Repeal cause could be seriously and effectively prosecuted only by means of a popular insurrection, which would bring destruction upon the South of Ireland, and which would not, after all, succeed; but although these gentlemen do not hesitate to give their sanction to the movement, and to hound on the people to their ruin, nothing is further from their intentions than to risk their own necks and fortunes. When the time arrives for showing colours (if, which God forbid, it ever should arrive), the poor deluded people will be astonished at the number of influential persons upon whom they now count, who will pair off with the government. If the gentlemen alluded to wish to preserve a character for common honesty and good faith, they will side with the people in the case supposed; but as they joined the movement from the selfish motive of obtaining for themselves a temporary popularity, they may be expected to prefer their own safety, and to sacrifice the people, when it comes to the point. I do not like the plan of giving unprincipled or foolish ambitious persons the opportunity of reaping the honours, without suffering the pains of martyrdom. It is desirable that no martyrs at all should be made; but if they must be made, let them at least be real martyrs.

There is another estate in the repeal ranks, of the existence of which people in England have no notion. These are the Young men of Dublin. They profess to be Irish politicians of the Emmett and Lord Edward Fitzgerald school; and as far as the difference in the circumstances of the two countries admits, they answer to the *Jeunes gens de Paris*. They are public-spirited, enthusiastic young men, possessed of that description of crude and imperfect information on political subjects, which induced several of our present Whig and Conservative leaders to be violent Radicals in their youth. These Young men of Dublin supply all the good writing, and history and political philosophy, such as it is, of the party: They also supply the poetry; and in order to give some idea of the spirit of it, I will quote an entire piece, which, although it goes the whole length of open warfare, falls far short of many other of their productions in point of bitterness and virulence, both against the English nation and their own landlords and other obnoxious persons.

I.

"Can the depths of the ocean afford you not graves,
That you come thus to perish afar o'er the waves;
To redden and swell the wild torrents that flow
Through the valley of vengeance, the dark Abarlow?

II.

"The clangour of conflict o'erburdens the breeze,
From the stormy Slieve Bloom to the stately Galtees;
Your caverns and torrents are purple with gore,
Slievenamon, Glencoloe, and sublime Galtymore!

III.

"The sun-burst that slumber'd embalm'd in our tears,
Tipperary! Shall wave o'er thy tall mountaineers!
And the dark hill shall bristle with sabre and spear,
While one tyrant remains to forge manacles here.

IV.

"The riderless war-steed careers o'er the plain,
With a shaft in his flank and a blood-dripping mane,
His gallant breast labours, and glare his wild eyes;
He plunges in torture—falls—shivers—and dies.

V.

"Let the trumpets ring triumph! The tyrant is slain:
He reels o'er his charger deep pierced through the brain;
And his myriads are flying like leaves on the gale,
But who shall escape from our hills with the tale?

VI.

"For the arrows of vengance are show'ring like rain,
And choke the strong rivers with islands of slain,
Till thy waves, 'lordly Shannon,' all crimsonly flow,
Like the billows of hell with the blood of the foe.

VII.

"Ay! The foemen are flying, but vainly they fly—
Revenge with the fleetness of lightning can vie:
And the septs from the mountains spring up from each rock,
And rush down the ravines like wolves on the flock.

VIII.

"And who shall pass over the stormy Slieve Bloom,
To tell the pale Saxon of tyranny's doom;
When, like tigers from ambush, our fierce mountaineers,
Leap along from the crags with their death-dealing spears?

IX.

"They came with high boasting to bind us as slaves
But the glen and the torrent have yawned for their graves—
From the gloomy Ardfinaan to wild Templemore—
From the Suir to the Shannon—is red with their gore.

X.

"By the sould of Heremon! Our warriors may smile,
To remember the march of the foe through our isle;
Their banners and harness were costly and gay,
And proudly they flash'd in the summer sun's ray;

XI.

"The hilts of their falchions were crusted with gold,
And the gems on their helmets were bright to behold,
By Saint Bride of Kildare! But they moved in fair show—
To gorge the young eagles of dark Abarlow!"

Popular ballads from the same workshop, of the same general description, but of a coarser and simpler kind, are openly sung in the streets of the towns and villages, and form not the least important part of the system of measures which has been adopted for the purpose of inflaming the people.

I shall resume this subject on Monday,
October 11, 1843.
PHILALETHES.

TREVELYAN LETTER PART TWO

To the EDITOR of the MORNING CHRONICLE.
The most serious fact of all connected with the present agitation has yet to be mentioned. There cannot be a doubt that the great body of the Roman Catholic priests have gone into the movement in the worst, that is, in the rebellious sense. Many of the priests of the old school, who had been educated in France and had seen the world, held out for a time; but they were given to understand that if they continued to take this line, the shepherd would be deserted by his flock, and they were forced to yield. Two or three splendid instances are still mentioned of priests openly professing their determination to submit to any consequences rather than give their sanction to a movement which they know to be of the most dangerous and pernicious character: but the curates and young priests brought up at Maynooth have gone into it heartily, almost to a man. Those young men are generally the sons of small farmers and other persons of a similar rank in life. They, therefore, bring with them strong feelings and limited and one-sided information from home, and at Maynooth they are brought up, like our young Newmanite clergy at Oxford, to

regard THE CHURCH as the sole object for which they are to live, and think, and act. They have no property, no families of their own, to be compromised by a rebellion; and as it would be inconsistent with the character of their sacred profession to appear at the head of their flocks in the field of battle, they run no personal risk. They may gain, but they cannot well lose, by the result of a conflict. Some, more heady and enthusiastic than the rest, might even lead their flocks to battle; but whatever their conduct in this respect might be, there cannot be a doubt that the prevailing spirit of the priesthood is correctly represented by the following expressions, extracted from the speech of the Rev. Mr. Cantwell, parish priest of Tramore, at the last monster meeting at Lismore: "He could support O'Connell with his voice, but he would support him with more. Look at that arm (said the reverend gentleman, stretching forth his right arm). After the magnificent scene I have this day witnessed, I'll die a death, or see Ireland free [tremendous cheering, waving of hats, &c]." The priests have given to the repeal movement all the weight of a religious cause in the eyes of a superstitious people. They form the medium through which an understanding is kept up among all classes of Repealers, and through which the practical instructions are conveyed to the people. The women and children are sent out of chapel after the service is over, and the men are lectured on political subjects, and have treasonable papers read to them, often for an hour together. I did not consider the movement as really alarming, until the conviction was forced upon me that the priests had gone into it in the worst sense.

The primary object of the priests is, no doubt, to get the temporalities of the Established Church; but they have also a further object, which lies much nearer their heart, which is to make Ireland a Catholic country. Everybody in the south of Ireland, both Protestant and Catholic, admits that if an insurrection were to succeed, the Protestants must either conform, or quit the country. O'Connell does his utmost to keep the religious character of the movement in the back ground. The same was done by the leaders in the movement of 1798; but the moment the rebellion broke out, it assumed the character of a religious war, and the few Protestants who had been inclined to join it, at once withdrew.

The object of the people is to get plenty of work, and to obtain a favourable permanent settlement of their rents; but they have a further object, which they took to as the inevitable result of a successful insurrection, which is to get rid of the landlords altogether, and to divide the land among themselves—not merely the forfeited estates, but all the land; at least all which is in the possession of persons not thoroughly devoted to their cause.

The result is, that we are standing on the verge of a religious and agrarian war, which would unite the horrors of the Jacquerie and St. Bartholomew.

O'Connell has for some time past been aware of this fact, and nobody has been more alarmed at it than he has been. He has whipped his horses until they have run away with him, and now, to his dismay, he finds that he is not his own coachman. He has a gentleman on the box, dressed in black. If any of the more moderate lay Repealers are asked what is the ground of the confidence expressed by them that there will be no outbreak, they can only refer you to the priests. O'Connell himself is now really as much in the hands of the priests, as far as this question is concerned, as we are ourselves. He has evoked a spirit which is too strong for him.

Nevertheless, he has lately done his best to set bounds to the torrent. The following expressions, extracted from his speech at Lismore, will convey some idea of his real position: "My heart is filled with delight at the scene that has been exhibited before us all this day [hear, hear]. It proves that I ought to change my position; I ought to become a different person from what I was. Heretofore I was an agitator, stimulating and exciting to exertion, and endeavouring to persuade every person by argument that they ought to exert themselves to the very utmost [hear, hear]. I think I must give this up, and become one of the Moderates [laughter]. Yes, the people and the priests are going beyond me [renewed laughter and cheers]. Did you ever hear two such agitators as my reverend friends who preceded me [hear, hear]? They are outrunning me altogether, and I have become like the heavy schoolboy in the race. My own pupils are beating me [great laughter and cheering]. I am to be the drag on the wheel that it may go down steadily the plane of liberty [hear]. It is my duty now to restrain. It was my duty formerly to excite. My reverent colleagues have left their trade of preaching for agitating, and I now take up the gowns which they have thrown from off their shoulders and set about sermonizing you.

O'Connell, although the author of all this mischief, is, nevertheless, now our chief ground of reliance for the preservation of the peace. As an English gentleman was lately driving in the neighbourhood of Dublin his attention was attracted by G.P.O. (from the *General Post-office*) on all the mile stones, and he asked his car driver what it meant. "Oh, sir, don't you know what that means? *God Preserve O'Connell* to be sure," a prayer in which I heartily join.

The danger is, that O'Connell has so filled the imagination of the people with the idea of their Parliament in College-green, that the only way in which he is now able to keep them quiet is by confirming the delusion; or, in other words, by assuring them that he will not flinch, and that they shall have their Parliament whole and entire. He ought to have recollected Wolsey's dying advice to Mr. Kingstone: "He is a Prince of royal courage, and hath a princely heart; and rather than he will miss or want any part of his will or pleasure, he will endanger the loss of the one-half of his realm. For I assure you I have often kneeled before him, the space sometimes of three hours, to persuade him from his will and appetite; but I could never dissuade him therefrom. Therefore, Mr. Kingstone I warn you if it chance you hereafter to be of his Privy Council, as for you wisdom you are very meat, be well assured and advised what ye put in his head, for ye shall never put it out again."

One of the greatest of the delusions which have been put into the heads of the peasantry is that they are a *nation*. The idea has been sedulously inculcated: "We are many." "Whatever a nation wills, must be."

The poor people forget, or they have never heard, that although positively many, they are comparatively few. The Roman Catholic peasantry of the south of Ireland are greatly outnumbered by the rest of their countrymen, including the loyal well-affected Catholics and Protestants of Ireland, and the great body of the English and Scotch people.

But mere numbers form only one, and by no means the most important, element in a military question.

The sea is entirely at the command of the British government. No part of Ireland is much more than 50 miles from the sea. Our ships of war and steamers would command the maritime towns and coast, and convey troops to the flank or rear of any rebel force that might be assembled in any part of the country. There is no part of Ireland in which an insurrectionary force could take up its position, and say, "We are safe here."

The country is, also, for the most part, very open and weak, in a military point of view; there are no fences which would oppose a serious obstacle to the manoeuvres of regular infantry, and in most parts of the country cavalry might act in numbers sufficient for a contest of this description. The island is, also, now perforated in every direction by good roads; it is true that there are some mountainous districts in the west which would afford strong positions; but the question would not be decided in the mountains. As far as that district is concerned, it would be sufficient to watch any rebel force that might assemble there, and it must soon melt away of itself for want of provisions.

All the strongholds of the country are in the hands of the government and its officers and troops are fully prepared.

It is a vain expectation of the Roman Catholic peasantry of the south that the Protestants of the north would not declare against them. As surely as the south rose in rebellion against the government, the north would rise in support of the government. The spirit which prompted the ever memorable defence of Londonderry, and excited the Enniskilliners always to rush to the attack with the ferocity and exultation of a tiger bounding upon his prey, is by no means extinct. All minor differences will be absorbed by the portentous consideration of the maintenance of their religion and liberties. The northerns are quite as ready to fall on as the Roman Catholic peasantry of the south; and it will be seen that such is the case the moment the restraint which is at present imposed upon them by the government is removed. They declare that, if the government would only leave them to themselves, they would conquer the rest of Ireland without any assistance; and those who know the intelligence, the vigour, the dogged perseverance, the high and courageous spirit of this class of people, will not consider this so empty a boast as it might at first sight appear. They possess all the high qualities of the English and Scotch nations, with the addition of the determined, and it may be, in some instances the ferocious spirit which an unsettled state of society, and the frequent contemplation of danger, naturally produce. To let loose this power is certainly a dreadful alternative; but it would be far more dreadful that our well-affected countrymen in the south should be left to have their throats cut at the leisure of the insurgents, and that a destructive warfare should be allowed to be protracted.

But, say the southerns, we mean to carry on a guerrilla warfare, and we shall accomplish our objects without anywhere opposing a front to your troops.

This is the greatest delusion of all. The ignorant people think that the loss of a million or two of their number is the utmost extent of the sacrifice which they would have to make—that they would wear us out by delay, and that the survivors would be left better off than they were before.

The actual loss of life is the least of the evils which is entailed by a popular war; when the contest is merely between the governments, the people look on while the regular armies fight it out; and, after a campaign or two, the matter is decided without much injury to either party. Even in our own civil wars, although infinite evils were entailed upon England, the contest was in the main between the regular armies on each side. But if an insurrection breaks out in Ireland, the struggle will be between the people and with the people. Every town, every village, every farmhouse will be a scene of conflict; the industry of the country will be suspended, the stock of food and the means of further production will be destroyed—within six months there will be a famine, and within six months more there will be a pestilence, to say nothing of the widows and orphans. There is no European country which would suffer so severely from the effects of a popular war as Ireland, because none is more populous and none less provided with varied resources. In order to find a parallel to the effects of such a warfare in Ireland, it would be necessary to go to those districts of India which have been the scene of murderous and long-continued contests. In the struggle carried on in the south of Ireland in the reign of Elizabeth, which is known by the name of the Desmond War, the people died by hundreds in the ditches, with grass in their mouths, with which they vainly endeavoured to satisfy the cravings of hunger. This has been repeatedly referred to by O'Connell, as a proof of the atrocious cruelty of the English. It was no such thing. The Desmond War was a strictly popular war, such as we are now threatened with; and the necessary consequence of such a war, in a country circumstanced as Ireland, is that the sources whence life is sustained are dried up. In such a case the miserable people have no choice given them between famine, pestilence, and the sword. They fall under all three. Will it now be said that the loss of a million or two of lives would be the only sacrifice which the people would have to make, and that the survivors would be benefited by the change?

Even the most sanguine cannot expect that France and America will fall on the moment the peasantry in the south of Ireland choose to rise. Before the French and Americans became sufficiently excited to force their governments into the contest, if they ever reached that point, the contest would be decided in Ireland. They who rest their hopes on foreign assistance greatly underrate the spirit and power of England. England maintained her ground for many years against nearly the whole world in arms, and she is prepared to do so again, if the occasion requires it. If the south of Ireland were to rebel, the loyal and well-affected Britons, both at home and in many of the dependencies of the empire, would take the preservation of the peace into their own hands. The great bulk of the British army would be precipitated on the south of Ireland. The shores of Ireland would be surrounded with ships and steamers of war; and such is the trust reposed by capitalists in the good faith and resources of the government of the United Kingdom, that any sum of money which might be necessary for carrying on the war for any length of time would be forthcoming on demand.

And let not these poor deluded people count on the British soldier abandoning his colours. Some drunken men, who have had liquor given them by the Repealers, may roll down the street, shouting out in the frolicsome thoughtless style of such people, "Hurrah for Repeal!" but it came to be a question whether they would be true to their Sovereign, and to their own pledged faith, even those persons would do their duty perhaps as effectually as their more steady comrades; and as soon as the first blood is spilt, see who will be the greater tiger of the two.

And will there be no defections in the rebel camp? They are now all apparently united, because the popular current runs so strongly in one direction that all are obliged to yield at least an outward conformity to the prevailing idea. But wait, I say again, till the time comes for showing colours, and see how many of the gentlemen who now cheer you on to the brink of the precipice will jump down with you. Are you so mad as to imagine that several persons whose names will at once occur to you, will ever dream of hoisting the white cockade? Even among those who will jump down with you. Even among those who will break out with you, is it to be expected that all will remain true? There is an old Irish adage, "Roast an Irishman on the spit, and you will be sure to get another turn him." Many will soon weary of the contest. Others will begin to doubt whether it may be eventually attended with success; and there will be no want of persons who will gladly avail themselves of any opportunity that may offer to making their peace with the government at the expense of their former associates.

Oct. 11, 1843.
PHILALETHES.

APPENDIX 2

AVERAGE ANNUAL RATES OF EXCESS MORTALITY BY COUNTY, 1846–1851 (PER THOUSAND)

Statistics from J. Moykr as quoted by James S. Donnelly Jr., *The Great Irish Potato Famine* (Phoenix Mill, Gloucestershire: Sutton Publishing, 2001)

County	Rate	County	Rate
Mayo	58.4	King's	18.0
Sligo	52.1	Meath	15.8
Roscommon	49.5	Armagh	15.3
Galway	46.1	Tyrone	15.2
Leitrim	42.9	Antrim	15.0
Cavan	42.7	Kilkenny	12.5
Cork	32.0	Wicklow	10.8
Clare	31.5	Donegal	10.7
Fermanagh	29.2	Limerick	10.0
Monaghan	28.6	Louth	8.2
Tipperary	23.8	Kildare	7.3
Kerry	22.4	Down	6.7
Queen's	21.6	Londonderry	5.7
Waterford	20.8	Carlow	2.7
Longford	20.2	Wexford	1.7
Westmeath	20.0	Dublin	−2.1

IRISH COUNTIES DURING THE FAMINE

APPENDIX 3

FOLKLORE QUESTIONNAIRE CONCERNING THE GREAT FAMINE OF 1845–1852

THE GREAT FAMINE OF 1845–1852

1. Are there any local traditions about the manner in which the blight first appeared? How was the crop affected (while growing, before being dug, or when stored)? Did the blight return on successive years at that time?

2. Please write down any stories or traditions you can find locally about the following: Famine deaths, burials, graves, graveyards. The Cholera in your district; local fever hospitals at that time.

3. Can you give any accounts of the dissolution of individual local families during the Famine (or soon afterwards) by death or migration (to other districts) or emigration (to other countries)? Where did those who left the district go to? Passage-money; emigrant ships.

4. Local evictions during or soon after the Famine. What was the attitude of the local landlords, merchants and shopkeepers, well-to-do families and priests to the people during the Famine; alma, credits, mortgages on land, seizures, evictions etc. Local "Poor-houses." Homeless individuals.

5. Food during the Famine: types of food available locally; uses made of special foods (herbs etc.). Food-centres set up by the Government and various societies; local soup-kitchens: how run, individuals associated with them; conditions (if any) attached to the receipt of food at some of those centres. Souperism and proselytism in your district during the Famine (it is necessary to distinguish between centres at which proselytism was carried on and those at which it was not). Any accounts of the forcible taking of food (crops, cattle etc.) and of means taken to counter it (man-traps etc.).

6. Accounts of local relief-schemes during the Famine (road-making, drainage etc.). Financing of these schemes, pay, stewards, choice of workers, value of the work done. Attitude of the people generally and of the well-to-do farmers to relief schemes.

APPENDIX 4

UN CONVENTION ON THE PREVENTION AND PUNISHMENT OF THE CRIME OF GENOCIDE

Retrieved from http://www.hrweb.org/legal/genocide.html. Created on August 16, 1994 / Last edited on January 27, 1997.

Adopted by Resolution 260 (III) A of the United Nations General Assembly on December 9, 1948.

ARTICLE 1

The Contracting Parties confirm that genocide, whether committed in time of peace or in time of war, is a crime under international law which they undertake to prevent and to punish.

ARTICLE 2

In the present Convention, genocide means any of the following acts committed with intent to destroy, in whole or in part, a national, ethnical, racial or religious group, as such:

(a) Killing members of the group;
(b) Causing serious bodily or mental harm to members of the group;
(c) Deliberately inflicting on the group conditions of life calculated to bring about its physical destruction in whole or in part;
(d) Imposing measures intended to prevent births within the group;
(e) Forcibly transferring children of the group to another group.

ARTICLE 3

The following acts shall be punishable:

(a) Genocide;
(b) Conspiracy to commit genocide;
(c) Direct and public incitement to commit genocide;
(d) Attempt to commit genocide;
(e) Complicity in genocide.

ARTICLE 4

Persons committing genocide or any of the other acts enumerated in Article 3 shall be punished, whether they are constitutionally responsible rulers, public officials or private individuals.

ARTICLE 5

The Contracting Parties undertake to enact, in accordance with their respective Constitutions, the necessary legislation to give effect to the provisions of the present Convention and, in particular, to provide effective penalties for persons guilty of genocide or any of the other acts enumerated in Article 3.

ARTICLE 6

Persons charged with genocide or any of the other acts enumerated in Article 3 shall be tried by a competent tribunal of the State in the territory of which the act was committed, or by such international penal tribunal as may have jurisdiction with respect to those Contracting Parties which shall have accepted its jurisdiction.

ARTICLE 7

Genocide and the other acts enumerated in Article 3 shall not be considered as political crimes for the purpose of extradition.

The Contracting Parties pledge themselves in such cases to grant extradition in accordance with their laws and treaties in force.

ARTICLE 8

Any Contracting Party may call upon the competent organs of the United Nations to take such action under the Charter of the United Nations as they consider appropriate for the prevention and suppression of acts of genocide or any of the other acts enumerated in Article 3.

ARTICLE 9

Disputes between the Contracting Parties relating to the interpretation, application or fulfilment of the present Convention, including those relating to the responsibility of a State for genocide or any of the other acts enumerated in Article 3, shall be submitted to the International Court of Justice at the request of any of the parties to the dispute.

ARTICLE 10

The present Convention, of which the Chinese, English, French, Russian and Spanish texts are equally authentic, shall bear the date of 9 December 1948.

ARTICLE 11

The present Convention shall be open until 31 December 1949 for signature on behalf of any Member of the United Nations and of any non-member State to which an invitation to sign has been addressed by the General Assembly.

The present Convention shall be ratified, and the instruments of ratification shall be deposited with the Secretary-General of the United Nations.

After 1 January 1950, the present Convention may be acceded to on behalf of any Member of the United Nations and of any non-member State which has received an invitation as aforesaid.

Instruments of accession shall be deposited with the Secretary-General of the United Nations.

ARTICLE 12

Any Contracting Party may at any time, by notification addressed to the Secretary-General of the United Nations, extend the application of the present Convention to all or any of the territories for the conduct of whose foreign relations that Contracting Party is responsible.

ARTICLE 13

On the day when the first twenty instruments of ratification or accession have been deposited, the Secretary-General shall draw up a procès-verbal and transmit a copy of it to each Member of the United Nations and to each of the non-member States contemplated in Article 11.

The present Convention shall come into force on the ninetieth day following the date of deposit of the twentieth instrument of ratification or accession.

Any ratification or accession effected subsequent to the latter date shall become effective on the ninetieth day following the deposit of the instrument of ratification or accession.

ARTICLE 14

The present Convention shall remain in effect for a period of ten years as from the date of its coming into force.

It shall thereafter remain in force for successive periods of five years for such Contracting Parties as have not denounced it at least six months before the expiration of the current period.

Denunciation shall be effected by a written notification addressed to the Secretary-General of the United Nations.

ARTICLE 15

If, as a result of denunciations, the number of Parties to the present Convention should become less than sixteen, the Convention shall cease to be in force as from the date on which the last of these denunciations shall become effective.

ARTICLE 16

A request for the revision of the present Convention may be made at any time by any Contracting Party by means of a notification in writing addressed to the Secretary-General.

The General Assembly shall decide upon the steps, if any, to be taken in respect of such request.

ARTICLE 17

The Secretary-General of the United Nations shall notify all Members of the United Nations and the non-member States contemplated in Article 11 of the following:

(a) Signatures, ratifications and accessions received in accordance with Article 11;
(b) Notifications received in accordance with Article 12;
(c) The date upon which the present Convention comes into force in accordance with Article 13;
(d) Denunciations received in accordance with Article 14;
(e) The abrogation of the Convention in accordance with Article 15;
(f) Notifications received in accordance with Article 16.

ARTICLE 18

The original of the present Convention shall be deposited in the archives of the United Nations.

A certified copy of the Convention shall be transmitted to all Members of the United Nations and to the non-member States contemplated in Article 11.

ARTICLE 19

The present Convention shall be registered by the Secretary-General of the United Nations on the date of its coming into force.

APPENDIX 5

EXTRACT FROM A SPEECH BY EARL GREY IN THE HOUSE OF LORDS

(HANSARD. HOUSE OF LORDS, MARCH 23, 1846, 1345–7)

The state of Ireland is one which is notorious. We know the ordinary condition of that country to be one both of lawlessness and wretchedness. It is so described by every competent authority. There is not an intelligent foreigner coming to our shores, who turns his attention to the state of Ireland, but who bears back with him such a description. Ireland is the one weak place in the solid fabric of British power: Ireland is the one deep (I had almost said ineffaceable) blot upon the brightness of British honour. Ireland is our disgrace. It is the reproach, the standing disgrace, of this country that Ireland remains in the condition she is. It is so regarded throughout the whole civilized world. To ourselves we may palliate it if we will, and disguise the truth: but we cannot conceal it from others. There is not, as I have said, a foreigner— no matter when he comes, be it from France, Russia, Germany, or America—there is no native of any foreign country, different as their forms of government may be, who visits Ireland, and who on his return does not congratulate himself that he sees nothing comparable with the condition of that country at home.

If such be the state of things, how then does it arise, and what is its cause. My Lords, it is only by this government that such evils could have been produced: the mere fact that Ireland is in so deplorable and wretched a condition saves whole volumes of argument, and is of itself a complete and irrefutable proof of the misgovernment to which she has been subjected. Nor can we lay to our souls the "flattering unction" that this misgovernment was only of ancient date, and has not been our doing. It is not enough in our own excuse to say, "No wonder this state of things exists; the government of Ireland before the Union was the most ingeniously bad that was ever contrived in the face of the world: it was the government of a corrupt minority, sustained by the superior power of this great country in oppressing and tyrannizing over the great body of the nation: such a system of government could not fail to leave behind it a train of fearful evils from which we are still suffering at the present day.

To a certain extent, no doubt, this is true. No man has a stronger opinion than I regarding the iniquitous system of misgovernment in Ireland prior to the Union. But the Union is not an event of yesterday. It is nearly half a century since that measure passed. For nearly fifty years, now, Ireland has been under the immediate control of the Imperial parliament. Since it has been so, a whole generation has grown up, and is now passing away to be replaced by another: and in that time, I ask you, what impression has been made upon the evils of Ireland? It is true some good has been done. I gladly acknowledge that many useful measures have been adopted, which have, I hope, contributed in some respects to the improvement of Ireland, but none of these measures have gone to the root of the social disease to which Ireland is a prey, in the worst symptoms of which no amelioration whatever can be observed: the wretchedness and misery of the population have experienced no abatement. Upon that point I can quote high authority. I find that the commission presided over by a noble earl, whom I do not now see in his place [the Earl of Devon], reported the year before last, that "improvement was indeed beginning to take place in agriculture, but there had been corresponding advance in the condition and comforts of the labouring classes." By the report of that Commission we are informed that the agricultural labourers are still suffering the greatest privations and hardships, and still depend upon casual and precarious employment for their subsistence: that they are badly fed, badly clothed, badly housed, and badly paid for their labour; and the Commissioners conclude this part of their report by saying, "We cannot forbear expressing our strong sense of the patient endurance which the labouring classes have generally exhibited under sufferings greater, we believe, than the people of any other country have ever endured."

But there is another symptom of the condition of Ireland, which seems to me even more alarming than the prevalence of distress—I mean the general alienation of the whole mass of the nation from the institutions under which they live, and the existence in their minds of a strong deep feeling of hostility to the form of government under which they are placed. This feeling, which is the worst feature in the case, seems to be rather gaining strength than to be diminishing. I am led to that opinion by what I heard two years ago fall from the Secretary of State for the Home Department [Sir James Graham] in the House of Commons. I heard that right hon. Gentleman—and it was a statement which made a deep impression upon me—I heard the right hon. Gentleman, in answer to a speech made by a noble friend of mine, distinctly admit that we had military occupation of Ireland, but that in other sense could it be said to be governed: that it was occupied by troops, not governed like England. Such was the admission of the Secretary of State for the Home Department.

APPENDIX 6

TRANSACTIONS OF THE CENTRAL RELIEF COMMITTEE OF THE SOCIETY OF FRIENDS DURING THE FAMINE IN IRELAND IN 1846 AND 1847 (PUBLISHED IN 1852)

The Friends named the Famine as "A visitation of Divine Providence." Generally, what they found:

- "The calamity so extreme as to paralyse any general or united action"
- That the prevailing attitude was that the provision of food was a matter for government
- Little cooperation by independent individuals across all classes to help
- Few private offers of benevolence
- Insufficient accommodation in the Union Poor Houses
- Neglect of the most remote districts
- Inability to discover either the cause of or remedy for the blight
- That the Famine hit the poorest most
- Anomaly of food left in ports, markets, and warehouses
- That Ireland was not a country where either animal or vegetable food had failed before
- Reliance on the potato . . . "the failure of the crop was necessarily the failure of all"
- Some districts more heavily populated by the poor than others, "pauperism which has hitherto been the bane of the Irish peasantry"
- Rise in the price of corn and other crops
- The daily allowance on the public works scheme was totally insufficient to meet the needs of what were generally large families

- No outdoor relief
- Lack of permanent individual employment
- Absentee landlords
- Lack of proper fishing equipment and boats in coastal towns
- Cost of turf
- Lack of clothing
- Large tracts of land uncultivated and unclaimed
- Ignorance among the poor as to how to work the land
- Lack of seed, lack of money
- Lack of farming equipment
- Resident landlords who tried to help, as rents stopped, became overburdened themselves
- Deplorable discrepancies between the rich and the poor
- Enormous rates charged under the conacre system
- Work available in many instances in areas too distant for the weak to walk to
- Wages from public works often left unpaid or delayed
- Lack of depots, retail stores, services to remote areas
- Hucksters inflating price of meal as against market prices
- Pawnshops that bought fishing nets, clothes, and furniture closed because there were no buyers
- Pawnbrokers wouldn't take the coarse woollen clothes issued by the relief committees because they were stamped
- Lack of authority figures to distribute supplies when they were sent
- Abject suffering in the West
- Reluctance to go to the poor houses because it meant giving up the home
- Imposters taking advantage of the charities
- Prevalence of favor and faction—petty patronage, or old grudges, or desire to serve friends or own tenants first
- The spirit of "a little brief authority" in some areas
- Instances where the lands of well-meaning proprietors were in Chancery, leaving them with no means to assist with relief efforts
- Awful suffering during the delay in bringing in the Temporary Relief Act because the soup kitchens were, by then, closed
- People with over 1/4 acre of land were excluded from relief
- Reliance on relief stifled industry
- Instances of clearances by landlords as ex officio poor law guardians refusing to recommend their tenants to outdoor relief unless they gave up their holdings
- Dead left unburied, "so contrary to the Irish reverence for funeral rites"
- Landlords not interested in taking advantage of the Improvement Act to get their lands drained
- Only the able-bodied men and boys could participate in the government's public works scheme—the aged, infirm, widowed, disabled were excluded
- Apart from the problem of absentee landlords and lack of resident gentry in some areas, towns owned by the Ecclesiastical Commission were precluded by an act of parliament from granting aid and these suffered terribly

NOTES

INTRODUCTION

1. Caitlín Ní Houlihan was the poetic name given to Ireland by the Nobel laureate poet W. B. Yeats.
2. Figures supplied by Shane MacThomais, Glasnevin Cemetery; J. S. Donnelly Jr., *The Great Irish Potato Famine* (Port Stroud, Gloucestershire: The History Press, 2010).
3. In a review of *The Great Hunger* by Cecil Woodham-Smith in *The New Statesman*, London, 1962.
4. Joseph Lee, "The Famine as History," in *Famine 150: Commemorative Lecture Series*, by Cormac Ó Gráda (Dublin: University College, 1997).
5. Donnelly, *The Great Irish Potato Famine*.
6. Joel Mokyr, *Why Ireland Starved: A Quantitative and Analytical History of the Irish Economy, 1800-50* (London: Allen and Unwin, 1983 [revised 1985]).
7. Yeast is an essential component in the manufacture of Guinness.
8. Avril Doyle, speech reported in *Irish Australian*, April 1996.
9. Tony Blair, at the Famine Commemoration event, Millstreet, County Cork, June 1997.

CHAPTER 1: SETTING THE SCENE

1. Joe Mokyr and Cormac Ó Grada, *Famine Disease and Famine Mortality: Lessons from the Irish Experience, 1845-1850*, Working Paper WP99/12, June 1999; and Cecil Woodham-Smith, *The Great Hunger: Ireland, 1845-1849* (New York: Old Town Books, 1962).
2. Original version written in Irish:

   > *Fág uaim do eaglais ghalla*
   > *Is do chreideamh gan bonn gan bhrí*
   > *Mar gurb é is cloch bonn dóibh*
   > *Magairlí Anraí Rí*
   >   —Anthony Raftery, 1779-1835

2. English Viceroy Arthur Chichester writing to Elizabeth I's chief advisor, November 1601.
3. M. A. Busteed and R. I. Hodgson, *A Geographical Journal* 162, part 2 (July 1996).
4. Ibid.
5. T. Pakenham, *The Scramble for Africa* (London: Abacus, 1992).

CHAPTER 2: BORN TO FILTH

1. M. Murphy, ed., *Ireland's Welcome to the Stranger* (Dublin, 2002).
2. E. Larkin, ed., *Alexis de Tocqueville's Journey in Ireland—July-August, 1835* (Dublin: Wolfhound Press, 1990).
3. Evidence given to the Devon Commission (1843-1845) by Mayo clergy, quoted by Liam Swords in *The Famine in North Connacht* (Dublin: Columba Press, 1999). Reports

of select committees of the House of Commons published even before the Devon Commission reported in 1830 gave graphic descriptions of the extreme poverty of the peasantry.

4. L. O'Flaherty, *The Life of Tim Healy* (London: Jonathan Cape, 1927).
5. G. de Beaumont and W. C. Taylor, eds., *Ireland: Social, Political, and Religious,* 2 vols. (London: Richard Bentley, 1839).
6. C. Maxwell, *Dublin under the Georges* (London: Faber and Faber, 1956).
7. Ibid.
8. Ibid.

CHAPTER 3: A MILLION DEATHS OF NO USE

1. "Scarcity in Ireland," between the years 1822 and 1839, presented to Parliament, London, 1846.
2. As quoted by Cormac Ó Gráda, *Black '47 and Beyond: The Great Irish Famine in History, Economy and Memory* (Princeton, NJ: Princeton University Press, 1999).
3. Peter Gray, *Famine, Land and Politics: British Government and Irish Society, 1843-50* (Dublin: Irish Academic Press, 1999).
4. A. Smith, *The Wealth of Nations* (London: Methuen, 1904).
5. Gray, *Famine, Land and Politics.*
6. Ibid.
7. Edmund Burke, *Thoughts and Details on Scarcity*, quoted by C. Kinealy, *This Great Calamity* (Boulder, CO: Roberts Rinehart, 1995).
8. Ibid.
9. Ibid.

CHAPTER 4: FIVE ACTORS AND THE ORCHARDS OF HELL

1. Dublin paper quoted in Noel Kissane, ed., *The Irish Famine: A Documentary History* (Dublin: National Library of Ireland, 1995).
2. Patrick M. Geoghegan, *Liberator: The Life and Death of Daniel O'Connell, 1830-1847* (Dublin: Gill and Macmillan, 2010).
3. Cecil Woodham-Smith, *The Great Hunger: Ireland, 1845-1849* (New York: Old Town Books, 1962).
4. Kissane, *The Irish Famine.*
5. Woodham-Smith, *The Great Hunger.*
6. B. Coogan, *The Big Wind* (New York: Doubleday, 1969).
7. *Thom's Irish Almanac*, 1851 edition, the official directory used by the post office, legal agencies, and banking, for statistics and other information, founded by Alexander Thom and published annually since 1844.
8. Ibid.
9. Ibid.
10. Ibid.
11. Ibid.
12. Peter Gray, *Famine, Land, and Politics: British Government and Irish Society, 1843-1850* (Dublin: Irish Academic Press, 1999).
13. Thomas Cahill, *How the Irish Saved Civilization: The Untold Story of Ireland's Heroic Role from the Fall of Rome to the Rise of Medieval Europe* (New York: Anchor Books, 1996).
14. J. S. Donnelly Jr., *The Land and the People of Nineteenth Century Cork: The Rural Economy and the Land Question* (London: Routledge and Kegan Paul, 1975).
15. "The Municipal Gallery Revisited," in W. B. Yeats, *Yeats's Poems*, ed. A. Norman Jeffares (Dublin: Gill and Macmillan, 1989).
16. J. M. Hernon, "A Victorian Cromwell: Sir Charles Trevelyan, the Famine and the Age of Improvement," in *Éire-Ireland* 22 (1987).
17. Ibid.
18. Douglas Hurd, *Robert Peel: A Biography* (London: Phoenix, 2008).

CHAPTER 5: MEAL USE

1. John Boyle O'Reilly, *In Bohemia* (Boston: Pilot Publishing, 1886).
2. Cecil Woodham-Smith gives an account of the Heytesbury meeting based on the highly critical report of the *Freeman's Journal* and on a respected work published some twenty-five years after the Famine ended, John O'Rourke's *The History of the Great Irish Famine of 1847: With Notices of Earlier Irish Famines* (Dublin: Duffy, 1902).
3. James Donnelly Jr., *The Land and the People of Nineteenth Century Cork: The Rural Economy and the Land Question* (London: Routledge and Kegan Paul, 1975).
4. Cecil Woodham-Smith, *The Great Hunger: Ireland, 1845-1849* (New York: Old Town Books, 1962).
5. Ibid.
6. Ibid.
7. Ibid.
8. Cormac Ó Gráda, *Black '47 and Beyond: The Great Irish Famine in History, Economy and Memory* (Princeton, NJ: Princeton University Press, 2000).
9. David P. Nally, *Human Encumbrances: Political Violence and the Great Irish Famine* (Notre Dame, IN: University of Notre Dame Press, 2011).
10. Murray Papers, Dublin Diocesan Archives, April 6, 1849.
11. Relief Commission Papers, National Archives of Ireland, 1884.
12. Woodham-Smith, *The Great Hunger*.
13. Ibid.
14. Ibid.
15. Ibid.
16. Ibid.
17. Ibid.
18. Douglas Hurd, *Robert Peel: A Biography* (London: Phoenix, 2008).
19. Donnelly, *The Land and the People of Nineteenth Century Cork*.
20. Ibid.
21. Distress papers are readily available in archives such as the National Library of Ireland. The selection printed in this chapter was taken from Noel Kissane, ed., *The Irish Famine: A Documentary History* (Dublin: National Library of Ireland, 1995).
22. Woodham-Smith, *The Great Hunger*.
23. Ibid.
24. Ibid.
25. Kissane, *The Irish Famine*.

CHAPTER 6: EVICTIONS

1. John Mitchel, *The Last Conquest of Ireland (Perhaps)*, ed. Patrick Maume (Dublin: University College Dublin Press, 2005).
2. Cecil Woodham-Smith, *The Great Hunger: Ireland, 1845-1849* (New York: Old Town Books, 1962).
3. Ibid.
4. Ibid.
5. Ibid.
6. Noel Kissane, ed., *The Irish Famine: A Documentary History* (Dublin: National Library of Ireland, 1995).
7. Ibid.
8. James Donnelly Jr., *The Land and the People of Nineteenth Century Cork: The Rural Economy and the Land Question* (London: Routledge and Kegan Paul, 1975).
9. Tyler Anbinder, "From Famine to Five Points: Lord Lansdowne's Irish Tenants Encounter North America's Most Notorious Slum," *The American Historical Review* 107, no. 2 (April 2, 2002).
10. Peter Gray, *Famine, Land, and Politics: British Government and Irish Society, 1843-1850* (Dublin: Irish Academic Press, 1999).

11. Ibid.

CHAPTER 7: THE WORK SCHEMES

1. Liam Swords, *In Their Own Words: The Famine in North Connacht, 1845-1849* (Dublin: Columba Press, 1999).
2. Noel Kissane, ed., *The Irish Famine: A Documentary History* (Dublin: National Library of Ireland, 1995).
3. Ciarán Ó Murchadha, *The Great Famine: Ireland's Agony, 1845-1852* (London: Continuum, 2011).
4. Captain Edmond Wynne, quoted in Ó Murchadha, *The Great Famine*.
5. Cecil Woodham-Smith, *The Great Hunger: Ireland, 1845-1849* (New York: Old Town Books, 1962).
6. Ibid.
7. James Donnelly Jr., *The Land and the People of Nineteenth Century Cork: The Rural Economy and the Land Question* (London: Routledge and Kegan Paul, 1975).
8. Liam Swords, *A Dominant Church: The Diocese of Achonry, 1818-1960* (Dublin: Columba Press, 2004).
9. Donnelly, *The Land and the People of Nineteenth Century Cork*.
10. Ibid.
11. Ibid.
12. Ibid.
13. Swords, *In Their Own Words*.
14. Ibid.
15. Laurence M. Geary, "What People Died of during the Famine," in *Famine 150: Commemorative Lecture Series*, by Cormac Ó Gráda (Dublin: University College, 1997).

CHAPTER 8: THE WORKHOUSE

1. Monteagle Papers, MS 13,387/11, National Library of Ireland, collection list no. 122.
2. Cathal Póirtéir, ed., *The Great Irish Famine*, Thomas Davis Lecture Series (Dublin: Mercier Press, 1995).
3. Cited by Professor Cormac Ó Grada, UCD, at a New York conference on world hunger at Fordham University and reported on by Niall O'Dowd in *Irish Central*, May 15, 2012.
4. "The State of Ballinrobe," *Ballina Chronicle*, May 23, 1849.
5. Ibid.
6. James Mahoney, "Sketches in the West of Ireland," published in *Illustrated London News*, 1847.
7. Ibid.
8. Ibid.
9. Ibid.
10. Ibid.
11. *Northern Whig*, January 1847.
12. R. Dudley Edwards and Thomas Desmond Williams, eds., *The Great Famine: Studies in Irish History, 1845-52* (Dublin: Lilliput Press, 1956).
13. Laurence M. Geary, "What People Died of during the Famine," in *Famine 150: Commemorative Lecture Series*, by Cormac Ó Gráda (Dublin: University College, 1997), 95-111; Joe Mokyr and Cormac Ó Grada, *Famine Disease and Famine Mortality: Lessons from the Irish Experience, 1845-1850*, Working Paper WP99/12, June 1999; and Cecil Woodham-Smith, *The Great Hunger: Ireland, 1845-1849* (New York: Old Town Books, 1962).
14. Quoted in Joseph Robins, *The Lost Children* (Dublin: Institute of Public Administration, 1980).
15. Ned McHugh, *Drogheda before the Famine* (Dublin: Irish Academic Press, 1998).
16. Quoted in Robins, *The Lost Children*.
17. Noel Kissane, ed., *The Irish Famine: A Documentary History* (Dublin: National Library of Ireland, 1995).

CHAPTER 9: SOUP AND SOUPERISM

1. Noel Kissane, ed., *The Irish Famine: A Documentary History* (Dublin: National Library of Ireland, 1995).
2. Central Relief Committee of the Society of Friends, *Transactions of the Central Relief Committee of the Society of Friends during the Famine in Ireland, in 1846 and 1847* (Dublin: Hodges and Smith, 1852).
3. T. P. O'Neill, "The Organisation and Administration of Relief, 1845-52," in *The Great Famine: Studies in Irish History, 1845-52*, ed. R. Dudley Edwards and Thomas Desmond Williams (Dublin: Lilliput Press, 1956). At the meeting at which it was decided, the Quakers took a formal decision that there was to be no religious discrimination in the distribution of food.
4. Kissane, *The Irish Famine.*
5. Ibid.
6. Ibid.
7. Ibid.
8. Central Relief Committee of the Society of Friends, *Transactions of the Central Relief Committee of the Society of Friends during the Famine in Ireland, in 1846 and 1847.*
9. The lord lieutenant, as the king's principal representative in Ireland, was regarded as having viceregal status, and his official residence in Dublin's Phoenix Park was known as the Vice Regal Lodge. Hence the use of the term "viceroy."
10. Peter Gray, *Famine, Land, and Politics: British Government and Irish Society, 1843-1850* (Dublin: Irish Academic Press, 1999).
11. Rates are a tax on property, the proceeds of which are supposed to provide local services.
12. James Donnelly Jr., *The Land and the People of Nineteenth Century Cork: The Rural Economy and the Land Question* (London: Routledge and Kegan Paul, 1975).
13. Christine Kinealy, *This Great Calamity: The Irish Famine, 1845-52* (Boulder, CO: Roberts Rinehart, 1995).
14. Patrick Sarsfield O'Hegarty, *A History of Ireland under the Union, 1801-1922* (London: Methuen, 1952).
15. For an authoritative and dispassionate account of Nangle's life, see Edward Nangle and The Achill Island Mission, *History Ireland,* issue 3 (Autumn 2000).
16. Kissane, *The Irish Famine.*
17. Miriam Moffitt, *Soupers and Jumpers: The Protestant Missions in Connemara, 1848-1937* (Dublin: Nonsuch, 2008).
18. Mrs. D. P. Thompson, *A Brief Account of the Rise and Progress of the Change in Religious Opinion Now Taking Place in Dingle and the West of the County of Kerry* (London: Seeley, 1847).
19. J. H. Murphy, "The Role of Vincentian Parish Missions in the 'Irish Counter-Reformation' of the Mid-Nineteenth Century," *Irish Historical Studies* 24 (1984): 152-171.
20. O'Hegarty, *A History of Ireland under the Union.*
21. Asenath Nicholson, *Ireland's Welcome to the Stranger; or, An Excursion through Ireland in 1844 and 1845: For the Purpose of Personally Investigating the Condition of the Poor* (New York: Baker and Scribner, 1847).
22. S. C. Hall, *Hall's Ireland: Mr and Mrs Hall's Tour of 1840* (London: Hall, Virtue, 1841), ed. Michael Scott (London: Sphere Books, 1984).
23. Thompson, *A Brief Account of the Rise and Progress of the Change in Religious Opinion.*
24. Kieran Waldron, *The Archbishops of Tuam, 1700-2000* (Tuam: Nordlaw Books, 2008).
25. Murphy, "The Role of Vincentian Parish Missions in the 'Irish Counter-Reformation' of the Mid-Nineteenth Century."

CHAPTER 10: THE POOR LAW COMETH

1. Peter Gray, *Famine, Land, and Politics: British Government and Irish Society, 1843-1850* (Dublin: Irish Academic Press, 1999).
2. Quoted in Cecil Woodham-Smith, *The Great Hunger: Ireland, 1845-1849* (New York: Old Town Books, 1962).

3. Ibid.
4. Ibid.
5. Ibid.
6. Ibid.
7. Ibid.
8. Ibid.
9. Tim Robinson, foreword in *Connemara after the Famine: Journal of a Survey of the Martin Estate, 1853*, by Thomas Colville Scott (Dublin: Lilliput Press, 1995).
10. Woodham-Smith, *The Great Hunger*.
11. Ibid.
12. Ibid.
13. Ibid.
14. Ibid.
15. Ibid.
16. Clarendon State Papers, vol. iii, at the Bodleian Library, Oxford University.
17. Ibid.
18. Woodham-Smith, *The Great Hunger*.
19. Ibid.
20. Ibid.
21. Quoted in Gray, *Famine, Land, and Politics*.
22. Woodham-Smith, *The Great Hunger*.
23. The Vatican designated areas where it had once held sway but that had subsequently fallen into the hands of new conquerors as *partibus infidelium*, literally "in the lands of the unbelievers."
24. Woodham-Smith, *The Great Hunger*.
25. Ibid.
26. Ibid.
27. Ibid.
28. Ibid.
29. Ibid.
30. Ibid.
31. Ibid.
32. Ibid.
33. Ibid.

CHAPTER 11: LANDLORDS TARGETED

1. Peter Gray, *Famine, Land, and Politics: British Government and Irish Society, 1843-1850* (Dublin: Irish Academic Press, 1999).
2. James Donnelly Jr., *The Land and the People of Nineteenth Century Cork: The Rural Economy and the Land Question* (London: Routledge and Kegan Paul, 1975).
3. Ibid.
4. "To the Right Hon, the Earl of Shrewsbury," *Sydney Chronicle*, June 3, 1848, 2, http://nla.gov.au/nla.news-article31756865.
5. Quoted in Cecil Woodham-Smith, *The Great Hunger: Ireland, 1845-1849* (New York: Old Town Books, 1962).
6. Ibid.
7. Ibid.
8. C. Kinealy, *A Death-Dealing Famine: The Great Hunger in Ireland* (London: Pluto Press, 1997).

CHAPTER 12: EMIGRATION: ESCAPE BY COFFIN SHIP

1. Cecil Woodham-Smith, *The Great Hunger: Ireland, 1845-1849* (New York: Old Town Books, 1962).
2. Ibid.

3. Ibid.
4. Ibid.
5. Ibid.
6. Like the Turkish grain episode, some apologues for the Gore Booth family have challenged the coffin ship story on the basis that no record of the ship having been registered exists. However, like the reported landing of the Turkish grain at Drogheda, there may have been a clandestine element to Sir Robert Gore Booth's chartering of the vessel (through fear of public opinion) and normal records would not have been kept.
7. Peter Gray, *Famine, Land and Politics: British Government and Irish Society, 1843-1850* (Dublin: Irish Academic Press, 1999).
8. Woodham-Smith, *The Great Hunger.*
9. Ibid.
10. Ibid.
11. R. J. Scally, *The End of Hidden Ireland: Rebellion, Famine, and Emigration* (New York: Oxford University Press, 1995).
12. Gerard J. Lyne, *The Lansdowne Estate in Kerry under the Agency of William Steuart Trench, 1849-72* (Dublin: Geography Publications 2001).
13. Tyler Anbinder, "From Famine to Five Points: Lord Lansdowne's Irish Tenants Encounter North America's Most Notorious Slum," *American Historical Review* 107, no. 2 (April 2002).
14. Ibid.
15. Ibid.
16. Ibid.
17. Ibid.
18. Ibid.
19. Quoted in Tim Pat Coogan, *Wherever Green Is Worn: The Story of the Irish Diaspora* (New York: Palgrave Macmillan, 2000).
20. Ibid.
21. Ibid.
22. Noel Ignatiev, *How the Irish Became White* (New York: Routledge, 1995).
23. Woodham-Smith, *The Great Hunger.*
24. Report of Special Committee of the Board of Aldermen Relating to Back Bay, July 2, 1847, Boston City Documents, Document No. 36.
25. Ibid.
26. Report of The Society for the Prevention of Pauperism, *Journal,* April 1849.
27. Woodham-Smith, *The Great Hunger.*
28. Coogan, *Wherever Green Is Worn.*
29. Ibid.
30. Robert O'Driscoll and Lorna Reynolds, eds., *The Untold Story: The Irish in Canada,* vol. 1 (Toronto: Celtic Arts of Canada, 1988).
31. Kevin Murphy and Una Walsh, *A Famine Link: The "Hannah"—South Armagh to Ontario* (Mullaghbane Community Association, 2006).
32. Ibid.
33. Woodham-Smith, *The Great Hunger.*
34. Coogan, *Wherever Green Is Worn.*

CHAPTER 13: THE PROPAGANDA OF FAMINE

1. Central Relief Committee of the Society of Friends, *Transactions of the Central Relief Committee of the Society of Friends during the Famine in Ireland, in 1846 and 1847* (Hodges and Smith, 1852).
2. Charles E. Trevelyan, *The Irish Crisis* (London: Longman, Brown, Green and Longmans, 1848).
3. *The Times,* March 31, 1851.
4. Sir Adolphus William Ward, ed., *The Cambridge History of English Literature,* vol. 1, *From the Beginnings to the Cycles of Romance* (Cambridge: The University Press, 1920).

5. Quoted in John Mitchel, *The Last Conquest of Ireland (Perhaps)*, ed. Patrick Maume (London: University College Dublin Press, 2005).
6. Ibid.
7. Kenneth Bourne, *Palmerston: The Early Years, 1784-1841* (London: Allen Lane, 1982).
8. Daniel T. Dorrity, "Monkeys in a Menagerie: The Imagery of Unionist Opposition to Home Rule, 1886-1893," *Eire-Ireland* 12 (1977): 5-22.
9. R. F. Foster, *Paddy and Mr Punch: Connections in Irish and English History* (London: Allen Lane, 1993).
10. M. A. Busteed and R. I. Hodgson, "Irish Migrant Responses to Urban Life in Early Nineteenth-Century Manchester," *Geographical Journal* 162, no. 2 (July 1996): 139-153.
11. L. Perry Curtis, *Anglo-Saxons and Celts: A Study of Anti-Irish Prejudice in Victorian England* (New York: New York University, 1968).
12. Robert Knox, *The Races of Men: A Fragment* (Philadelphia: Lea and Blanchard, 1850).
13. Curtis, *Anglo-Saxons and Celts*.
14. Cecil Woodham-Smith, *The Great Hunger: Ireland, 1845-1849* (New York: Old Town Books, 1962).
15. Ibid.
16. Ibid.
17. Ibid.
18. Mitchel, *The Last Conquest of Ireland*.
19. Woodham-Smith, *The Great Hunger*.
20. Tom Morley, "The Arcana of That Great Machine: Politicians and *The Times* in the Late 1840s," *History* 73 (February 1988).
21. Ibid.
22. Ibid.
23. Ibid.
24. *The Times*, February 10, 1849.
25. Thomas Campbell Foster, Esq., *Letters on the Condition of the People of Ireland* (London: Chapman and Hall, 1846).
26. *The Times*, March 31, 1846.
27. *The Times*, November 3, 1845.
28. C. E. Trevelyan, *The Irish Crisis* (London: Longman, Brown, Green and Longmans, 1848).
29. *The Times*, September 22, 1846.
30. Monteagle Papers, MS 13,387/11, National Library of Ireland, collection list no. 122.
31. Peter Gray, *Famine, Land and Politics: British Government and Irish Society, 1843-1850* (Dublin: Irish Academic Press, 1999).
32. Adopted by Resolution 260 (111)A, United Nations General Assembly, December 9, 1948.

EPILOGUE

1. David P. Nally, *Human Encumbrances: Political Violence and the Great Irish Famine* (Notre Dame, IN: University of Notre Dame Press, 2011).

BIBLIOGRAPHY

BOOKS

Amory, J. *The Life of Joseph Chamberlain.* 6 volumes. London: Macmillan, 1952-1963.

Bourne, K. *Palmerston: The Early Years, 1784-1841.* London: Allen Lane, 1982.

Cahill, T. *How the Irish Saved Civilization: The Untold Story of Ireland's Heroic Role from the Fall of Rome to the Rise of Medieval Europe.* New York: Anchor Books, 1996.

Coogan, B. *The Big Wind.* New York: Doubleday, 1969.

Coogan, T. P. *De Valera.* London: Hutchinson, 1993.

———. *Wherever Green Is Worn: The Story of the Irish Diaspora.* London: Arrow, 2002.

Cullen, L. M. *An Economic History of Ireland since 1660.* London: B. T. Batsford, 1976.

———. *Life in Ireland.* London: B. T. Batsford, 1979.

Curtis, L. *Anglo-Saxons and Celts: A Study of Anti-Irish Prejudice in Victorian England.* New York: New York University Press, 1968.

———. *Ireland, the Propaganda War: The British Media and the Battle for Hearts and Minds.* London: Pluto Press, 1984.

Dangerfield, G. *The Damnable Question: A Study in Anglo-Irish Relations.* London: Quartet Books, 1979.

De Beaumont, G., and W. C. Taylor, eds. *Ireland: Social, Political, and Religious.* 2 volumes. London: Richard Bentley, 1839.

Doherty, J. E., and D. J. Hickey. *A Chronology of Irish History since 1500.* Dublin: Gill and Macmillan, 1989.

Dolan, J. P. *The Immigrant Church: New York's Irish and German Catholics, 1815-1865.* Baltimore: John Hopkins University Press, 1975.

Donnelly, J. S., Jr. *The Land and the People of Nineteenth Century Cork: The Rural Economy and the Land Question.* London: Routledge and Kegan Paul, 1975.

———. *The Great Irish Potato Famine.* Port Stroud, Gloucestershire: The History Press, 2010.

Drinkwater, C. *The Hunger, My Story: An Irish Girl's Diary, 1845-1847.* London: Scholastic Children's Books, 2008.

Dudley Edwards, R., and T. D. Williams, eds. *The Great Famine Studies in Irish History, 1845-52.* Dublin: Lilliput Press, 1956.

Erie, S. P. *Rainbow's End: Irish-Americans and the Dilemmas of Urban Machine Politics, 1840-1985.* Los Angeles: University of California Press, 1988.

Europe Central Relief Committee of the Society of Friends. *Transactions of the Central Relief Committee of the Society of Friends during the Famine in Ireland.* Dublin: Edmund Burke Publisher, 1852.

Flood Davin, N. *The Irishman in Canada.* Shannon: Irish University Press, 1968.

Foster, R. F. *Paddy and Mr Punch: Connections in Irish and English History.* London: Allen Lane, Penguin Press, 1993.

Foynes, P. *The Great Famine in Skibbereen.* Cork: Irish Famine Commemoration Skibbereen, 2004.

Gallagher, T. *Paddy's Lament: Ireland, 1846-1847: Prelude to Hatred.* Swords: Poolbeg, 1988.

Geary, L. M. *What People Died of during the Famine.* In *Famine 150: Commemorative Lecture Series.* Dublin: Teagasc, 1997.

Geoghegan, P. *Liberator: The Life and Death of Daniel O'Connell, 1830-1847.* Dublin: Gill and Macmillan, 2010.

Grace, Robert J. *The Irish in Quebec: An Introduction to the Historiography.* Québec: Institut Québécois de Recherche sur la Culture, 1993.

Gray, P. *Famine, Land and Politics: British Government and Irish Society, 1843-1850.* Dublin: Irish Academic Press, 1999.

Hackett Fischer, D. *Albion's Seed: Four British Folkways in America.* New York: Oxford University Press, 1989.

Haines, R. F. *Charles Trevelyan and the Great Irish Famine.* Dublin: Four Courts Press, 2004.

Hayden, T., ed. *Irish Hunger: Personal Reflections on the Legacy of the Famine.* Boulder, CO: Roberts Rinehart, 1997.

Helps, A. *Leaves: Journal of Our Life in the Highlands from 1848 to 1861.* Vol. 1. London: Smith, Elder, 1868.

Houston, C. J., and Smyth, W. J. *Irish Emigration and Canadian Settlement: Patterns, Links and Letters.* Toronto: University of Toronto Press, 1990.

Hurd, D. *Robert Peel: A Biography.* London: Phoenix, 2007.

Ignatiev, N. *How the Irish Became White.* New York: Routledge, 1995.

Jeffares, N., ed. *Yeats's Poems.* Dublin: Gill and Macmillan, 1989.

Kelly, L., G. Lucid, and M. O'Sullivan. *Blennerville: Gateway to Tralee's Past.* Kilkenny: Beothius, 1989.

Kenealy, T. *The Great Shame.* London: Vintage Books, 1999.

Kinealy, C. *A Death-Dealing Famine: The Great Hunger in Ireland.* London: Pluto Press, 1997.

———. *A New History of Ireland.* Gloucestershire: Sutton Publishing, 2008.

———. *This Great Calamity: The Irish Famine, 1845-52.* Boulder, CO: Roberts Rinehart, 1995.

Kissane, N., ed. *The Irish Famine: A Documentary History.* Dublin: National Library of Ireland, 1995.

Langan-Egan, M. *Women in Mayo, 1821-1851: A Historical Perspective.* Galway: National University of Ireland, 1986.

Larkin, E., ed. *Alexis de Tocqueville's Journey in Ireland—July-August, 1835.* Dublin: Wolfhound Press, 1990.

Laxton, E. *The Famine Ships: Irish Exodus to America, 1846-51.* London: Bloomsbury, 1996.

Lee, J. *The Famine as History.* In *Famine 150: Commemorative Lecture Series,* by Cormac Ó Gráda. Dublin: Teagasc/UCD, 1997.

Leyburn, J. G. *The Scotch-Irish: A Social History.* Chapel Hill: University of North Carolina Press, 1962.

Lymington, V. *Famine in England.* London: H. F. & G. Witherby, 1938.

MacKay, D. *Flight from Famine: The Coming of the Irish to Canada.* Toronto: McClelland and Stewart, 1990.

Maxwell, C. *Dublin under the Georges.* London: Faber and Faber, 1937.

McHugh, N. *Drogheda before the Famine: Urban Poverty in the Shadow of Privilege, 1826-45.* Dublin: Irish Academic Press, 1998.

McWhiney, G. *Cracker Culture, Celtic Ways in the Old South.* Tuscaloosa: University of Alabama Press, 1988.

Metress, S. P. *Outlines in Irish History: Eight Hundred Years of Struggle.* Detroit: Connolly Books, 1995.

Mitchel, J. *The Last Conquest of Ireland (Perhaps).* Dublin: University College Dublin Press, 2005.

Moffitt, M. *Soupers and Jumpers: The Protestant Missions in Connemara, 1848-1937.* Dublin: Nonsuch Publishing, 2008.

Mokyr, Joel. *Why Ireland Starved: A Quantitative and Analytical History of the Irish Economy, 1800-50.* London: Allen and Unwin, 1983 (revised 1985).

Murphy, K., and U. Walsh. *A Famine Link: The "Hannah"—South Armagh to Ontario.* Mullaghbane Community Association, 2006.

Murphy, M. *Mining Cultures: Men, Women, and Leisure in Butte, 1914–41*. Urbana: University of Illinois Press, 1997.

Nally, D. P. *Human Encumbrances: Political Violence and the Great Irish Famine*. Notre Dame, IN: University of Notre Dame, 2011.

Ó Cathaoir, B. *Famine Diary*. Dublin: Irish Academic Press, 2011.

O'Donnell, L. A. *Irish Voice and Organized Labor in America*. London: Greenwood Press, 1997.

O'Driscoll, R., and L. Reynolds, eds. *The Untold Story: The Irish in Canada*. 2 volumes. Toronto: Celtic Arts of Canada, 1988.

Ó Gráda, C. *Black '47 and Beyond: The Great Irish Famine in History, Economy and Memory*. Princeton, NJ: Princeton University Press, 2000.

———. *Famine: A Short History*. Princeton, NJ: Princeton University Press, 2009.

———. *The Great Irish Famine*. London: Macmillan, and Dublin: Gill and Macmillan, 1989.

O'Hegarty, P. S. *A History of Ireland under the Union, 1801–1922*. London: Methuen, 1952.

O'Laughlin, Michael C. *Irish Settlers on the American Frontier*. Kansas City, MO: Irish Genealogical Foundation, 1984.

Ó Murchadha, C. *The Great Famine: Ireland's Agony, 1845–1852*. London: Continuum, 2011.

Pórtéir, C., ed. *The Great Irish Famine*. The Thomas Davis Lecture Series. Dublin: RTE/Mercier, 1995.

Robins, J. *The Lost Children*. Dublin: Dublin's Institute of Public Administration, 1980.

Scally, R. J. *The End of Hidden Ireland: Rebellion, Famine, and Emigration*. New York: Oxford University Press, 1995.

Schrier, A. *Ireland and the American Emigration, 1850–1900*. Chester Springs, PA: Dufour Editions, 1997.

Scott, M., ed. *Hall's Ireland: Mr & Mrs Hall's Tour of 1840* [abridged]. London: Hall, Virtue, 1841.

Scott, T. C. *Connemara after the Famine: Journal of a Survey of the Martin Estate*. Dublin: Lilliput Press, 1995.

Sweeney, E. *Down Down Deeper and Down: Ireland in the 70s and 80s*. Dublin: Gill and Macmillan, 2010.

Swords, L. *A Dominant Church: The Diocese of Achonry, 1818–1960*. Dublin: Columba Press, 2004.

———. *In Their Own Words: The Famine in North Connacht, 1845–1849*. Dublin: Columba Press, 1999.

Thompson, Mrs. D. P. *A Brief Account of the Rise and Progress of the Change in Religious Opinion Now Taking Place in Dingle, and the West of the County of Kerry, Ireland*. London: Seeley, 1847.

Tóibín, C., and D. Ferriter. *The Irish Famine*. London: Profile Books, 2004.

Waldron, K. *The Archbishops of Tuam, 1700–2000*. Tuam: Nordlaw Books, 2008.

Wallace, Martin. *A Little History of Ireland: Henry Grattan's Parliament*. Belfast: Appletree Press, 1994.

Woodham-Smith, C. *The Great Hunger: Ireland, 1845–1849*. New York: Old Town Books, 1962.

JOURNALS, PERIODICALS, WEBSITES, AND NEWSPAPER ARTICLES

Anbinder, Tyler. "From Famine to Five Points: Lord Lansdowne's Irish Tenants Encounter North America's Most Notorious Slum." *American Historical Review* 107, no. 2 (April 2002).

Dorrity, D. "Monkeys in a Menagerie: The Imagery of Unionist Opposition to Home Rule." *Éire-Ireland* 12, 18 (1977): 5–22.

Hernon, J. M. "A Victorian Cromwell: Sir Charles Trevelyan, the Famine and the Age of Improvement." *Éire-Ireland* 22 (1987).

Mahony, J. "Sketches in the West of Ireland." *Illustrated London News*, 1847.

Mokyr, J., & C. Ó Gráda. *Famine Disease and Famine Mortality: Lessons from Ireland, 1845–1850*. Northwestern University and University College Dublin (June 1999).

Morley, T. "The Arcana of That Great Machine: Politicians and *The Times* in the Late 1840s." *The Journal of the Historical Association* 73, no. 237 (1988).

Murphy, J. H. "The Role of Vincentian Parish Missions in the 'Irish Counter-Reformation' of the Mid-Nineteenth Century." *Irish Historical Studies* 24, no. 94 (November 1984).

RECOMMENDED READING

Abel, Anne Heloise, and Frank J. Klingberg. "The Tappan Papers." *The Journal of Negro History* 12, no. 2 (April 1927).

"Achill Island History, Co. Mayo, Ireland: A Brief History of Achill." www.Achilltourism.com/history.

"After the Famine." *The History Place Irish Potato Famine.* www.historyplace.com.

Anbinder, Tyler. "From Famine to Five Points: Lord Lansdowne's Irish Tenants Encounter North America's Most Notorious Slum." *The American Historical Review* 107, no. 2 (April 2002).

An Irish American. "'Coffin Ship' to 'Atlantic Greyhound.'" *The Irish Review* 4, no. 37 (March 1914).

Branach, Niall R. "Edward Nangle and the Achill Island Mission." *History Ireland* 8, no. 3 (Autumn 2000): 35-38.

Brasbie, Father, and Pádraig de Brun. *Journal of the Kerry Archaeological and Historical Society,* no. 3 (1970).

Cahalane, Patrick. "An Economic Study of the Great Famine." *Studies: An Irish Quarterly Review* 6, no. 21 (March 1917).

"Caricature or Racism?" www.fathom.com.

"Condition of Ireland: Illustrations of the New Poor-Law: The Famine in Clare." *Illustrated London News* (December 22, 1849).

Deane, John F. "Slievemore Village on Achill." *Studies: An Irish Quarterly Review* 65, no. 258 (Summer 1976).

Dickson, David. "The Other Great Irish Famine." In *The Great Irish Famine,* ed. Cathal Poirteir. Cork: Mercier Press, 1995.

Donnelly, Brian. "The Great Famine and the Literary Imagination." *An Irish Quarterly Review* 69, no. 275/276 (Autumn-Winter 1980).

Donnelly, James S., Jr. "The Great Famine: Its Interpreters, Old and New." *History Ireland* 1, no. 3 (Autumn 1993).

Edwards, R. Dudley, and T. Desmond Williams, eds. *The Great Famine Studies in Irish History.* Dublin: Browne and Nolan, 1956.

Enright, Flan. "Pre-famine Clare—Society in Crisis." *Canadian Vindicator,* no. 5.

Gannon, P. "A Sidelight on Souperism." *The Irish Monthly* 51, no. 595 (January 1923).

Ghabhann, Gillian Ní. "A Critical Examination of a Selection of Travel Writing Produced during the Great Famine." www.ucc.ie/chronicon/smith.htm.

Gibbons, Margaret. "Margaret Aylward, Foundress, Holy Faith Sisters." *The Irish Monthly* 55, no. 654 (December 1927).

Gray, Peter. "Famine and Land in Ireland and India, 1845-1880." *The Historical Journal* 49, no. 1 (March 2006).

Green, Alice Stopford, Harold Barbour, Douglas Hyde, and Alec Wilson. "The Connemara Islands." *Irish Review* 4, no. 39 (May 1914).

Hernon, J. M. "A Victorian Cromwell: Sir Charles Trevelyan, the Famine and the Age of Improvement." *Eire-Ireland* 22 (1987).

Hillan King, Sophia. "Pictures Drawn from Memory: William Carleton's Experience of Famine." *The Irish Review,* no. 17/18 (Winter 1995).

Hood, Susan. "The Famine in the Strokestown Park Archive." *The Irish Review,* no.17/18 (Winter 1995).

"Irish Identity, Famine in the West Cork." *The Southern Star* (November 2004).

"The Irish Potato Famine, 1847." www.eyewitnesstohistory.com/irishfamine.htm.

Jenkins, Lee. "Beyond the Pale: Frederick Douglass in Cork." *The Irish Review,* no. 24 (Autumn 1999).

Keogh, Jackie. "The Great Irish Famine: Remember Skibbereen." *The Southern Star* (August 1, 2009).

Knightly, John. "The Godfrey Estate during the Great Famine." *Journal of the Kerry Archaeological and Historical Society,* series 2 (5) (2005).

Leerssen, Joep. "Theory, History and Ireland." *The Irish Review,* no. 17/18 (Winter 1995).

Lochlainn, A. Mac. "The Famine in Gaelic Tradition." *The Irish Review*, no. 17/18 (Winter 1995).

Lord Dufferin and The Hon. G. G. Boyle. "Narrative of a Journey from Oxford to Skibbereen during the Year of the Irish Famine." http://adminstaff.vassar.edu/sttaylor/FAMINE/Journey/Frontispiece.html.

Lysaght, Patricia. "Perspectives on Women during the Famine." *Bealoideas* (1995/97).

Marks, Kathy. "Blair Issues Apology for Irish Potato Famine." *The Independent* (June 2, 1997).

Maynard, Douglas H. "The World's Anti-Slavery Convention of 1840." *The Mississippi Valley Historical Review* 47, no. 3 (December 1960).

"Memorial Notes XVIII: Dr. Russell of Maynooth." *The Irish Monthly* 21, no. 243 (September 1893).

Moore, George Henry. *The Irish Review* 4, no. 38 (April 1914).

Morash, Chris. "Entering the Abyss." *The Irish Review*, no. 17/18 (Winter 1995).

———. "Spectres of the Famine." *The Irish Review*, no. 17/18 (Winter 1995).

Nelson, Bruce. "My Countrymen Are All Mankind." *Field Day Review* 4 (2008).

O'Ciosain, Michael. "Cead Bliain, 1871-1971." Muinitir Phiarias, Baile an Fheirtearaigh, 1973.

O'Ciosain, Niall. "Approaching a Folklore Archive." *Folklore* 115, no. 2 (August 2004).

"Official British Intent." www.irishholocaust.org (Fogarty, 1995).

Ó Gráda, Cormac. *The Great Irish Famine*. Princeton University Press, 1999.

O'Neill, Thomas P. "The Scientific Investigation of the Failure of the Potato Crop in Ireland, 1845-6." *Irish Historical Studies* 5, no. 18 (September 1946).

———. "The Society of Friends and the Great Famine." *Studies: An Irish Quarterly Review* 39, no. 154 (June 1950).

O'Neill, William J. "Ireland and Her Agitators." Dublin: John Browne, 1845 (New York Public Library 281306B).

"Persecution of Protestants in the Year 1845, as Detailed in a Full and Correct Report of the Trial at Tralee on Thursday, March 20, 1845 for a Libel on the Rev. Charles Gayer." Dublin: Philip Dixon Hardy and Sons, 1845.

Purcell, Richard J. "The New York Commissioners of Emigration and Irish Immigrants, 1847-1860." *Studies: An Irish Quarterly Review* 37, no. 145 (March 1948).

Quinlan, Carmel. "A Punishment from God: The Famine in the Centenary Folklore Questionnaire." *The Irish Review*, no. 19 (Spring-Summer 1996).

Quinn, Eileen Moore. "Entextualizing Famine, Reconstituting Self: Testimonial Narratives from Ireland." *Anthropological Quarterly* 74, no. 2 (April 2001).

"The 'Rambler' on Bread-and Butter Catholics." *The Catholic Layman* 7, no. 77 (May 19, 1858).

Regan, John M. "Irish Nationalism as a Historical Problem." *The Historical Journal* 50, no. 1 (2007).

Riach, Douglas C. "Daniel O'Connell and American Anti-Slavery." *Irish Historical Studies* 20, no. 77 (March 1976).

"The Role of Vincentian Parish Missions in the 'Irish Counter-Reformation' of the Nineteenth Century." *Irish Historical Studies* 24, no. 94 (November 1984).

Russell, C. W., and W. E. Gladstone. "Correspondence with Lord O'Hagan." *Irish Jesuit Province*.

Russell, Geo. W. "The Problem of Rural Life." *The Irish Review* 1, no. 1 (March 1911).

Sarbaugh, Timothy Jerome. "A Moral Spectacle: American Relief and the Famine, 1845-1849."

Scott, Thomas Colville. *Connemara after the Famine: Journal of a Survey of the Martin Estate, 1853*. Dublin: Lilliput Press, 1995.

Sherwin, Oscar. "Ignoble Ease and Peaceful Sloth, Not Peace." *Phylon* 9, no. 4 (1948).

Silke, John J. "A Survey of Recent Historiography." *Studia Hibernica*, no. 15 (1975).

Stitt, Sean. "This Blessed Famine." *Insight*. http://homepage.eircom.net/~archaeology/two/famine.htm.

Usherwood, Paul. "Lady Butler's Irish Pictures." *Irish Arts Review* 4, no. 4 (Winter 1987).

INDEX

Act of Union
    agriculture and, 22–24
    attempts to repeal, 46–47, 175
    Coercion Bill and, 57, 193
    Corn Laws and, 65
    dissolution of Irish parliament, ix, 17
    Earl Grey and, 18
    economic elite and, 28–29
    economic relief and, 39, 65
    effects on Ireland's economy, 18, 28–29, 202
    O'Connell and, 46–47
    slums and, 202
    White Boys and, 27
Affre, Denis-Auguste, 186
agrarian violence, 24–26, 57, 63, 215, 243
alcohol, 2, 30, 47, 235, 238, 240, 247
Alts, Terry, 27
American Revolution, 15
Anglican Church, 15, 45, 132, 153, 207, 219
Archbishop Hughes of New York, 46
Archbishop of Armagh, 25
Archbishop of Dublin, 71, 132, 137, 150, 153
Archbishop of Tuam, 149, 181
Ascendancy, 15, 28, 30, 155, 178
"averted births," 10

Ballyveagh Strand, 24
Bennett, William, 101, 114
Bentham, Jeremy, 36
Bentinck, Lord George, 109–10
Bishop Berkeley, 29
Bishop Doyle, 22, 32, 37
Blair, Tony, 3, 7–8
Boleyn, Anne, 11
Bordeaux Mixture, 54
Boston, 93, 201, 203–5, 210

British Relief Association, x, 68, 91, 175
Burgoyne, John, 143–44, 166, 171–72, 221
Burke, Edmund, 36, 229
Burke, Joseph, 134
Busteed, M.A., 13, 218
Butler, Sir William, 177
Butterfield, Herbert, 6
Byrne, James, 158
Byrne, Robert, 158

cannibalism, 119–21
Captain Rock, 26
Carlyle, Thomas, 219–20
Catholics
    Bible reading and, 147, 149
    clergy, 24–25
    discrimination against, 45, 210, 219
    Disraeli and, 57
    emigration and, 190, 201, 205
    famine and, 3, 125, 234
    Irish identity and, 12–14
    Mahon murder and, 180–81
    O'Connell and, 17–18, 22, 43–48
    Parliament and, 45
    peasantry and, 14, 29, 190, 210
    Peel and, 49
    population, 23–24
    propaganda against, 130
    Protestants and, 25, 29–30, 35, 125
    rebellion and, 184–86
    Relief Commission and, 68
    Roman Catholic Church and, 71
    social welfare and, 132
    souperism and, 150–61
    Society of United Irishmen and, 15–16, 26
    Trevelyan and, 60, 62–66, 97, 103, 237–41, 243–46

violence against, 16–17, 230
Young Irelanders and, 185
see also Catholic Emancipation
Catholic Emancipation, 17–18, 45–46, 49, 66,
  94, 154, 158–59, 215
cholera, xi, 126, 131, 196, 206, 210
Coercion Bill, 57, 193
Corn Laws, x, 49–50, 55–57, 65–67, 76, 225,
  229
Crawford, William Sharman, 37
Cromwell, Oliver, ix, 12, 59, 97, 166, 180,
  195, 230
croppy, 16
Cullen, Paul, 160

Dasent, George Webbe, 225
Davitt, Michael, 233
de Beaumont, Gustave, 26–28
de Lamartine, Alphonse, 185
Delane, John Thadeus, 170, 225
Devon Commission, 32, 50, 68, 226–27
Dillon, John Blake, 185
Dingle, County Kerry, viii, 151–60, 189
Disraeli, Benjamin, 48, 57
Donnelly, James Jr., 6, 7, 58, 67, 147, 248
Dublin Castle, 24, 32, 47–48, 54, 68, 74, 139,
  186
Duffy, Charles Gavan, 184, 220
Duffy's Cut, 210
Duke of Leinster, 15, 65
Duke of Wellington, 56, 186
dysentery, x, 73, 76, 116, 131, 196–97, 221

Earl Grey, 9, 18, 194, 254–55
Edinburgh Review, The, 33
Edwards, Dudley, 4–7
emigration
  evictions and, 191–93
  landlords and, 199, 204, 206, 210
  Peel and, 198
  Trevelyan and, 190, 193, 209
  Wood and, 192–93, 230
Emperor Theodorus, 35
Encumbered Estates Act (1848), xi, 94, 233
Eureka Stockade uprising, 185
Evicted, 127
evictions
  Ballinglass and, 88–89, 93–94
  Butler and, 177–78
  Catholics and, 94–95, 152
  Connemara, 216–17

Delphi Lodge, 92
Devon Commission and, 226
Doolough Lake incident, 91–92
elections and, 222
emigration and, 191–93
Encumbered Estates Act and, xi
Gregory Clause and, 111
James Hack Tuke and, 87, 143
landlords and, 87–91, 93–96, 98–99, 115,
  176–77
laws and, 96–97
legality of, 95–96
Lord Lucan and, 88, 112, 176
Mahon and, 180–81
Mayo County, 92–93
media and, 227
memories of, 119
Mullaroghue and, 90–91
nighttime, 90–91, 93, 100
potato famine and, 107
Russell and, 98–99
"scalps" and, 89
Silgo and, 176–77
Tory Lord Brogham on, 87, 93
Trevelyan and, 85, 97–98
violence against landlords and, 27
U.S. and, 204
Walshe and, 90–91
weather and, 114–15, 166–67
extermination, 174

faction fighting, 24–25, 47, 239
Ferrie, Adam, 194
Fever Act (1847), x
Five Points neighborhood, 99, 196
Flannelly, Father William, 137, 150
food riots, 69
Forrester, James Edward, 143
Fox, Charles, 193
Foxites, 193
French Revolution, 15–16

Gangs of New York, 25, 199
genocide, 31, 67, 229–31, 250–53
Gombeen Men, 26
Gore Booth, Robert, 191–92, 263
Goulburn, Henry, 109
Graham, James, 60–61, 76, 255
Grattan, Henry, 14–15, 65
Great Hunger, The (Woodham-Smith), 3, 7,
  189

Gregory Clause, 42, 94, 96, 111, 144
Grey, George, 44, 104, 168
Gubbins, George, 152

Hack Tuke, James, 87, 90–91, 143, 166–67
Hamilton (inspector), 90–91
Hearts of Oak Association, 26
Hearts of Steel, 26
Hernan, Joseph M., 59
Hodgson, R.I., 13, 218
House of Commons
    Coercion Bill and, 57
    extermination and, 174
    famine and, 22, 74–76
    Ireland and, 32, 38, 67
    landlords and, 95, 99
    O'Connell and, 44–48
    Poor Law Committee, 121
    providentialism and, 228
    rate collection and, 165
    relief and, 84, 110
    soup kitchens and, 145
    Temporary Relief Act, 143
House of Lords, 9, 18, 39, 57, 89, 173, 181,
    190–91, 254–55
Hurd, Douglas, 77, 105

Improvement Act, 112
industrialization, 32, 49, 228
Irish Republican Army (IRA), 4, 48, 184, 234
Irish Reform Act (1832), 58, 67

Jackson, George Vaughn, 168
Jervis, Sir John, 96
John of Salisbury, 11

Kane, Robert, 53–54, 68
Kennedy, John Pitt, 68
Kinealy, Christine, 41, 147
"King Dan"
    see O'Connell, Daniel
King George III, 17
King Henry II, 11
King Henry VIII, 11–12, 195
King James II, 13
King Louis XIV, 13
King of Connemara, 40
Kingsley, Charles, 219
Kingstown, 81, 222

Lalor, James Fintan, 184–85, 234

Land Improvement Act, 233
landlordism, 154, 159, 227–28
landlords
    absentee, 23, 105, 256
    anger with, 215, 222
    buy out by British government, 234
    Clanricarde and, 193
    Corn Laws and, 49
    criticism of, 33
    Devon Commission and, 226
    Doonass and, 82
    emigration and, 199, 204, 206, 210
    employment and, 72, 74–76
    evictions and, 87–91, 93–96, 98–99, 115,
        176–77
    famine relief and, 142–43, 167–68
    farming and, 176–77, 190–91
    Grattan and, 14–15
    Improvement Act and, 111–12
    land grabs and, 119
    Nassau Senior and, 33
    Peel and, 55, 72–75
    place in Irish society, 138
    Poor Laws and, 38–41, 82, 167
    power, 19–20, 25–27
    Protestantism and, 151–52, 238
    rate collection and, 145, 172–73
    road schemes and, 106
    stringency and, 41–42
    studies of, 195
    subsidies and, 105
    taxes and, 66
    tenant rights and, 37
    Trevelyan and, 108–9, 242, 244
    violence against, 27, 174–75, 178, 179–87,
        224
"lazy beds," 20, 33
learned helplessness, 28, 235
Lee, Beoum-Seok, 148
Lee, Joseph, 4–6
Lissadell, 192
Lichfield Compact, 58
London Political Club, 55–56, 62
London Reform Club, 58, 220
Lord Ashburton, 194
Lord Brougham, 87, 93
Lord Carnarvon, 177–78
Lord Charlemont, 15
Lord Chichester, 12
Lord Clarendon, 99, 145, 166, 170, 179, 183,
    193, 216

Lord Clarincarde, 176, 193, 234
Lord Clements, 81
Lord Cloncurry, 28, 65
Lord Farnham, 181
Lord Heytesbury, 50, 65–66, 259
Lord Landsowne, 98, 195
Lord Londonderry, 94
Lord Lucan, 88, 112, 176
Lord Melbourne, 58
Lord Monteagle, 55, 76, 97, 99, 117, 130,
　　176, 190, 228
Lord Mountbatten, 48
Lord Mountcashel, 173
Lord Palmerston, 88, 98, 104, 176, 193,
　　216–17
Lord Sligo, 168, 176
Lord Ventry, 151–52
Louisburgh, 73, 91–92, 226
Lyne, Gerard J., vii, 195

MacAleese, Mary, 71
Mahon, Denis, 180–81, 194
Mahoney, James, 126–30
Malthus, Thomas, 36–38, 56, 130
Manifest Destiny, 33, 97
Mapas, John, 14
marriage, 2, 20–21, 235
Martin, "Humanity Dick," 40, 167
Martin, Thomas, 216
McAteer, Hugh, 184
McCarthy, Margaret, 199–200
McDermot, Father, 180–81
McHale, John, 149–51
McHughes, Roger, 5
McKie, Major, 95
McMurragh, Diarmuid, 11
McNamara, Thomas, 160
Melville, Herman, 9
Moderates, 193, 244
Mokyr, Joel, 5–6, 10
"monster meetings," 47–48, 172, 239, 244
Moody, T.W., 6
Moore, David, 51
Moore, Tom, 58, 99
Moralists, 193
Murphy, James H., 153, 158
Murphy, John, 208
Murphy, Michael J., 118
Murphy, Mike, 7
Murray, Daniel (Archbishop of Dublin), 71,
　　137, 150

Nangle, Edward, 150
Nassau Senior, William, 33–34, 36–39, 153
Navigation Acts (1847), 200
New York City, 99, 192, 194, 196–203,
　　210–11
Nicholls, George, 37–39, 41, 132
Nicholson, Asenath, 19, 153–54
Northern Whig, 130, 155
Nowlan, Kevin, 6–7

O'Connell, Daniel
　　Catholic Emanicpation and, 17–18, 43–48
　　Clontarf meeting and, 60–61
　　famine and, 22
　　House of Commons and, 22, 32, 38
　　Irish parliament and, 17
　　landlords and, 184–85
　　meal use and, 65–67
　　"monster meetings" and, 47–48
　　Peel and, 43–48
　　Poor Laws and, 172, 174
　　Russell and, 58
　　Select Committee on Ireland and, 22, 32
　　soup kitchens and, 151, 154, 158–59
　　Trevelyan and, 61–63, 237–38, 240,
　　　　244–45, 247
　　work schemes and, 103
O'Connor, Feargus, 45
O'Connor, Mary, 200
O'Cuív, Éamon, 123
O'Flaherty, Liam, 26, 222–23
O'Grada, Cormac, 5, 10, 69–70
O'Hara, Charles, 142
O'Higgins, Kevin, 59
O'Neill, T.P., 6–7, 138
O'Reilly, John Boyle, 65
O'Shaughnessy, 121
O'Sullivan, John, 196
Obama, Barack, 46
Orange Order, 26

Parnell, Charles Stuart, 234
Pataki, George, 200
Peel, Sir Robert
　　Clontarf and, 48–49
　　Coercion Bills and, 57–58
　　Corn Laws and, 49–50, 55–57, 225
　　emigration and, 198
　　evictions and, 95
　　landlords and, 184
　　meal use and, 65–68, 72, 74–78, 80, 82–83

O'Connell and, 43–44, 47
ouster from office, x
propaganda and, 214
Relief Commission and, ix
soup kitchens and, 154–55
studies of blight, 53
Trevelyan and, 60–61
work schemes and, 105–6, 108, 110,
    115–16
workhouses and, 50–51
Penal Laws, 45, 74
Petty, Sir William, 195
Piggot, David, 158
Pine-Coffin, Edward, 68, 105
pigs, 76, 81, 106–7, 202–3
pitch capping, 16
Pitt, William, 16
Pitt, William the Younger, 17, 224
Political Economy Club, 34–35, 37
Poor Laws
    British debate over, 37–39
    evictions and, 90
    Gregory Clause and, 42
    landlords and, 38–41, 82, 167, 191, 257
    Peel and, 67
    Poor Law Act (1834), 33, 37
    Poor Law Act (1838), 132
    Poor Law Extension Act (1847), 163, 165,
        169, 182
    Poor Law Unions, x, 81
    relief efforts and, 90–92, 111
    stringency and, 41
    Trevelyan and, 163, 165–67, 169–75
    Twistleton and, 71–72
    workhouses and, 117, 121, 132, 134–35
Poor Relief Act, x
Pope Adrian IV, 11, 70–71
Pope Gregory XIII, 152
Pope Innocent XI, 13
popery, 49, 151, 154, 215
Presbyterians, 17, 23, 45, 185, 239
Prince Albert, xi, 225
providentialism, 33, 35–36, 88, 97, 215

Quakers, x, xi, 37, 68, 90, 111, 134, 137–44,
    154, 161, 166, 173–74, 192, 214, 261
    see also Society of Friends Relief
        Committee
Queen Elizabeth I, ix, 12, 32, 132, 152, 246
Queen Elizabeth II, 124, 221
Queen Victoria, xi, 56, 70, 72, 198, 221

Querist, The (Berkeley), 29

Raleigh, Sir Walter, 152
rate collection, 164–65, 172
Redington, T.N., 167
ribbon men, 26
road schemes, 106, 169
rockites, 26
Routh, Randolph, 67, 69, 74, 77–78, 83–84,
    107, 143–44, 165
Russell, Lord John
    attitude toward Ireland, 58
    Clarendon and, 172–73, 224–25
    Corn Laws and, 49
    evictions and, 98–100
    Irish clergy and, 181
    landlords and, 179, 182–83
    Nassau Senior and, 38
    Peel and, 49, 56–58
    Political Economy Club and, 35
    Poor Laws and, 34
    Quakers and, 143, 173–74
    relief and, 43–44, 58, 166
    soup kitchens and, 145
    Trevelyan and, 83–84, 110–11, 175
    work scheme and, 164

Scorsese, Martin, 25, 199
Scotland, 17, 39, 69, 90, 106, 172, 226, 239
Scrope, George, 36, 95
Seligman, Martin, 28
sex, 20
Smith, Adam, 35, 37, 56, 229
Smith, William J., 7
Smith O'Brien, William, 76, 184–87
Society of Friends Relief Committee, x, 91,
    111, 214, 255–56
Society of the United Irishmen, 15–16
Soup Kitchen Act (1846), 138, 143–45, 163
soup kitchens, x, 116, 118, 124, 137–47, 154,
    163, 165, 169, 220–21, 257
souperism, viii, 147–51, 153, 159–61, 221
Soyer, Alexis, 220–21
"squireocracy," 49
stringency, 41–42, 110
Swift, Dean, 29
Swift, Jonathan, 185

Temporary Relief Act (1847), 143, 257
Tocqueville, Alexis de, 19, 28, 33–34
Tone, Wolfe, 15–17

Tories, 44, 49, 57, 158
Trench, William Steuart, 195, 197–200,
    233–34
Trevelyan, Charles
    Act of Union and, 47
    Adam Smith and, 35–36
    attitude toward Ireland, 44, 47, 60–64, 155
    background, 59–60
    Catholics and, 63–64
    emigration and, 190, 193, 209
    famine relief efforts and, 68–70, 74, 91,
        107–9
    in "Famine Road," 120
    grain shipments and, 77–79, 83–85
    historical view of, 101–4
    landlords and, 107–8, 182, 184
    letter (October 11, 1843), 237–47
    morality and, 97
    personality, 60–61
    Poor Laws and, 163, 165–67, 169–75
    propaganda and, 98, 214–16, 220, 227–30
    providentialism and, 88, 155, 233
    Quakers and, 139
    on relief for the poor, 117
    Temporary Relief Act and, 143–44
    unions and, 96
    Wood and, 83
    work schemes and, 101–4, 107–14
    workhouses and, 132
Twisleton, Edward, 67, 167, 170–71, 173–75

unions, 39–40, 96, 117, 125, 134, 138,
    171–72, 175, 226

Vincentian Fathers, 158–60, 189
Viscount Morpeth, 37, 143
Volunteer Army, 15, 72

Wales, 17, 39, 106, 172, 226, 239
Washington, George, 46
Wealth of Nations, The (Smith), 35, 229
Whately, Richard, 38, 132, 153
Whately, Thomas, 37
Whig Party
    1841 elections and, 44
    1846 elections and, x

Corn Laws and, 49
Disraeli and, 57
food riots and, 69
House of Commons and, 44
Lichfield Compact and, 58
Palmerston and, 104
Peel and, x, 56–57, 80
policy, 101, 103, 129, 143–44, 146,
    229–31
public opinion of Irish and, 6, 33, 187, 214,
    220, 224–25, 229–31, 233
Quakers and, 37
rate collection and, 165
Trevelyan and, 78, 83–84, 101, 103–4,
    109–11, 143–44, 193
White Boys, 26–27, 49, 146, 178, 234
Whitelaw, James, 30
Wilberforce, William, 59
William of Orange, ix, 13, 21, 49
Williams, Desmond, 6–7
Wood, Charles
    British press and, 214
    Carlyle and, 220
    Clarendon and, 169–72
    Delane and, 225
    emigration and, 192–93, 230
    famine relief and, 70, 96, 110, 143–44
    Gore Booth and, 192–93
    grain shipments to Ireland and, 83–84
    Monteagle and, 190
    potato blight and, 174
    providentialism and, 88, 98, 216, 228
    Quakers and, 139
    rate collection and, 165–67, 172
    Russell and, 143
    Trevelyan and, 44, 83–84, 104, 110,
        174–75
Woodham-Smith, Cecil, 3, 7, 60, 63, 76, 101,
    127, 189
workhouses, 4, 37–42, 50, 55, 66, 72, 78, 93,
    108, 117–36, 146, 163–64, 167, 171,
    173, 176–77, 180, 191, 196, 199, 220
Wynne, Edmond, 108

Young Ireland, xi, 65, 174, 181, 184–87, 189,
    215, 217, 220